Drones – Future of Aviation Law?

Ius, Lex et Res Publica
Studies in Law, Philosophy and Political Cultures

Edited by Barbara Janusz-Pohl and Anna Jaroń

Volume 24

PETER LANG

Piotr Kasprzyk / Anna Konert

Drones – Future of Aviation Law?

Interference of Public Law in Private Law

PETER LANG

Bibliographic Information published by the Deutsche Nationalbibliothek
The Deutsche Nationalbibliothek lists this publication
in the Deutsche Nationalbibliografie; detailed bibliographic
data is available online at http://dnb.d-nb.de.

Library of Congress Cataloging-in-Publication Data
A CIP catalog record for this book has been applied for at the
Library of Congress.

This publication was financially supported by the Lazarski University.

ISSN 2191-3250
ISBN 978-3-631-89527-6 (Print)
E-ISBN 978-3-631-89187-2 (E-Book)
E-ISBN 978-3-631-89702-7 (EPUB)
DOI 10.3726/b20554

Peter Lang – Berlin· Lausanne · Bruxelles · New York ·
Oxford · Warszawa · Wien

www.peterlang.com

Table of Contents

Acknowledgement

We would like to express our gratitude to Mateusz Kotliński for the guidance and instruction he provided us throughout our book.
The opinions and conclusions expressed herein are those of the author. They are not intended to and should not be thought to represent official ideas, attitudes, or policies of the International Civil Aviation Organization (ICAO), the ICAO Council, or other bodies of the Organization, or any ICAO Member State(s).

Introduction – Drone as new technology. Drone law

A decade ago, unmanned aircraft (UA) were talked about mainly in the context of their military applications. First, it was just reconnaissance missions. Then, UA were being used in combat scenarios, especially during the wars in Iraq and Afghanistan[1]. It seemed that development of unmanned aircraft and technological development on the modern-day battlefield were intertwined. Manned aviation was perfecting aircraft designs and the automation of aircraft systems and subsystems was progressing year after year. Satellite technology enabled the development of navigation systems, as well as better data transfer over long distances. Add to that was the miniaturization of equipment necessary to conduct, for example, remote observations from the air. At the end of the 1990s, American and Israeli armed forces began using UA systems for reconnaissance activities on a large scale. It was just a matter of time before they started using them as combat platforms. After the 9/11 attacks, the US military and intelligence agencies carried out the world's first attacks using UA armed with laser-guided missiles. That was when the first unmanned aircraft systems designed for combat saw the light of the day. In the following years, the use of unmanned aircraft for so-called *selective elimination* drew many controversies, including legal ones[2]. Nevertheless, this new technology not only changed the modern-day battlefield, but also military doctrines. Along with these changes, it became difficult to separate technological progress from politics, as new technology allowed for combat operations to be conducted in a way that minimized risk to human life, leading to a lower, politically accepted threshold for the use of force[3].

Today, we are seeing numerous civil applications for drones. There are solar-powered drones, which have giant wingspans and can be used as mobile Internet

---

1 See e.g. John David Blom Unmanned Aerial Systems: A Historical Perspective, 2010. For Polish publications see e.g. J.M. Brzezina, Atak Dronów, Warsaw, 2013.

2 See e.g. E. Di Nucci, F. Santoni de Sio, Drones and responsibility: legal, philosophical and socio-technical perspectives on remotely controlled weapons, 2016, A. Bodnar, I. Pacho, Targeted Killings (Drone Strikes) and The European Convention on Human Rights, XXXII Polish Yearbook of International Law, 2013.

3 Sarah E. Kreps, Drony. Wprowadzenie. Technologie. Zastosowania, PWN 2019, p. 54.

access points since they don't need to land for months[4]. Medium-sized drones can be used in logistics and transport services, fleet management, electronic media, in the movie and entertainment industries and even in agriculture (in the inventory of crops, forests, animals, etc.). Moreover, drones can support local government units and municipal economies in areas including geodesy and spatial management, crisis management, public safety (urban surveillance, mass events, command systems support, atypical event detection, law enforcement support, search and rescue operations), infrastructure inspection (flood embankments, rivers, monitoring of critical infrastructure), construction inspections and support for logistics work in the construction sector, environmental protection (location and air quality check-ups, illegal landfill detection), ground and surface waters inspections, transport management support, etc. And finally, drones can also be the size of an insect. For example, scientists at Harvard have created miniature RoboBees, which use so-called *swarm intelligence* to search for victims of natural disasters, pollinate plants, monitor road traffic or enable research to be carried out in environments too hostile for humans.[5]

The general development of unmanned aircraft has been closely related to technological development in many other fields, but the popularization of lithium-ion batteries was a key factor for its widespread expansion. This solution enabled the construction of electrically powered flying devices, which, combined with device miniaturization and satellite navigation positioning, led to the popularization of the new technology. The first unmanned devices used by civilians brought on the development of the very first legal regulations concerning their use. These regulations focused on UA operations conducted within an operator's visual line of sight, and applied to aircraft weighing less than 25 kg. Denmark was one of the first countries to adopt such regulations in 1986,[6] when UA were commonly referred to as consumer drones. However, contrary to their name, they were often used for commercial purposes, for example for filming videos or taking photos. Tech companies design and manufacture such devices on a mass scale. The Chinese company DJI turned out to be particularly successful in this segment, taking a 70% share in the global consumer drone market within the span of just a couple of years[7].

---

4 R. Kuchta, Trzy przykłady nowych robotów, Robotyka, Warsaw, 2015, p. 11: https://newtech.law/wp-content/uploads/2017/08/Wardynski-i-Wspolnicy_raport-robotyka.pdf [access: October 23, 2019].

5 Ibidem, p. 11.

6 Source: A. Masutti, F. Tomasello, International…, p. 4.

7 https://technode.com/2018/01/03/worlds-top-drone-seller-dji-made-2-7-billion-2017/

People have been working on more complex UA systems for over a decade. These systems are intended to perform operations beyond an operator's line of sight and are designed with commercial services in mind, including the transport of goods and the provision of services for the public sector. For example, at the beginning of 2020, trade media informed about UA test flights being carried out in the area of cargo shipping (Japan Airlines[8]), search and rescue operations for British state services[9], or stratospheric UA flights (pseudo-satellites)[10].

Numerous reports indicate that drones will gradually replace "traditional" (manned) aviation in such fields as aerial photography, search and rescue operations, transmission network monitoring or precise aerial application activity[11]. The costs of using unmanned systems are incomparable to those incurred through manned aviation. Various services can be provided both remotely, i.e. with an operator (pilot) remotely controlling a UA, or autonomously in a pre-programmed manner without an operator's (pilot's) intervention or with their role simply limited to system supervision. Some believe that unmanned aircraft systems could result in the creation of completely new types of services which would stem from their ability to operate at very low altitudes and in urban areas. They could be used to provide emergency medical services[12] or deliver parcels. Some groups are also working on replacing satellites with solar energy-powered UA operating at very high altitudes (HAPS; *High-Altitude Pseudo Satellite*), which are capable of carrying out long-term missions without having to land to refuel. Such platforms can be used, for example, to transmit ICT data.

---

https://time.com/collection/genius-companies-2018/5412498/dji/

8 https://www.flightglobal.com/civil-uavs/jal-trials-transporting-fresh-fish-with-uavs/136922.article [access February 28, 2020]

9 https://www.flightglobal.com/civil-uavs/elbit-to-fly-hermes-900-for-uk-search-and-rescue-trials/136554.article [access February 28, 2020].

10 https://www.flightglobal.com/aerospace/bae-joins-high-altitude-race-with-maiden-phasa-35-flight/136767.article [access February 28, 2020].

11 See e.g. "Clarity from above, PwC global report on the commercial applications of drone technology". Available at https://www.pwc.pl/en/publikacje/2016/clarity-from-above.html

12 A. Konert, et al. The Use of Drones in Emergency Medicine: Practical and Legal Aspects.

It is estimated that the changes brought about by this new technology will be comparable to those that took place in the service sector after the widespread development of computer technology, the Internet and mobile phones[13].

The dynamics of UA technology development are best illustrated by economic data and forecasts. It is estimated that the global value of the civil application sector of the drone market in the years 2017–2026 will amount to nearly USD 73.5 billion, including USD 3.3 billion in Poland[14]. However, it is quite difficult to rely on data from estimates and forecasts as these tend to change. For example, according to forecasts prepared at the request of the European Commission in 2016, it was estimated that there would be around 7 million consumer drones and 400,000 specialized drones in use in EU countries by 2050[15]. Meanwhile, according to the data provided by the European Commission in 2019[16], the total number of consumer drones around the world will reach approx. 35 million in 2022, 25% of which will be in Europe. At the same time, it is estimated that the number of specialized drones (used in BVLOS operations) will reach 9 million worldwide by 2022.

Concrete data on the number of UA and their users seems a lot more reliable than forecasts. According to conservative estimates from 2016, there were about 1–1.5 million consumer drones and about 10,000 specialized drones in the EU at the time[17]. It is worth noting that as new EU regulations requiring the registration of operators of drones with a mass of over 250 g enter into force (in December 2020), these numbers regarding individual EU Member States will change. It will be possible to actually see not just estimates, but rather real-life data on the actual total number of drone operators and their devices.

For example, in the USA at the end of 2018, there were[18]:

---

13 Communication from the Commission to the European Parliament, the Council, The European Economic and Social Committee and the Committee of the Regions An Aviation Strategy for Europe COM/2015/0598 final.

14 Biała Księga Rynku Bezzałogowych Statków Powietrznych, Warsaw, 2019.

15 SESAR JU. European Drones Outlook Study. Unlocking the value for Europe. 2016.

16 EC representative speaks at the World ATM Conference, Madrid, 2019. https://issuu.com/airtrafficcontrolassociation/docs/watmc_2019_keynote_speech_henrik_ho [access February 28, 2020].

17 SESAR JU. European Drones Outlook Study. Unlocking the value for Europe. 2016

18 FAA Aerospace Forecast, Fiscal Years 2019–2039.

1. over 900,000 registered owners of so-called models, i.e. drones weighing up to 25 kg (55 lbs.) used for recreational or hobby purposes, estimating the number of such drones at over 1.25 million,
2. over 277,000 registered drones weighing up to 25 kg (55 lbs.) used for commercial purposes.

Based on the dynamics of UA registration in the US, the FAA forecasts that the number of models will increase to approx. 1.4 million registered devices by 2023. However, it is estimated that the number of drones (with a mass of up to 25 kg) used for commercial purposes could grow threefold and reach up to 835,000 (from today's 277,000) by around the same time.

Interestingly, the categorizations of unmanned aircraft into consumer and specialized (adopted in the EU) and into model and commercial (adopted in the US) do not coincide. Moreover, consulting companies use different types of classification in their UA sales estimates.

Consulting firm Gartner estimates that there will be 500,000 drones sold worldwide in 2020. This would signify a 50% jump in sales compared to 2019[19]. And this number is expected to reach 1.3 million in 2023. Experts also predict the construction industry to be the sector with the widest range of UA applications. One of the tasks that drones are being used for in this industry is BIM (*Building Information Modeling*). It is estimated that the total number of drones sold for monitoring construction work will increase from 141,000 in 2019 to over 510,000 in 2023. Subsequently, it is believed that UA will be purchased more and more often for purposes related to fire protection, public safety (police services), logistics services, or for the purposes of performing damage assessments in liquidation proceedings.

It is safe to say that UA technology has been developing very dynamically in recent years. Therefore, it can be argued on reasonable ground that, based on the number of UA in use and estimates on the industry's development in the coming years, a new type of aviation activity has been created and requires strong regulatory action.

This publication was borne of research-based intentions – an attempt to show the framework of aviation law and to analyze and distinguish manned aviation regulations and define the scope of their application in unmanned aviation. However, an analysis of these regulations, as well as an observation of the

19 https://www.gartner.com/en/newsroom/press-releases/2019-12-04-gartner-forecasts-global-iot-enterprise-drone-shipmen [access February 28, 2020].

technological development of unmanned aerial systems, led to one question – namely, are we on the brink of a new era in aviation law? An era that started because of the development of a new type of flying device? One thing is for certain – we still don't know how UA should be treated (like next-generation flying devices or regular aircraft?) due to their specific characteristics, various types, range of sizes, methods of use, and means of control (such as through artificial intelligence systems, etc.).

The main research problem is establishing a legal classification for drones. This concept is understood in many different ways. On the one hand, drones are defined as unmanned aircraft. But on the other hand, some say they should be considered robots[20]. Public law defines UA as aircraft that fall within the scope of aviation law, and only sometimes need new, special regulations that go beyond the framework of traditional aviation law. However, from the point of view of private law, especially civil liability, classifying drones into one or another category is of great importance. This issue is part of a larger discussion on new technologies, including robotics, that has been ongoing for years. The main research thesis is that we are now facing the creation of a new "branch of law" which is the Drone law.

The pace of development of UA technology in recent years rightly gives grounds to say that we are dealing with *disruptive technology*[21]. The disruptiveness of this technology should be considered in two aspects. First, it creates new possibilities as UA are designed to carry out operations (in most cases) at very low altitudes and in a completely different manner than manned aviation. Second, the development of this technology necessitates its integration with manned aviation – particularly commercial transport, taking into consideration its statistically high levels of safety. This new technology can only be allowed to develop if it can be demonstrated that UA are capable of flying in the same airspace as manned aviation without jeopardizing the safety and efficiency of

---

20 Mikromakro Institute's report "Człowiek – maszyna – bezpieczeństwo", 2013; Mikromakro Institute's report "Roboty w przestrzeni publicznej", 2014; Mikromakro Institute's report "Rynek dronów w Polsce. Księga popytu i podaży", 2015; Mikromakro Institute's report "Rynek dronów w Polsce. Świt w dolinie śmierci", 2017; Mikromakro Institute's report "Rynek dronów w Polsce. Jutrzenka", 2018 and R. Kuchta, Trzy przykłady nowych robotów, Robotyka, Warsaw, 2015, p. 10: https://newtech.law/wp-content/uploads/2017/08/Wardynski-i-Wspolnicy_raport-robotyka.pdf [access: October 23, 2019].

21 A. Masutti, F. Tomasello, International Regulation of Non-Military Drones, 2018, p. 7.

aviation as a whole[22]. Therefore, from a legal viewpoint, the safety of UA operations is the most fundamental issue in question, and should be looked into by authorities, but from a dual perspective. First of all, UA could engage in accidents and thus jeopardize the safety of people and property on the ground. Second, if a drone collides with a manned airplane, the safety of the passengers and crew members on board might be endangered. This publication addresses the issue of unmanned aircraft operation safety regulations and the issue of manned aviation safety regulations in the context of integrating the two.

It is based on an analysis of the ever-growing number of publications and studies regarding the development of unmanned aviation and its integration with manned aviation, relying mainly on documents published at an institutional level, including those published by public authorities performing a regulatory role. Such studies constitute as the basis for drafting new laws and regulations regarding UA operations.

The authors draw upon the growing number of scientific studies on new UA technologies, as well as on different aspects of its development, including regulatory (legal) considerations. Over the years, a wealth of scientific literature, including numerous post-conference studies, countless presentations, as well studies and reports compiled by various organizations, institutions, and private companies have been made available.

An analysis of the available material, the amount and degree of detail of which increases in proportion to one's interest in the subject, leads to the following research questions in terms of safety of unmanned aircraft operations and the development of regulations in this field.

First off, what are the consequences of recognizing unmanned aircraft as aircraft? The term "aircraft" is central in aviation law and aviation safety regulations – regulations that, for over a century now, have assumed that there is always a crew on board any aircraft, and which only allow for the introduction of new rules if they ensure a current or higher level of safety. An unmanned aircraft, although it is also an aircraft, will not meet these requirements by design. So, what approach should be adopted regarding UA safety regulations? Should we just modify existing rules on manned aviation and adjust them to unmanned aviation? Or should we create completely new regulations dedicated to new types of operations, loosely based on those found in manned aviation?

22 Communication from the Commission to the European Parliament and the Council "A new era for aviation. Opening the aviation market to the civil use of remotely piloted aircraft systems in a safe and sustainable manner" COM (2014) 207 final.

In order to answer these questions, it is essential to better understand the differences between manned and unmanned aviation operations. The possibility of carrying out operations without a crew on board results from the use of new technologies, many of which are already known in manned aviation. Automation, miniaturization, satellite navigation, and motion detection systems are, after all, used as solutions that raise levels of safety and efficiency in manned aviation operations. However, unmanned aviation operations differ so much that there is no point in talking about their safety without a sufficient understanding of their nature. Understanding technical, operational and organizational issues is also important since it is necessary to identify the challenges (and solutions) that affect the safety and effectiveness of UA operations, if only to assess whether the current state and availability of unmanned aviation technology allows regulators to precisely determine the safety requirements present.

The main research question of this publication in the scope of public law is whether UA operations can be treated equally alongside manned aviation operations from the point of view of aviation safety regulations? In other words, is an unmanned aircraft simply a new type of aircraft, or is it a more complex system, one of the components of which is an aircraft without a pilot on board?

The first possible take on this is that unmanned aircraft are a new type of aviation activity, so maintaining a uniform regulatory regime for aviation as a whole, including both manned and unmanned aircraft, is justifiable.

A second perspective states that the differences resulting from the lack of a crew on board are so far-reaching that unmanned aviation is a completely new type of activity in itself. Moreover, it is so different from manned aviation that it is necessary to create new safety regulations dedicated to this type of activity.

In both cases, it will be necessary to introduce amendments to existing aviation laws in order to allow for UA technology to grow. These amendments include air traffic regulations or the organization of airspace, which as of now limits UA operations to designated zones only and does not address the capability of carrying out operations at very low altitudes, in airspace in which manned aircraft simply do not operate.

What's more, this publication seeks to identify the main issues related to the development potential of UA and their integration with manned aviation, focusing on the safety aspects of unmanned and manned aviation.

These issues are identified and clarified by analyzing safety regulations and documents that preceded adopting official laws. New technologies require new regulations, but their adoption is not an easy process and must be preceded, in most cases, by analyses, reports, studies, and conceptual and analytical documents. Oftentimes, the process itself is quite innovative – making some new technologies even more disruptive. However, we should bear in mind that aviation safety regulations are quite conservative. The introduction of any regulations other than existing ones (and their mitigation in particular) has to ensure the continuation of at least the current level of safety, if not better. Moreover, meeting most aviation safety requirements can be clearly assessed, since they are regulated in great detail in specialized documents that are based on good practice and research.

On the one hand, this publication focuses on the safety of UA operations on the assumption that safety is a priority and the purpose of safety requirements is to ensure the protection of the overarching values of human life and health. On the other hand, it deals with issues related to all kinds of human concerns posed by this new technology, as seen from the public's viewpoint, i.e. issues related to the protection of the right to privacy or the processing of personal data, the protection of property, liability for damage, insurance, the protection of public security, the capability to carry out autonomous operations, as well as the use of artificial intelligence systems to support these types of operations.

The main research thesis in the field of private law is that it is not possible to unambiguously qualify drones as aircraft. A drone falls within the traditional legal definition of an aircraft (public law); however, if we do recognize a drone as an aircraft, more questions appear as aircraft laws are all based on the assumption that there is a crew on board. In addition, many aspects related to the use of unmanned aircraft remain outside the scope of specific regulations. Therefore, one should follow the general rules, some of which were created in the 1960s or even as early as the 1930s. As current regulations mostly do not recognize drones at all, their scope and enforcement may be unclear or even impossible in some cases. This publication also features an analysis of existing civil liability regulations related to drone classification.

The authors point to a strong integration between public and private law, especially in terms of applying the provisions of public law on the use of drones (including those that ensure the safety of UAS operations) to determine the scope of liability for damages they may cause. These regulations should always be taken into account when determining liability for damages caused by UAS operations. When it comes to strict liability, a better understanding of public law, and in consequence the specifics of drone-related activities, ensures a better understanding of the risks of potential damages that could be caused by specific types of activity. Public law sets the rules for civil liability (especially liability for damages), which are necessary to establish the illegality of a specific action. These regulations not only allow to determine fault (illegality), for example in the case of drone-to-drone collisions, but also to establish fault-based liability of a party, for example, a tech-support provider, as well as assess the possibility of recourse by an insurer or the contribution of the injured party to the occurrence of damage. They also regulate the issue of exemption from liability – for example, in order to prove the exclusive fault of the injured party, the operator should follow the provisions of public law. Moreover, it should be stressed that if an operator is found to have committed a crime, the limitation period for civil claims is extended. Furthermore, being aware of the laws that regulate new types of activity can be useful in interpreting the provisions of public law, particularly those on liability without fault.

Chapter 1 Terminology and classifications

1. Terminological ambiguities

The most commonly used terms for drones are model aircraft, pilotless aircraft, autonomous aircraft, unmanned aircraft (UA), unmanned aircraft system (UAS), unmanned aerial vehicle (UAV), remotely piloted aircraft system (RPAS), remotely piloted aircraft (RPA), or remotely piloted vehicle (RPV).

The word "drone" has not caught on in professional terminology, where it only appears occasionally. Interestingly enough, back in 2015, EASA proposed that the term be used as a basic definition in bills, laws, and regulations concerning unmanned aircraft[23]. However, the organization quickly abandoned this idea and decided to use the term solely for the purpose of communicating with the public[24].

1.1 Etymology

The most common term to describe unmanned aerial vehicles is "drone" – it has been and is continually used in both the media and in numerous research papers. One should note, however, that it is a colloquial word. The English term "drone" means a male bee.

The term drone was first used to refer to honeybees (*Apis mellifera*), an all too familiar species which can be classified into three categories: queens, workers, and drones.[25] To put it simply, the queen has complete control over her hive and is surrounded by helpers. She sends out messages using "messenger bees", which may control many of the hive's actions.

Bearing a slight resemblance to what we know as drones today, a widely known concept in 1918 included so-called "air torpedoes" or "flying bombs" – American maneuvering missiles built with a wooden frame and papier-mâché coating (Kettering Bug).

In 1935, US Admiral William H. Standley saw a British demonstration of the Royal Navy's new remote-control aircraft for target exercise – the DH 82B Queen Bee. After returning home, he ordered Commander Delmer Fahrney to

---

23 EASA A-NPA-2015.

24 EASA, Technical Opinion to A-NPA-2015, p. 5.

25 K. Harris, Drones: Proposed Standards of Liability. Santa Clara High Technology Law Journal, Vol. 31, Issue 1, 2018, p. 99.

develop a similar machine for the American Navy and adopted the name "drone" in tribute to the Queen Bee. The drone could only function under the control of an operator on the ground.[26]

In recent history, when faced with the potential risk of seeing bees become extinct, humans developed drone bees that pollinate flowers. Japanese scientists have transformed these robot insects into artificial pollinators by using a sticky gel and horsehair.[27] It seems that history has come full circle.

What's more, engineers at Harvard's microrobotics laboratory have created a RoboBee microdrone that weighs just 60 mg, the wings of which are capable of performing 120 strokes per second. It is even equipped with a flight control system that stabilizes the work of each wing separately.[28]

"Drone", the oldest and most commonly used word to describe an UAV, was first used in the 1930s[29]. However, the term and its rich history have led to certain doubts when it comes to the use of proper terminology. Even EASA used the word in its 2015 document entitled *Advanced Notice of Proposed Amendment "Introduction of a Regulatory Framework for the Operation of Drones"*[30]. Most recently, the term is seen as unprofessional and is losing popularity as people begin to favor more technical terms.[31] It is no longer used in EU or ICAO documents.[32] EASA also officially dropped the term in favor of another one – "*unmanned*

26 Ibidem, p. 101.

27 The experiment was described in: S. A. Chechetka, Y. Yu, M. Tange I E. Miyako, Materially Engineered Artificial Pollinators. Chem, Vol. 2, Issue 2, 2017, pp. 153–310.

28 Pszczoły roboty zapylą kwiaty, a komary drony będą nas szpiegować (Robo-bees will pollinate flowers and mosquito-drones will spy on us), Rzeczpospolita's article: February 15, 2018: https://www.rp.pl/Plus-Minus/302159928-Pszczoly-roboty-zapyla-kwiaty-a-komary-drony-beda-nas-szpiegowac.html [access: November 1, 2019].

29 L.R. Newcome, Unmanned Aviation: A Brief History of Unmanned Aerial Vehicles, American Institute of Aeronautics and Astronautics, 2004.

30 A-NPA: 2015-10—RMT.0230—18.12.2015.

31 M. Peterson, The UAV and the Current and Future Regulatory Construct for Integration into the National Airspace System. Journal of Air Law and Commerce, Vol. 71, 2006, p. 528.

32 See e.g. Communication from the Commission to the European Parliament and the Council "A new era for aviation. Opening the aviation market to the civil use of remotely piloted aircraft systems in a safe and sustainable manner" COM (2014) 207 final, Brussels, April 8, 2014; ICAO, Unmanned Aircraft Systems (UAS), Cir 328 AN/190, 2011.

aircraft / UA".[33] The term "drone" was seen as implying that the device in question may not necessarily be an aircraft.

1.2 Drones as robots

As time passed, people started to have negative connotations with the word, as it was associated with the use of drones in military operations – this was one of the reasons why the term faded away in favor of more technical terminology[34], but it wasn't the only one. The name seems to imply that the object is not an aircraft but some other type of device[35]. In particular, "drone" may signify a type of robot or a highly automated machine. Such connotations give rise to concern amongst the public, as is common whenever any type of autonomous technology is involved.

The term "robot" has many definitions. While robots are often viewed as machines, they are often associated with having human-like capabilities, such as being aware of their surroundings, or being able to act on their own accord.

The word "robot" was first used in Karel Čapek's 1921 play entitled "Rossumovi Universal Roboti," which tells the story of mechanical men who had been created to work on factory assembly lines and eventually rebelled against their human masters. They got their name from a Czech word that can either mean slave, hard work, or effort.

In 1928, engineer Alan H. Reffel molded the stereotypical features of a robot in his work known as Eric Robot. This became the starting point for classic Hollywood horror films which depicted robots as human-controlled contraptions with stiff, motorized movements, an aluminum body, and a distorted, electronic voice. As rightly pointed out by K. Harris, these pop culture images influenced a very misleading perception of both robots and drones.[36] A drone is a programmed machine that performs tasks with a limited degree of human

---

33 Technical Opinion tto A-NPA 2015–10.

34 M. Peterson, The UAV and the Current and Future Regulatory Construct for Integration into the National Airspace System. Journal of Air Law and Commerce, Vol. 71, 2006, p. 528; https://www.wsj.com/articles/why-some-drone-makers-hate-the-word-drone-and-want-to-change-it-1412821801

35 See B.I. Scott, Terminology, Definitions and Classifications, w: B.I. Scott (red.), The Law of Unmanned Aircraft Systems. An Introduction to the Current and Future Regulation under National, Regional and International Law, Kluwer Law International BV, The Netherlands, 2016, p. 9 and n.

36 Harris, Drones: Proposed Standards of Liability. p. 104.

interaction. However, should drones capable of flying independently be treated as aircraft or as robots? While browsing literature on the subject, one may encounter the opinion that drones are robots that somewhat resemble autonomous cars, which are capable of remaining airborne and perform certain tasks through the use of appropriate software.[37]

With human assistance, a plane can choose its own flight route, estimate airspace conflict, and select its own vectors to guide or track other aircraft. So, what if a drone could select a flight route or an aiming vector on its own? Could a robot or a drone then decide whether to take people's lives or not? If that were the case, who would grant the drone the right to make such a decision? Should autonomous weaponized drones be qualified as drones or robots? This issue concerns autonomous weapons more than drones themselves.[38]

Claiming that artificial intelligence has a certain degree of freedom of choice raises the question of whether it will mimic human thinking. However, in order to be considered fully autonomous, a machine must operate independently – without interference from an operator. In this regard, "robots" are more drone–robot hybrids. Robotics has a limited degree of decision-making capabilities and interactions with the environment, and remains under human control.[39] Robots are commonly perceived as technical devices designed to perform certain motor tasks for humans. They have a specific energy, information, and machine intelligence level i.e. they can achieve operation autonomy, but only in certain environments.[40]

Similar to robots, drones receive commands and, using their central processing unit, act upon them. A robot is a physical shell with the appearance of a mechanical machine. However, if a robot is equipped with an autonomous machine learning algorithm, it cannot be identified as a drone in accordance with the proposed definition.[41]

---

37 David K. Beyer, Donna A. Dulo, Gale A. Townsley, and Stephen S. Wu, Risk, Product Liability Trends, Triggers, and Insurance in Commercial Aerial Robots, WE ROBOT Conference on Legal & Policy Issues Relating to Robotics University of Miami School of Law, April 4 & 5, 2014; S.Wu, Unmanned Vehicles and US Product Liability Law. Journal of Law, Information and Science, Vol. 21, Issue 2, 2012, s.234; R. Kuchta, Trzy przykłady nowych robotów, Robotyka, Warsaw, 2015, p. 10: https://newtech.law/wp-content/uploads/2017/08/Wardynski-i-Wspolnicy_raport-robotyka.pdf [access: October 10, 2019]

38 See https://autonomousweapons.org/ (access: June 16, 2020).

39 Harris, Drones: Proposed Standards of Liability, p. 103.

40 Ibidem.

41 Ibidem, p. 105.

We can often observe a lack of consistency when using the terms "drone" and "robot". This is most likely caused by a lack of knowledge when it comes to using the term "drone" itself.[42]

Considering the above, there are many similarities between drones and robots – especially those that remain under human control with limited decision-making capabilities (not fully autonomous).

Lately, there have been works on creating fully autonomous robots, for example mobile autonomous robots which would explore their environment and independently choose the most efficient routes to their destination points using data from cameras, built-in sensors, laser scanners, and advanced software.[43] It seems that the fine line of differences between autonomous drones and robots is becoming blurred.

1.3. Unmanned aircraft classification

Upon applying various criteria, we can classify unmanned aircraft in the following ways[44]:

Criterion – flight control method:

- Remotely Piloted Aircraft or Remotely Piloted Aircraft System (RPAS) – an aircraft that is piloted and controlled by an operator/pilot;
- Autonomous aircraft – devices that do not allow for pilot intervention during flight. An operator may be present, but they can do nothing to change the flight parameters.

Criterion – type of operation:

- operations within Visual Line of Sight (VLOS) – if the UA remains within an operator's line of sight;
- Beyond Visual Line of Sight (BVLOS) operations – if the UA does not remain within the operator's line of sight; distance plays no role here, as the UA may

---

42 Pszczoły roboty zapylą kwiaty, a komary drony będą nas szpiegować (Robo-bees will pollinate flowers and mosquito-drones will spy on us), Rzeczpospolita's article: February 15, 2018: https://www.rp.pl/Plus-Minus/302159928-Pszczoly-roboty-zapyla-kwiaty-a-komary-drony-beda-nas-szpiegowac.html (access: November 1, 2019).

43 https://automatykab2b.pl/prezentacje/51126-autonomiczne-i-wspolpracujace-roboty-mobilne-mir-przyszlosc-transportu-wewnetrznego (access: June 3, 2020).

44 For more, see A. Masutti, F. Tomasello, International Regulation of Non-Military Drones, Edward Elgar, 2018, p. 50. The authors rightly point out that regulations often refer to one or more criteria, e.g. regulations on VLOS of up to 25 kg.

be nearby, but an obstacle obstructs the operator's view of it and they cannot see it;
- FPV (First Person View) operation – operations with a first-person view. Operations in which the operator controls the UA without maintaining direct eye contact with it, determining its position in the airspace through video data transmitted to them in real time by devices mounted onboard the UA;

Criterion – purpose of use:

- flying model / model aircraft – unmanned aircraft used for recreational or sports purposes;
- UAV – unmanned aircraft used for purposes other than recreation or sports (e.g. commercial purposes); also called models;

Criterion – operating mass:

- UA weighing less than 600 g
- UA weighing less than 25 kg
- UA weighing more than 25 kg and below 150 kg

1.4. Unmanned Aircraft

Nowadays, the term "*unmanned aircraft*" (UA) is gaining popularity and is widely used. It has been officially recommended by ICAO and adopted by the EU and EASA. ICAO uses the term UAV, but as a broad definition including autonomous drones. However, it focuses on regulating only those that fall into the RPA category, since the presence of a pilot is a guarantee of safety. Both ICAO and EASA have ceased to use the term *unmanned aerial vehicle* (UAV) in favor of the term *unmanned aircraft* (UA). Therefore professional terminology hasn't acknowledged the term UAV. Actually, the term used to be quite common. It is even found in Poland's Aviation Law to describe UA. However, the term "UAV" was not widely accepted as, similarly to "drone", it suggested a device that differs from an aircraft. An analysis of ICAO and EASA dossiers indicates that they stopped using the term at around the same time (2005–2007). The main reason for this decision was efforts to standardize terminology with that used by technical organizations that deal with standardization in aviation (EUROCAE, RTCA)[45].

45 Cir. 328, note 1.4.

It should be underlined that an UAV meets the technical requirements necessary for it to be considered an aircraft, as it is a device capable of maintaining flight through the use of forces other than those that bounce air off the ground (Art. 2 point 1 of Poland's Aviation Law Act, Annexes to the Chicago Convention). Therefore, in the scope of public law, a drone is an aircraft intended for use without a pilot on board. In the absence of specific regulations concerning UA, it should meet the requirements for regular aircraft, which in practice is not possible. The century-old system of regulations in the field of civil aviation safety (at an international level, and consequently also at a European and national level) is based on the assumption that there is a flight crew on board, directing or supervising a flight.[46]

Subject literature indicates that only 30% of currently existing regulations in the field of aviation safety are fully applicable to UA, that 54% are partially applicable once necessary changes have been made, and that 16% are not applicable at all.[47]

1.5. Remote-controlled or autonomous?

The broad definition of UA includes both remote-controlled vehicles and those automatically following a pre-programmed route. If a UA flight is carried out by a pilot, then it is referred to as a Remotely Piloted Aircraft (RPA) or a Remotely Piloted Aircraft System (RPAS). It is possible to fly along a pre-programmed route during such flights, but the pilot-in-command always has the possibility of taking full control (automatic flights). Automatic flights must be distinguished from autonomous flights. Unmanned vehicles capable of flying without human involvement (including intervention) are referred to as autonomous aircraft, although this term refers to a type of operation (autonomous operation). Remotely controlled UA are also capable of carrying out certain operations in an autonomous mode, i.e. without a pilot's intervention[48].

ICAO and EASA include both RPAs and autonomous aircraft capable of carrying out operations along a pre-programmed route in their broad definitions of UA. While it can be assumed that remotely controlled UA will be integrated into

---

46 P. Kasprzyk, A. Konert, Bezzałogowe statki powietrzne. Nowa era w dziejach lotnictwa. Nowa era w prawie lotniczym? , księga pamiątkowa XX-lecia Wydziału Prawa i Administracji. Przyszłość prawa, Warsaw, 2017, p. 523.

47 K.P. Valavanis, G.J. Vachtsevanos (eds.), Handbook of Unmanned Aerial Vehicles, Springer International Publishing, 2018, p. 359 and 360.

48 See ICAO 10019, pp. 1–4, JARUS GLOSSARY 0.7, p. 33.

manned aviation in the foreseeable future, the future of autonomous flights is not that clear. For this reason, ICAO documents concerning this topic explicitly narrow the term down to remotely controlled UA[49]. On the other hand, annexes to the Chicago Convention only use the terms RPA/RPAS. EU regulations broadly defined UA as aircraft carrying out or designed to carry out operations without a pilot on board, adding that the definition includes both autonomous and remotely controlled flights[50]. However, executory provisions explicitly stipulate that autonomous operations are only permissible within a specific or certified category. Therefore, in practice, autonomous operations will require prior authorization every time. They must be preceded by a risk analysis, ergo proof that despite the fact that the operation is autonomous, operational safety is still ensured at an acceptable level. In other words, it can be assumed that in the coming years, autonomous flights will only concern those operations carried out as part of research and development projects. EASA's advisory materials explicitly indicate that, at present, no universally accepted standards for autonomous operations have been developed[51]. There are ongoing discussions of such fundamental issues as the concept of autonomy itself or its levels. This discussion doesn't necessarily concern UA in particular, but rather autonomous vehicles in general. Vehicle autonomy, understood as a vehicle's capability to move without human involvement, goes far beyond the issue of automated vehicles operated under direct human supervision[52]. Interestingly, some argue that the development of autonomous vehicle technology and the social acceptance of it, for example, in the field of road transport, are closely related to the social acceptance of the development of unmanned aviation[53]. From the perspective of attempting to regulate UA operational safety, one can put the following thesis forward: unmanned aviation must develop gradually. It is one thing to have an aircraft flying without a crew and maintaining full control over it, but to completely rule out the possibility of human intervention in autonomous flights is an entirely different story. From the perspective of safety, remote-controlled and autonomous operations differ in the fundamental operational tenet itself. Key risk factors are therefore different and require a different approach, also in terms of safety regulations.

---

49 See e.g., Unmanned Aircraft Systems (UAS), Cir 328 AN / 190, note 2.2.

50 EU Regulation 2018/1139, Art. 3, p. 30.

51 See GM1 to UAS.SPEC.050 (1) (b).

52 For more see Autonomiczny Transport Przyszłości. Polish Economic Institute. April 2020.

53 SESAR, Drone outlook study, 2016, p. 26.

For this reason, the issue of autonomous UA is not raised in this publication. This subject would require a separate study. Given the current state of development of unmanned aviation, ensuring human control over remotely controlled aircraft flights remains one of the key elements of ensuring their safe operations. Manned aviation safety regulations should be used as a starting point for drafting safety regulations for unmanned aviation, as long as human control over aircraft is ensured. However, it seems necessary to create new regulations that adequately take into account the nature and risks of autonomous operations[54]. Also, the need to establish integration between manned and unmanned aviation makes widespread autonomous flights a long-term project[55]. Meanwhile, it is still difficult to imagine that the widespread use of drones – having them operate at low altitudes in urban areas – could ever take place without dependence on technology that facilitates such autonomous operations. Still, it remains more of a vision, and rather a distant one, than reality that should be taken into account while drafting safety laws. For this reason, solutions adopted at an EU level that allow for autonomous operations as a special separate category should be perceived as positive. These will allow for testing, research, and development while maintaining a required minimum level of safety. Safety certification will require that necessary competences and risk awareness studies are performed by aviation authorities granting authorization for these types of flights. However, it should be emphasized that regardless of autonomous operations, many issues related to automation will be closely related to the use of remotely controlled UA. Many functions and elements of remotely controlled UA systems are already based on advanced automation[56], such as the support of flight control systems with appropriate software. Carrying out remote-controlled UA flights along pre-programmed routes or mandatory systems that force UA to return home in emergency situations are also a standard.

1.6. The model aircraft concept

The concept of a model aircraft has been used over the years to refer to traditional models that mirror (albeit on a smaller scale) civilian or military aircraft. Due to the relatively limited scale of this phenomenon, as well as the fact that modeling activity usually remains the domain of hobbyist communities and organizations, no specific aviation safety regulations for models have been developed. Over the

---

54 See Autonomiczny Transport Przyszłości. p. 33.

55 K. Dalamagkidis, et al. op. cit., p. 201.

56 B. Custers (ed.), The future of drone use, 2016, p. 41.

years, this branch has grown much like the market for small, unmanned UA has. These are not models of classic manned aircraft anymore, but rather a new category of flying devices that are most often used for hobby, recreational, and sports purposes. Naturally, in the first years of the emerging UA market, the greatest interest in this new technology came from modeling enthusiasts.

The use of the term "model aircraft" as an UA used for recreational purposes can be noted at an international level[57]. These types of UA operations are irrelevant to international air navigation (except for the use of models around airports). However, a tendency to enact separate (simpler) regulations for models and separate (more comprehensive) regulations for UA used for commercial purposes has grown at a national regulatory level. For example, in the USA, the concept of a model aircraft was introduced into aviation safety law in 2012. A model aircraft is defined as "an UA that is capable of sustained flight in the atmosphere, flown within visual line of sight of the person operating the aircraft, and flown for hobby or recreational purposes"[58]. Models can be used based on fairly simple rules that are directly related to this definition. The aforementioned definition was confirmed in 2018 when the obligation to register UA was extended to include UA used for recreational purposes[59]. Poland uses a similar distinction. In 2011, the statutory requirement for having a "pilot model aircraft operator" certificate was replaced by an "operator of an UA used for purposes other than recreation and sports". This distinction was then applied in executory provisions for UA operations. Then, in 2016, separate annexes to these executory provisions were introduced. One concerned UA used for purposes other than recreation and sports – called model aircraft – and the other concerned other types of UA. The EU hasn't adopted such a distinction in its UA regulations. Instead, it has based its definition and approach on the potential risk posed by an operation to third parties and other users. The risk does not depend on the purpose of the operation. However, there are a few exceptions for modeling clubs and aviation associations who use UA, as the purpose of their operations is to carry out recreational, demo, or sports flights.

The distinction based on the operational purpose of an UA was justified in the early stage of UA safety regulation development. EU regulations no longer

57 ICAO Cir 328, note 2.4, ICAO Doc 11019, note 2.3.6.

58 US Congress, Public Law 112-95 112th Congress, FAA Modernization and Reform Act of 2012.

59 US Congress, Public Law 115-254 115th Congress, FAA Modernization and Reform Act of 2018.

distinguish between the purpose of individual operations, as they address most of the risks associated with a given UA operation in great detail. Before such regulations were created, it was possible to differentiate UA according to their use – the use of UA for purposes other than recreation meant that they were being used for business purposes which, for example, could influence how often it is exploited. So, it was justified to introduce higher standards and requirements with regard to such operations. On the other hand, the distinction of different types of flights helps limit possible "scenarios" to situations in which risk is minimized (e.g. through the establishment of no-fly zones, the obligation to maintain minimum distances, etc.).

Anyhow, even EU legislators used the term "model aircraft" before introducing regulations based on operational risk level distinction. Definitions of model aircraft and toy aircraft introduced in 2016 into the Uniform Air Traffic Regulations are great examples[60]. These were introduced to confirm that air traffic rules did not apply to these devices. Model aircraft are "unmanned aircraft, other than toy aircraft, having an operating mass not exceeding limits prescribed by the competent authority, that is capable of sustained flight in the atmosphere and that is used exclusively for display or recreational activities".

1.7. Unmanned Aircraft System

Due to the fact that UA flights are combined of many other elements rather than just the aircraft itself (i.e. a control station/remote-control station – RPS, communications systems, navigation systems, transponders, software, autopilot, etc.) people often use a broader term to describe UAs. The term is "*unmanned aircraft system*" (UAS)[61]. The evolution of this terminology can be observed in international[62] and European[63] documents. However, Polish documents still mostly use

60 COMMISSION IMPLEMENTING REGULATION (EU) 2016/1185 of 20 July 2016 amending Implementing Regulation (EU) No 923/2012 as regards the update and completion of the common rules of the air and operational provisions regarding services and procedures in air navigation (SERA Part C) and repealing Regulation (EC) No 730/2006, UE Journal of Laws, L 196 from July 21st, 2016.

61 P. Kasprzyk, A. Konert, Bezzałogowe statki powietrzne. Nowa era w dziejach lotnictwa. Nowa era w prawie lotniczym?, p. 525.

62 See e.g. Unmanned Aircraft Systems (UAS), Cir 328 AN/190. In 2011, ICAO introduced the term "RC Aircraft" to the Circular 328 – RPA, which is part of the "Remotely Piloted Aircraft System" – RPAS.

63 See e.g. EASA document NPA-2017-05.

the term "unmanned aerial vehicle" (UAV)[64]. Extending the terms "unmanned aircraft" and "remotely piloted aircraft" so they include the term "system" may have legal consequences. First of all, a system includes several components and it would be necessary to determine which of them are part of the aircraft itself and which are not. This is related to legal regulations in the field of airworthiness standards. Second of all, different parts of a system may be located in different places, including in different countries. So, which state should be competent to oversee such a system, including the creation of safety rules etc.? Moreover, individual components of such a system can be easily and quickly removed and replaced, unlike in manned aviation. Therefore, should a system undergo a certification process every time a component is swapped or replaced etc.? [65]It seems that without defining a "system", a legal loophole arises which may result in practical problems, including those related to private law and civil liability for damages caused by such a "system".

The European Commission's Implementing Regulation (EU) 2019/947[66] defines a "privately-built UAS" as a UAS assembled or manufactured for the builder's own use, not including a UAS assembled from sets of parts available on the market as a single ready-to-assemble kit.

Apart from the issue of using UA for recreational purposes, the adopted direction in which safety regulations concerning UA operations are being developed is quite clear – UA are recognized as aircraft. However, due to the fact that the system that regulates aircraft safety practically never took into account the possibility of flying without a crew on board, a significant part of UA regulations need to be developed from scratch, i.e. taking into account the characteristics and development of this new technology. The best example of this is the definition of the Unmanned Aircraft System, which is already commonly used in UA regulations.

The concept of an Unmanned Aircraft System (UAS) or a Remotely Piloted Aircraft System (RPAS) does not just refer to UA as devices capable of flight,

---

64 See e.g. Report of the Civil Aviation Authority of 2013 http://ulc.gov.pl/pl/drony/409-raporty/2739-raport-o-aktualny-stanie-prawnym-odnoszacym-sie-do-bezzalogowych-statkow-powietrznych [access May 20, 2017]. For detailed comments on the problems in defining unmanned aircrafts, see B.I. Scott, Terminology, Definitions and Classifications, in: B.I. Scott (ed.), The Law of Unmanned Aircraft Systems. An Introduction to the Current and Future Regulation under National, Regional and International Law, Kluwer Law International BV, The Netherlands, 2016, p. 9 et seq.

65 M. Huttunen, Unmanned, Remotely Piloted or Something Else?, p. 364.

66 Journal of Laws L 152/45, June 11, 2019.

but also includes the necessary elements that are functionally interlinked with UA. These elements are referred to as "devices necessary for maintaining remote control of unmanned aircraft"[67]. In particular, this concerns a remote-control station as well as a command and control link system that ensures data transfer between the control station and a UA[68]. However, a UAS understood in this way may also include other elements, such as[69]:

1. navigation devices that provide a UA's location,
2. devices used to contact air traffic services,
3. emergency systems activated in emergency situations (e.g. parachutes),
4. devices that support UA takeoffs and landings,
5. data quality monitoring systems,
6. flight support systems, such as on-board computers or an autopilot.

67 Art. 2 point 1 of the EC Implementing Regulation 2019/947.
68 ICAO Doc 11019, note 2.2.
69 ICAO Doc 11019, note 2.6.

Chapter 2 Development of regulations in the field of unmanned aviation safety: Differences between manned and unmanned aviation

1. Introduction

The term aircraft is an essential component in any definition in aviation, and although the concept has not been specified at the level of international agreements, the Chicago Convention features a commonly accepted definition. Aircraft, as defined in Poland's Aviation Law Act, are devices capable of sustaining flight through the use of forces other than those that bounce air off the ground[70]. This key definition in terms of aviation law has been transposed into both EU and national laws[71]. Over the years, the development of the aviation industry and aviation law itself brought about the need for the introduction of detailed aircraft classification regulations. These serve specific purposes and differentiate aircraft in terms of their technical characteristics, operational purposes, or even by the means through which they generate lift. For example, for the purposes of aircraft certification and production, Annex 7 to the Chicago Convention distinguishes what are called large aircraft (Maximum Take-Off Mass – MTOM over 5,700 kg), small aircraft (MTOM between 750 kg and 5,700 kg), and helicopters[72]. With time, aviation authorities responsible for aircraft certification further refined these classifications. But one issue still remains – existing classification systems do not distinguish between manned and UA. Why? The answer is simple. Such a distinction has not been needed so far. It wasn't until UA and their use in the military that the technology began to grow. As mentioned in the introduction, civil entities quickly saw the possibility of adapting this new technology to even more areas. Their attempts, however, soon encountered several fundamental limitations.

70 M. Żylicz, Prawo lotnicze międzynarodowe, europejskie i krajowe, Warsaw, 2011, p. 25.

71 Art. 3 point 28 of the EU Regulation 2018/1138, Art. 2 point 1 of the Aviation Law.

72 See Announcement No. 10 of the President of the Polish Civil Aviation Authority, Journal of Laws, April 16, 2013, item 58.

First, they were *technical limitations* resulting from the level of development of UA technology. This technology is controversial and still gives rise to more questions than it does answers. Suffice it to point out that there is no data on the safety of UA operations, as there are no uniform standards for reporting dangerous events involving UA. Information that is available is often based on fragmentary data (e.g. from military UA operations) and indicates that most UA accidents are caused by technical errors. This situation mirrors the early days of manned aviation. In its case, however, the development of aviation technology and regulations brought about a reduction in the number of accidents caused by technical issues. To put it simply, one can say that UA technology is still taking its first baby steps. This is a rather widely known concept in aviation, whereby the introduction of any new technology causes unforeseeable problems[73]. In manned aviation, this applies at most to new models (types) of aircraft being brought into service and usually results from the implementation of some sort of new solutions. In the case of unmanned aviation, this applies to the technology in general, and as such, to the entire UA sector. There are no technical reliability standards for UA. This is not just about how reliable UA are in maintaining flight. In this regard, we could apply the same standards or requirements that are imposed on regular, manned aircraft. It's the issues that arise from the lack of crew on board that are key. There are at least two critical elements deriving from the nature of UA – the first is the need to ensure constant communications between the pilot, the control station, and the airborne aircraft. The second is motion detection and collision avoidance systems. Any further limitations result from, or are interdependent with, technological limitations.

Social limitations result from social acceptance (or a lack thereof) of UA technology, the development of which brings not only benefits but hazards as well. It is quite commonly indicated that legislators should take into account social concerns primarily related to safety, but also to the protection of privacy or even (and perhaps above all) the protection against noise pollution[74]. Research has shown that the noise generated by medium-sized UA can be much more of a nuisance than that generated by road traffic[75]. Therefore, society's attitudes toward the negative effects of UA technology remain uncertain. Widespread social

---

73 https://www.altair.com.pl/magazines/article?article_id=4176 [access: February 28, 2020].

74 https://www.easa.europa.eu/newsroom-and-events/press-releases/regulators-and-industry-unite-need-address-societal-concerns [access: February 28, 2020].

75 https://arc.aiaa.org/doi/10.2514/6.2017-4051 [access: February 28, 2020].

acceptance of UA technology depends on whether the benefits of this technology outweigh the negative consequences[76]. This statement is confirmed in practice – an increase in levels of social anxiety related to the use of drones can be linked with events like accidents or incidents. For example, a study conducted in England after the Gatwick airport incident (the airport was closed during the busy holiday season after its area was breached by unknown drones) showed that two-thirds of respondents were primarily concerned about the use of drones for illegal purposes[77]. This study seems to confirm another concept, one that is extremely important in terms of developing regulations on new technologies – namely, levels of social acceptance of accidents are lower for new technologies. Road accident statistics are the best example here. These have been observed and widely commented on in the area of automation in road vehicles[78]. Therefore, it is extremely important, especially in terms of social perception, that UA regulations ensure operational safety at a socially acceptable level.

Social restrictions are closely related to **legal restrictions**. Every new technology raises the same questions regarding its applications for business purposes. The lack of any principles regulating the rules of use of a new technology has some benefits, but these are often short-lived. Their development also depends on whether a given legal system recognizes (in the sphere of public regulation) the principle of "everything which is not forbidden is allowed". The lack of a regulatory framework undoubtedly allows for the development of a new technology. However, since widespread application is a condition for economic viability, and thus development, it requires a fairly clear legal framework. Therefore, when regulating a new technology or activities related to its use, legislators are forced to find a balance between what is acceptable and what is necessary to push development forward. It is obvious that the development of a new technology cannot take place at the expense of lowering levels of safety, i.e. preventing accidents in which someone may die or become injured. There are also other issues that need to be taken into account, such as public safety, protection of privacy, or the already mentioned protection against noise pollution and other annoyances. Due to the adopted purpose and scope of this study, further considerations are

---

76 A. Masutti, F. Tomasello, op. cit., p. 29. For more, see R. Bartsch, J. Coyne, K. Gray, Drones in Society, 2017.

77 https://www.pwc.co.uk/press-room/press-releases/public-concerns-remain-a-barrier-to-drone-adoption-pwc-research.html

78 See e.g. M. Maurer et al. Autonomous Driving. Technical, Legal and Social Aspects, 2016.

limited to issues related to safety. A common feature of both manned and unmanned aviation is that machines involved in such operations are inherently dangerous to their surrounding environment. An aircraft in flight constantly poses the risk of causing damage. The main difference here is that manned aviation has had decades to evolve, and as a result has become the safest means of transport. There is no doubt that we should draw conclusions from this process and use them for creating regulations to be applied to unmanned aviation. Quite naturally, it was manned aviation regulations that became the reference point for regulating unmanned aviation. This is mainly due to the fact that every UA meets the basic criteria to be classified as an aircraft. After all, they are devices capable of sustaining flight through the use of forces other than those that bounce air off the ground. Nevertheless, this rather simple fact carries with it the following consequences. In the absence of specific regulations regarding UA operations, they should meet the requirements applicable to all aircraft in terms of such issues as airworthiness, personnel requirements, operational requirements, or air traffic procedures. However, time has shown that this is not possible. The century-old system of civil aviation safety regulations is based on the assumption that there is always a crew on board an aircraft, directing or supervising its flight. Moreover, safety requirements are primarily aimed at ensuring the safety of passengers in aviation, which is achieved by applying the highest safety standards possible, such as costly and lengthy processes of aircraft or equipment certification. Therefore, it is not possible to carry out a UA flight in accordance with the same regulations, which were developed for aircraft with a crew on board. It is necessary to establish detailed solutions regarding a number of technical and operational issues so that unmanned flights (or autonomous flights) can become a reality. One of the goals of this publication is to identify these issues. However, the basic safety requirements that are applicable today remain the reference point here. Further parts of this publication will present basic aviation safety regulations and legal trends related to their development. Knowing how aviation safety systems work allows us to compare their requirements with the basic differences between manned and unmanned aviation. In turn, this allows for a better understanding of the direction in which UA safety regulations should be developed. It is always considered an added value to refer to whatever research is available to better illustrate the essence of a topic. It is estimated that the currently existing aviation safety regulations are[79]:

79 K. Dalamagkidis, et al. On Integrating Unmanned Aircraft Systems into the National Airspace System, 2012, p. 162, reference to a 2007 US study.

- 30% applicable to unmanned aircraft;
- 54% applicable to unmanned aircraft after necessary changes have been made;
- 16% completely inapplicable to unmanned aircraft.

2. Regulations in the field of aviation safety

Aviation safety regulations are complex, multiplanar and shaped on many levels. They are based on various sources of law (international, EU, and national) and have different subjective and objective scopes of application[80]. In addition, they are highly detailed in their reference to organizational, technical, and operational issues. Further parts of this publication present the general structure of these provisions and the assumptions behind detailed regulations. We can start by saying that aviation safety regulations are intended to regulate all aviation activities. Broadly speaking, these regulations apply to the following areas:

1. design, production, and certification of aircraft and any equipment or systems installed on them;
2. aviation personnel competences – including knowledge, skills, and experience requirements for persons involved in aviation activities;
3. technical and operational aircraft use and any organizational activities related to this;
4. use of airspace – including airspace organization, air traffic procedures, and air traffic service activities;
5. activities related to airports, i.e. their construction, equipment, operations, and staffing;
6. supervision of aviation activities through product and organization certification systems as well as personnel licensing;
7. air accident prevention – including preventive action, air accident investigations, air incident reporting, and aviation safety management.

2.1. International regulations

Aviation is by all means an international activity. This is why international regulations are essential in creating public law regulations that relate to aviation. The basic system of treaty law which regulates public law issues in aviation is based on the Convention on International Civil Aviation of 1944, more commonly

80 See M. Żylicz, op. cit., p. 26.

known as the Chicago Convention[81]. It established the International Civil Aviation Organization (ICAO) and defined its broad scope of activities. One of the primary responsibilities of ICAO member states is to facilitate international air navigation and to improve its efficiency and safety by following, whenever possible, international safety standards and recommendations provided by the organization[82]. We can find these Standards and Recommended Practices (SARPs) in the form of annexes to the Chicago Convention. As of today, there are 19 of them.

1. Annex 1 – Personnel Licensing,
2. Annex 2 – Rules of the Air,
3. Annex 3 – Meteorological Service for International Air Navigation,
4. Annex 4 – Aeronautical Charts,
5. Annex 5 – Units of Measurement to be Used in Air and Ground Operations,
6. Annex 6 – Operation of Aircraft,
7. Annex 7 – Aircraft Nationality and Registration Marks,
8. Annex 8 – Airworthiness of Aircraft,
9. Annex 9 – Facilitation,
10. Annex 10 – Aeronautical Telecommunications,
11. Annex 11 – Air Traffic Services,
12. Annex 12 – Search and Rescue,
13. Annex 13 – Aircraft Accident and Incident Investigation,
14. Annex 14 – Aerodromes
15. Annex 15 – Aeronautical Information Services,
16. Annex 16 – Environmental Protection,
17. Annex 17 – Security: Safeguarding International Civil Aviation Against Acts of Unlawful Interference,
18. Annex 18 – The Safe Transport of Dangerous Goods by Air,
19. Annex 19 – Safety Management.

The legal nature of ICAO SARPs is being covered by different sources[83]. Without going into details, it is sufficient to point out that only the standards are binding,

81 Convention on International Civil Aviation signed on December 7, 1944 in Chicago, ratified by Poland, Journal of Laws of 1959, No. 35, item 212 as amended.

82 This obligation is provided for in Art. 12 of the Chicago Convention, and Art. 37 regulates the procedure of adopting standards and recommendations.

83 For more on ICAO standards and recommendations, see M. Milde, Essential Air and Space Law, 2012, p. 169.

while the adoption of any recommendations is left to the discretion of member states. Therefore, national legislators who follow the principle of compliance with international laws should take the standards established by ICAO into account when adopting aviation regulations, at least when it comes to international aviation. However, any country may derogate from these standards, provided that the organization is notified about this in advance. The main problem with SARPs relates to compliancy. The ICAO, being a specialized agency of the United Nations, has limited powers to supervise whether the SARPs it introduces are properly implemented and complied with. Therefore, the international community undertakes activities such as audits to help member states comply with ICAO standards[84]. Although the results of these audits cannot be the basis for ICAO to impose any sanctions, some countries use them in regard to air carriers from countries subject to such audits as part of safety assessment activities. Despite these difficulties, the harmonization of worldwide aviation safety standards is undoubtedly ICAO's greatest achievement. The standards and recommendations established by this organization are a reference point for national legislators creating their own aviation laws.

That being said, one should note that the competences of national legislators in European Union Member States regarding aviation safety issues are rather limited. This is because of the process of transferring competences in the field of regulating aviation safety to the European Communities, which has been in motion since 2002. It should be emphasized that one of the main arguments for introducing aviation safety legislations at an EU level was the belief that the implementation of ICAO's SARPs would be more effective and beneficial if they were to be adopted at an EU level, and not at a national level.

The aims and objectives of the Organization are to develop the principles and techniques of international air navigation and foster the planning and development of international air transport so as to:

- Ensure the safe and orderly growth of international civil aviation throughout the world;
- Encourage the arts of aircraft design and operation for peaceful purposes;

84 The Universal Safety Oversight Audit Programme is mandatory audits in ICAO Member States, the purpose of which is to check the effectiveness of the implementation of the most important safety requirements resulting from ICAO standards. For more, see M. Bujnowski, Bezpieczeństwo lotnictwa cywilnego, Aspekty współpracy międzynarodowej, 2016, p. 106.

- Encourage the development of airways, airports, and air navigation facilities for international civil aviation;
- Meet the needs of the people of the world for safe, regular, efficient, and economical transport;
- Prevent economic waste caused by unreasonable competition;
- Ensure that the rights of contracting States are fully respected and that every contracting State has a fair opportunity to operate international airlines.

The above-mentioned objectives are still valid when unmanned aviation is concerned. The Chicago Convention also addressed unmanned aviation and to be precise "pilotless aircraft". Article 8 considers the pilotless aircraft operations. It states that "no aircraft capable of being flown without a pilot shall be flown without a pilot over the territory of a contracting State without the special authorization by that State and in accordance with the terms of such authorization. Each contracting State undertakes to insure that the flight of such aircraft without a pilot in regions open to civil aircraft shall be so controlled to obviate danger to civil aircraft".

The Chicago Convention also focuses on international aspect of the operations requiring a flight plan to be filled when the flight crosses the international borders[85] and the documents required when aircraft is engaged in international navigation such as certificate of registration, certificate of airworthiness, licenses for each crew member, journey log book, aircraft radio station license, passenger list, and manifest and detailed declarations of cargo[86].

The fast development of the new unmanned aviation branch introduced the need for distinction between the traditional approach to certification regarding the unmanned aviation. It also had its impact on ICAO's consideration of unmanned operations. ICAO's Standards and Recommended Practices regulate the Remotely Piloted Aircraft System (RPAS) operating in the Certified Category of operations where the full integration with conventional Instrumental Flight Procedure (IFR) traffic is expected. These are the operations when the obligations are similar to those for manned aircraft, including the documentation and certification. Those operations are meant to be conducted in the international IFR operations, controlled airspace, and aerodromes and aims for Remotely Piloted Aircraft to operate in the same airspace as manned aircraft in a predictable

85 Article 2 of the Chicago Convention.

86 Article 28 of the Chicago Convention.

manner and be cooperative like any other airspace users to support the global interoperability.

The certified category of RPAS operations is assumed to be covered by the Annexes to the Chicago Convention. Each Annex is or will be amended in order to cover specific elements of RPAS-related requirements. To name a few, Annex 1 Personnel Licensing to cover Remote Pilot License aspects, Annex 10: Aeronautical Telecommunications to cover C2 link and Detect and Avoid systems (DAA), and Annex 19 to cover Safety Management System for RPAS operators and operations. All 19 Annexes covering legacy aviation have also elements applicable to RPAS. ICAO in its early approach to the Remotely Piloted Aircraft Systems has put emphasis on cross-border operations having in mind the international aspect of the unmanned flights. Taking this fact into consideration, ICAO was focused mostly on large aircraft. The changing number of operations of smaller Unmanned Aircraft Systems (UAS) and generating different level of risks – Medium risk in the Specific Category and Low risk in Open Category – resulted in the establishment of ICAO Model UAS Regulations. It is worth noting that the Open, Specific, and Certified category differs in details from the requirements and definitions of respective categories in the European regulations[87]. However in general it is the same risk and operation-based approach to divide different level of operations based on risk.

The 39th Session of ICAO Assembly[88] has confirmed the leadership role of ICAO to develop guidance for harmonized UAS regulations and to develop UAS awareness and educational campaigns for users. The 13th Air Navigation Conference was also essential to establish the new role of ICAO in addressing UAS-related issues. The working paper 5 regarding very low altitude operations[89] provided recommendations for the Conference to:

- request ICAO to continue serving as the global facilitator and forum for States, industry, academia, and other interested stakeholders in the development of the UTM system, including by developing guidance for the identification, structuring, and implementation of necessary financing mechanisms such as public–private partnerships;

87 Commission Implementing Regulation (EU) 2019/947 of 24 May 2019 on the rules and procedures for the operation of unmanned aircraft.

88 39th ICAO Assembly held in September 2016.

89 https://www.icao.int/Meetings/anconf13/Documents/WP/wp_005_en.pdf [access: June 01, 2022].

- request ICAO to continue developing provisions for the proper harmonization and implementation of regulations on UAS;
- urge States to provide ICAO with dedicated financial and personnel support to undertake the expanded work program associated with UAS operations that remain outside of the international instrument flight rules (IFR) framework, with the development of the UTM system, and with other low altitude operations; and
- request ICAO to continue conducting awareness and educational activities amongst users, and to facilitate the exchange of information amongst States regarding their UAS regulations.

The 40th Session of ICAO Assembly reassured the need to accelerate full regulatory framework for UAS and UTM and to develop provisions and guidance material for safety risks of unauthorized presence of UA near aerodromes[90].

The ICAO's objectives concerning the ICAO Model UAS Regulations are:

- to harmonize the regulations
- to safely coordinate integration of UAS activities, and
- to assist ICAO Member States.

The ICAO Model UAS Regulations establish operational requirements for UA operations. Part 101 covers requirements for the Open Category operations and Part 102 for the Specific Category (applies if UA is operated other than in accordance with Part 101). Part 149 regulates the Approved Aviation Organisations (AAO) certification. ICAO has drafted other documents as part of ICAO Model UAS Regulations, such as Advisory Circulars[91] and Guidance Materials on U-AID and UTM. When guidelines on UTM are concerned, the *Unmanned Aircraft Systems Traffic Management (UTM) – A Common Framework with Core Principles for Global Harmonization, Edition 3* document is worth noting. This document provides framework and capabilities of a typical UTM system to States that are considering the implementation of UTM system. It lists the UTM principles, list of services, gaps, issues, and challenges. Few of the key assumptions that ICAO has provided in the document are:

90 Report on Technical Commission (A40-WP/609), https://www.icao.int/Meetings/a40/Documents/WP/wp_609_en.pdf [access: June 01, 2022].

91 AC 101-1, AC 102-1, AC 102-37

- Through UTM civil aviation authorities (CAAs) and ANSPs will be able to provide real-time information (…) directly or through a UTM service provider (USP).
- The primary means of communication and coordination between the ANSP(s), UAS operators, and remote pilots will be through a distributed network of highly automated systems and not between pilots and air traffic controllers via voice communication.
- In the immediate/near term, UTM is considered a separate system with an interface to ATM, while in the long term integration and potential convergence with ATM.

However there also few GAPS identified by ICAO such as:

- Airspace classification.

The documents states that the current airspace classification scheme as developed for manned aviation may not effectively support visual line-of-sight (VLOS) or BVLOS operations. This gap includes the potential modification of current classes of airspace or potentially creating new classes of airspace to accommodate the range of needs brought by UAS operations.

- -Rules of the Air.

Rules of the Air which specify flight rules, right-of-way, altitude above people and obstructions, distance from obstacles and types of flight rules, all of which, as written, are incompatible with the intended operations within UTM systems.

- -Operational procedures.

Procedures specific to the UTM system, including normal, contingency, and emergency scenarios, are needed. Such procedures would need to be harmonized with ATM systems whenever UAS operations are planned.

- -Interface between UTM and ATM.

There is a need to develop procedures and adequate tools to ensure the sharing of information, the interoperability of the two systems, and to identify roles, responsibilities, and limitations.

- -Communications.

Remote pilot interfaces as well as capabilities and performance requirements for communications with the UTM system must be developed. These include the ability to interface/communicate with ATC and pilots of manned aircraft.

ATC communication link type (e.g. VHF, telephone, data link); ATC communication link status[92].

The document stressed out as well that the UTM as a concept is still under development and the guidelines presented in the document are intended to support States in the implementation of the UTM systems. However the document itself shall be considered as a living document and will be subject to update with further developments in the UTM domain.

ICAO as an international organization has a paramount role in setting the path for world's unified regulations. It organizes the drone-focused event – Drone Enable, which is the UAS Industry Symposium gathering key stakeholders from industry, academia, government, and international organizations in the unmanned aviation sector to come together to exchange best practices, lessons learned, research material and discuss challenges related to the introduction of unmanned aircraft systems (UAS) and UAS traffic management (UTM). Every symposium is focused on different vital aspects of drone integration into the global aviation framework. In 2021 stakeholders presented the advancements in the UTM framework and showcased the commercial and non-commercial activities regarding UAS[93].

ICAO also work in specialized foras to support RPAS and UAS-related developments. The ICAO Panel, The Remotely Piloted Aircraft Systems Panel (RPASP), coordinates and develops ICAO Standards and Recommended Practices (SARPs), Procedures and Guidance material for remotely piloted aircraft systems (RPAS), to facilitate a safe, secure, and efficient integration of remotely piloted aircraft (RPA) into non-segregated airspace and aerodromes.

The RPAS Panel supports and collaborates with other expert groups, prepares studies and develops provisions to facilitate the safe, secure, and efficient integration of RPA into non-segregated airspace and aerodromes while maintaining the existing level of safety for manned aviation[94].

However the Unmanned Aircraft Systems Advisory Group (UAS-AG) established in 2015 supports the Secretariat in developing guidance material and expedites the development of provisions to be used by States to regulate

92 More: Unmanned Aircraft Systems Traffic Management (UTM) – A Common Framework with Core Principles for Global Harmonization, Edition 3.

93 https://www.icao.int/meetings/DRONEENABLE4/Pages/default.aspx

94 https://www.icao.int/safety/UA/Pages/Remotely-Piloted-Aircraft-Systems-Panel-(RPASP).aspx

unmanned aircraft systems (UAS), with its industry and international partners, as well as the Member States[95].

2.2. European Union Regulations

Until recently, Regulation (EC) No 216/2008 of the European Parliament and of the Council of 20 February 2008 on common rules in the field of civil aviation and establishing a European Aviation Safety Agency[96] (the so-called basic regulation) was the most basic legal act for European aviation law. The European Commission (EC) issued a number of implementing regulations covering individual aspects of aviation activity based on this regulation. Regulation 216/2008 was later replaced with Regulation (EU) 2018/1139 of the European Parliament and of the Council of 4 July 2018 on common rules in the field of civil aviation and establishing a European Union Aviation Safety Agency[97].

The main objective of these EU legislations is to establish and maintain a high and uniform level of civil aviation safety in Europe. Additional goals include promoting profitability in regulatory and certification processes and avoiding the duplication of efforts made at national and European levels. These goals are to be achieved primarily through effective legislation, i.e. provisions regulating aviation safety applied uniformly by all aviation authorities. To ensure this, the European Union established an independent European Union Aviation Safety Agency (EASA). The Agency's main task is to assist the EC in matters related to aviation safety, especially during legislative processes. Basically, this comes down to preparing executory provision drafts with regard to the basic regulation (in the form of so-called opinions) and supplementing materials necessary for the application of executory provisions (in the form of so-called acceptable means of compliance – AMC – and guidance materials - GM). To ensure the uniform application of these rules, EASA also conducts standardization inspections among Member States. The Agency has also been entrusted with some competences previously exercised by Member States' individual aviation authorities, although the vast majority of activities under the basic regulation and implementing regulations remain within their competences. Still, EASA is the competent body in cases where this is justified by the principle of proportionality. And so, the main "operational" competence of the Agency is, for example, issuing certificates

95 https://www.icao.int/safety/UA/Pages/Unmanned-Aircraft-Systems-Advisory-Group-(UAS-AG).aspx

96 OJEU L 079 of March 19, 2008.

97 OJEU L 212 of August 22, 2018.

(and conducting certification processes) for aviation products such as aircraft, engines, or propellers. A type certificate issued by EASA confirms that a given aviation product meets the specific safety requirements detailed in the so-called certification specifications defined by EASA for individual categories of aviation products.

Currently, European legislation regulates all the aspects of aviation activities that are related to civil aviation safety. As mentioned earlier, the EU started introducing these in 2002. An implementing regulation concerning design, production, and certification of aviation products and aircraft maintenance services was the first to be enforced. Subsequent regulations related to issues such as personnel licensing and the operational use of aircraft. Later, regulations in the fields of aerodrome activity, air traffic procedures, and air traffic services, including air traffic controller licensing, were also introduced. Together with the AMC guidelines published by EASA, the implementing regulations adopted by the EC on the basis of the basic regulation form a comprehensive and detailed regulatory system of aviation safety. The most important of the implementing regulations are listed below:

1. Commission Regulation (EU) No 748/2012 of 3 August 2012 laying down implementing rules for the airworthiness and environmental certification of aircraft and related products, parts and appliances, as well as for the certification of design and production organizations[98];
2. Commission Regulation (EU) No 1321/2014 of 26 November 2014 on the continuing airworthiness of aircraft and aeronautical products, parts, and appliances, and on the approval of organizations and personnel involved in these tasks[99];
3. Commission Regulation (EU) No 1178/2011 of 3 November 2011 laying down technical requirements and administrative procedures related to civil aviation aircrew pursuant to Regulation (EC) No 216/2008 of the European Parliament and of the Council[100];
4. Commission Regulation (EU) No 965/2012 of 5 October 2012 laying down technical requirements and administrative procedures related to air

98 OJEU L 224 of August 21, 2012 as amended.
99 OJEU L 362 of December 17, 2014 as amended.
100 OJEU L 311 of November 25, 2011 as amended.

operations pursuant to Regulation (EC) No 216/2008 of the European Parliament and of the Council[101];
5. Commission Regulation (EU) No 139/2014 of 12 February 2014 laying down requirements and administrative procedures related to aerodromes pursuant to Regulation (EC) No 216/2008 of the European Parliament and of the Council[102];
6. Commission Implementing Regulation (EU) No 923/2012 of 26 September 2012 laying down the common rules of the air and operational provisions regarding services and procedures in air navigation[103];
7. Commission Implementing Regulation (EU) 2017/373 of 1 March 2017 laying down common requirements for providers of air traffic management/air navigation services and other air traffic management network functions and their oversight[104];
8. Commission Regulation (EU) 2015/340 of 20 February 2015 laying down technical requirements and administrative procedures relating to air traffic controllers' licenses and certificates pursuant to Regulation (EC) No 216/2008 of the European Parliament and of the Council[105];
9. Commission Regulation (EU) No 452/2014 of 29 April 2014 laying down technical requirements and administrative procedures related to air operations of third country operators pursuant to Regulation (EC) No 216/2008 of the European Parliament and of the Council.[106]

However, it must be noted that the abovementioned regulations do not apply to UA. They were adopted on the basis of basic regulation 216/2008, which places unmanned aircraft weighing up to 150 kg beyond the EU's (EASA's) competences. It was only with the introduction of the new basic regulation 2018/1139 that it was possible to enact provisions that would regulate UA operations. The following chapters of this publication present how EU law has evolved in this area. In order to better understand the new basic regulation, it is necessary to consider the broader context of European safety regulations.

Ultimately, EU regulations regulate all aspects of aviation activities related to aviation safety in a detailed and comprehensive manner. What is important

101 OJEU L 296 of October 25, 2012 as amended.
102 OJEU L 44 of February 14, 2014 as amended.
103 OJEU L 281 of October 13, 2012 as amended.
104 OJEU L 62 of March 8, 2017 as amended.
105 OJEU UE L 63 of March 6, 2015 as amended.
106 OJEU L 133 of May 6, 2014 as amended.

is that the Chicago Convention, or rather its Annexes, are the basis for both the basic regulation(s) and implementing regulations. To simplify the issue, one could say that the basic regulation allowed for the EU to take over the obligation to implement international aviation standards and recommendations (resulting from the Chicago Convention) from Member States. However, the EU itself cannot accede to the Convention as it is not a country. The international community is closely observing the aviation safety system adopted at an EU level, which constitutes a unique supranational aviation safety organization[107].

The basic assumption of EU regulations related to aviation safety is that any aviation activity involves aircraft and other technical devices, aviation personnel, and aviation organizations. Therefore, these provisions mainly concern aviation products, including their design, production, rules of use and maintenance, as well as persons and organizations involved in these areas. The regulations also define personnel and organizational requirements related to the operation of aircraft. When it comes to aviation products such as aircraft, engines, propellers, and other aviation equipment, all of these must be evaluated from the point of view of aviation safety, which is later confirmed with the issuing of a so-called type certificate. The certification process diligently checks whether a product meets the safety requirements described in the detailed specifications. These specifications are based on previous experiences and assume a specific level of technical reliability. In simple terms, reliability is measured by the failure-free operation of a device (a ratio of the number of failures or incidents it has to the number of flight hours it operates). Also, each product already in use should have an appropriate document confirming its compliance with the previously approved type certificate. For example, with regard to aircraft, every one of them should have an airworthiness certificate, the validity of which depends on periodic airworthiness reviews. Aviation personnel are also subject to certain conditions. Both maintenance staff (mechanics) and personnel involved in flight operations (flight personnel, air traffic controllers, instructors) are required to meet specific requirements related to their knowledge and skills. In most cases, an appropriate license is a confirmation of meeting these requirements. In the case of organizations providing air services, it is assumed that any organization intending to carry out economic activity is subject to certification. Certification is the process during which aviation authorities check if an organization complies with all aviation safety regulations. If so, the organization is granted an appropriate

107 For more, see M. Ratajczyk, Regional Aviation Safety Organizations. Enhancing Air Transport Safety through Regional Cooperation, 2015.

certificate at the end of the process. As one of the basic requirements for obtaining a certificate, an organization must develop detailed operational instructions regulating the creation and operation of an internal management system. A supervisory authority, prior to issuing a relevant certificate, later approves these instructions. In addition, organizations are required to develop internal safety management and compliance (with regulations and internal procedures) monitoring systems. A holder of a certificate is subject to constant supervision by the competent aviation authority, the purpose of which is to ensure that the holder complies with all the aviation safety regulation requirements during the certificate's validity period.

The provisions discussed above are mainly of a regulatory nature. Safety is ensured by introducing detailed rules for undertaking and conducting aviation activities. The EU also adopted regulations on broadly understood safety management[108]. These are, first and foremost, regulations on air accident investigations carried out by independent state commissions, the purpose of which is to improve air transport safety. Safety recommendations resulting from accident investigations often provide an impetus to change regulatory provisions, similar to provisions on safety management and especially the obligation to report aviation incidents. Reporting incidents related to aviation safety allows for the identification of potential risk before an air accident occurs.

Finally, one must not forget the role of national law in the field of aviation safety. Due to the transfer of competences in this respect to the EU, the role played by national law is limited in Member States. However, it should be emphasized that national legislators have exclusive competences when regulating operations conducted by aircraft that are not subject to EU regulations. Until recently, this was the case with UA weighing up to 150 kg.

2.3. Safety and safety management in aviation

Aviation has always carried with it a risk of accidents – but since its global expansion over a century ago, this risk has been minimized to such an extent that currently air transport is the safest way to travel. Let us take a closer look at the safety statistics of operations involving large airplanes (MTOM over 5,700 kg). In 2018, there were 14 fatal air accidents worldwide which resulted in the death of 568 people[109]. In the same year, the total number of passenger transport

108 See Report from the Commission to the European Parliament and the Council – The European Aviation Safety Programme COM (2015) 599 final.

109 ICAO Safety Report 2019.

operations (scheduled traffic only) exceeded 37.8 million operations[110]. This means that 2.6 operations per one million end in a fatal air accident. In 2017, which was declared the safest year in the history of aviation, this rate stood at 2.4. In 2017, there were 5 fatal air accidents in which 50 people died[111]. The average death toll for the decade between 2008 and 2017 stands at 512 fatalities per year[112].

To better illustrate the level of safety in aviation and its evolution, let us refer to earlier statistics. These were a little different as they actually used the number of fatalities per 100 miles flown. In the first years after the Second World War, this indicator was app. 5. After about 20 years (1948–1968), this ratio decreased tenfold to 0.5. Another tenfold improvement was achieved over the following 30 years. After 1997, this ratio fell below 0.05 fatalities per 100 miles.[113]

This state of affairs is mainly due to the technical and organizational progress that has taken place in the aviation industry. The economic benefits brought about by the global operation of aircraft carried with them the development of newer and better airplane designs and engines, onboard devices and infrastructure, which all contributed to greatly increasing levels of safety. As these technologies continued to advance, so did society's perception of aviation safety. Literature on the subject indicates specific stages through which this evolution took place[114]. The period up to the 1960s is referred to as the "technical era" – safety was usually jeopardized by technical defects. Therefore, safety activities focused on researching and improving these factors. Technological development led to the introduction of safety requirements (regulations) and a decrease in the number of accidents. The industry introduced new devices and systems, methods of navigation, communication and pilot support (autopilot); computer technology was also used more widely. Traditional analog indicators were replaced with liquid crystal displays. Technological progress increased the efficiency of air operations and their safety. However, automation itself brought along new threats that had to be overcome. This takes us to the period between the 1970s and the late 1990s called the "era of the human factor". Aviation technology was

---

110 https://www.icao.int/annual-report-2018/Pages/the-world-of-air-transport-in-2018.aspx [access February 28, 2020].

111 Ibidem.

112 EASA Aviation Safety Report 2019.

113 EASA Aviation Safety Report 2006.

114 See ICAO Doc. 9859, Safety Management Manual, ed. 3, point 2.1.2. Guidelines of the President of the Civil Aviation Authority No. 13, CAA Journal of December 10, 2015, item 66.

now more reliable, so responsibility for safety shifted from technical factors to humans and their interactions with machines and automated systems. In the search for the causes of various aviation accidents, findings focused on aviation personnel and any mistakes they might have made. With time, it turned out that identifying human errors did not help prevent incidents. Identifying a human error usually allows for investigators to pinpoint when it may have taken place, but still this does not explain why it happened. Since the early 1990s, we began taking into account the fact that aircraft crew operate in complex environments and that their behavior is influenced by a number of factors, including organizational, systemic, and even cultural affairs. The ongoing "organizational era" began in the mid-1990s. Man and machine are now considered elements of an entire system, and aviation safety depends on the way this system is organized and how it runs.

The evolution of how we think about aviation safety is reflected in the evolution of aviation safety regulations.

Traditionally, the greatest importance is attached to regulations of an administrative nature, which regulate the principles of undertaking and conducting aviation activities. Such activities depend on meeting specific requirements, often confirmed by receiving certificates or licenses. Aviation authorities supervise compliance with these requirements and their violation is subject to criminal and administrative sanctions. Aviation law's organizational function still remains its most fundamental role. On the one hand, the system of legal regulations in the field of aviation law is very extensive. On the other, it often imposes quite general requirements on aviation entities. Aviation law regulations, by nature, rarely take into account the variety of conditions in which aviation entities operate. They are not and cannot be addressed to an individual organization. The essence of law is its universal application. The pursuit of more and more detailed regulations carries with it the risk of creating regulations that are too complicated, ineffective, or excessively expensive to implement. Therefore, there is a tendency to move away from so-called prescriptive describing of requirements toward risk-based and performance-based regulations. These trends are expressed at the level of legal regulations, which can be easily noted in the provisions of EU base regulation 2018/1139.

Regulations of an administrative nature are not the only regulations aimed at increasing levels of safety.

There are regulations on air accident investigation, the purpose of which is to prevent future accidents by, for example, issuing safety recommendations. Identifying the causes of accidents that have already occurred is a manifestation of a reactive approach to safety management.

There are also regulations which state that any air incident that may affect aviation safety must be reported to the appropriate authorities, even if it is not an accident. This, in turn, is a manifestation of a proactive approach. Incident reporting allows for the identification of potential threats that may materialize and cause air accidents. For example, reporting specific events at the level of aviation activity organization (e.g. unstable approaches, propulsion or system faults, etc.) allows for the identification of risks, their sources, and for taking appropriate action to eliminate them.

Third, there are regulations aimed at the development of an organized (systematic) approach to resolving issues related to aviation safety at national (civil aviation safety plans and programs) and aviation organization levels. These issues are dealt with in Annex 19 to the Chicago Convention[115]. As defined in this annex[116], aviation safety is a state in which risks associated with various types of aviation activities related to or directly supporting the operation of an aircraft are reduced to an acceptable level and kept under control. As indicated in ICAO guidelines, aviation will never be free from hazards and associated risks, although a complete elimination of accidents and serious incidents remains the ultimate goal. It is impossible to guarantee that human activity and human-made machines will be completely free from errors[117]. For this reason, it is necessary to take measures to control risks in aviation activities. For clarification, it should be stressed that the topic of safety discussed above is strictly related to aviation activities and the risks arising from them, and does not consider all threats related to aviation e.g. acts of unlawful interference.

The goal of aviation safety management is to continuously carry out activities that maintain the number of aviation incidents, and especially aviation accidents, at an acceptable level[118]. Aviation safety management is defined as a structured (systematic) approach to solving flight safety problems at an international, national, and aviation organization level[119]. Safety management at an organizational level is key – no one knows more about the specific conditions in which a given entity operates than the entity itself. The Safety Management System (SMS) is primarily designed to draw attention of appropriate

---

115 Announcement of the President of the Civil Aviation Authority No. 5, CAA Journal of March 29, 2017, item 471.

116 Ibidem.

117 ICAO Doc. 9859, Safety Management Manual, annotation 59.

118 E. Klich, Bezpieczeństwo lotów w transporcie lotniczym, Radom 2010, p. 214.

119 Ibidem, p. 213.

aviation organization managers (people in charge of staff, timesheets, finances, etc.) to undesirable events that may take place in a given environment. Identifying future threats is a much more effective form of management than just taking corrective and remedial actions. The latter take place after undesirable events have occurred and therefore cannot undo any of their negative effects. The goals of the SMS can be defined as follows: conducting air transport operations without accidents and serious incidents; reducing the death and injury count to the lowest extent possible; reducing damage to property and the environment to the lowest extent possible; focusing activities of all employees in a given organization on safety; avoiding hazardous and high-risk situations; reducing the level of risk to an acceptable level; and widespread application of risk management principles[120].

According to ICAO guidelines, an SMS in an aviation organization requires: (1) defining a safety policy, i.e. defining principles that constitute a safety culture that the organization's management is going to follow as well as the methods and processes to be used to achieve the desired levels of safety; (2) risk management, i.e. identifying and assessing threats, taking action to control and mitigate risks; (3) ensuring safety, i.e. assessing the results of safety management activities (through adopted safety measures and by managing changes that may affect operations); (4) promoting safety through appropriate training and communications within the organization. An SMS in an aviation organization should be correlated with safety management at a national or regional level. For this purpose, the aviation community, in accordance with Annex 19 to the Chicago Convention, has developed the following:

- at a national level – the National Civil Aviation Security Programme[121],
- at an EU level – the European Aviation Safety Program[122].

According to EU regulations implementing ICAO Annex 19's standards and recommendations, only organizations whose activities are subject to certification are required to implement an SMS. These are air carriers, aviation training organizations, units that manage public airports, air traffic service providers, as well as organizations in charge of managing the continuing airworthiness of

120 E. Klich, Bezpieczeństwo lotów w..., p. 231.

121 https://www.ulc.gov.pl/pl/zarzadzanie-bezpieczenstwem/program-bezpieczenstwa-w-lotnictwie-cywilnym/krajowy-program-bezpieczenstwa-w-lotnictwie-cywilnym-kpbwlc

122 See Report mentioned in footnote 28.

aircraft[123]. Currently, work is ongoing to develop SMS requirements for aircraft designers, manufacturers, and maintenance service providers.

2.4. Types of aviation subject to aviation law regulations

Aviation safety regulations are not (and cannot be) uniform for all types of aviation activity. The classification of aviation involves subjecting entities to differing legal regulations.

The most basic division in aviation is the division between **civil and state aviation**. State aviation considers aircraft used for military or public service purposes. Aviation safety rules have very limited applications here. Both ICAO and EU regulations do not apply to this branch of aviation[124] and national provisions are rather limited[125]. This division also applies to UA. However, it has far-reaching consequences resulting from the fact that state entities are deeply interested in UA technology. The issue of regulating UA operations will be discussed in further parts of this publication.

There are also different types of civil aviation[126]. Safety regulations primarily distinguish between air transport classified as either **commercial air transport**[127] (which must follow the highest safety standards resulting from the involvement of third parties such as passengers and other people at risk of air accidents) or **general aviation**, which is any aviation activity other than air transport. This includes business flights, private flights, as well as the training, sports, and recreational flights[128]. General aviation is subject to proportionally lower safety requirements. However, in situations where there is a need to increase the level of safety of flight personnel or third parties exposed to risk of an air accident, the safety requirements that general aviation is subject to may actually be stricter

123 A. Konert, P. Kasprzyk, P. Łaciński, Podstawy prawne zarządzania bezpieczeństwem w lotnictwie cywilnym (in) Zarządzanie Bezpieczeństwem w Lotnictwie Cywilnym, ed. K Łuczak, 2016.

124 Art. 3 of the Chicago Convention, Art. 2 sec. 3 letter a) of EU Regulation 2018/1139

125 Art. 1 sec. 4 of the Aviation Law, according to which the provisions of the Law do not apply to state aviation, except for certain strictly defined regulations.

126 On different types of aviation, see M. Żylicz, op. cit., pp. 26–27

127 "Commercial air transport" means aircraft operations carried out to transport passengers, cargo, or mail for remuneration or other valuable counter performance; see Annex 6, Volume I to the Chicago Convention, Art. 3 p. 24 of the EU Regulation 2018/1139, Art. 2 p. 13 of the Aviation Law

128 See Communication from the European Commission of January 11, 2008, on the development and future of general and business aviation COM (2007) 869.

than in the case of commercial air transport. These situations include training flights, aerial works (e.g. patrolling or agrotechnical services), or flights using aircraft that are considered difficult to operate for one's own needs (e.g. jet aircraft). Of course there are further subclassifications and divisions; however their detailed description would go beyond the aim of this publication.

From the point of view of safety regulations, unmanned aviation is also subject to various classifications depending on the technical characteristics of the UA involved or the type of operations being performed. Just as the concept of a manned aircraft includes an Airbus A380, the largest passenger plane, an ultra-light glider and everything in between, the concept of UA includes NATO's advanced Global Hawk system as well as a hobbyist DJI drone used for operations carried out within an operator's visual line of sight. However, the division into manned and unmanned aviation remains the reference point for the classification and division within unmanned aviation. This division is determined by the concept and definition of what constitutes an UA.

3. Differences between manned and unmanned aircraft

Regulations on the safety of UA operations must take into account the characteristics and properties of UA. To do so, it is necessary to highlight the several basic differences between manned and unmanned aircraft, through a certain level of generalization. Bearing in mind that just like the concept of manned aircraft includes the Airbus A380 and an ultra-light glider, the concept of UA includes the Global Hawk – a machine used by NATO and weighing several tons – as well as a DJI drone used for visual line of sight operations that can be purchased in almost any electronics store. The differences should be perceived from the perspective of the primary goal of aviation safety regulations, which is as follows: to achieve at least the same level of safety for unmanned aviation operations as the one achieved in manned aviation[129]. If we look at aviation safety as a situation in which the risks associated with certain activities are reduced to an acceptable level and controlled, then these risks must first be identified. Since various types of aviation operations can sometimes result in accidents or incidents, they can therefore be classified according to the risks involved:[130]

1. to people on the ground (death, bodily injury),

129 See e.g. Circular 328 ICAO, EC COM (2014) 207 final, or K. Dalmagkidis et al. op. cit., p. 91.

130 JARUS, 09 UAS Operational Categorization.

2. to people on board an aircraft (death, bodily injury resulting from an accident caused by a mid-air collision).
3. to critical infrastructure, the continuous functioning of which is important for society.

First of all, due to the lack of a crew on board UA, we must focus on the safety of people who are on the ground. One of the most important issues here is to ensure a certain degree of UA reliability and eliminate possible technical failures, but also avoid collisions with objects or people on the ground. Considering the need to integrate manned and unmanned aviation, it is also necessary to take into account the safety of people on board manned aircraft, and therefore prevent the possibility of collisions between the two types of aircraft.

Moving on, one can suggest that the key issues that arise when using unmanned aircraft stem from the lack of a crew on board. More precisely, these issues are not so much about the complete lack of a crew, but the mere fact that those in control are not on board the aircraft, but rather in a control station that is an entirely separate (and remotely located) device[131]. By describing UA in this way, the basic differences between an unmanned and a manned aircraft concern the following issues[132]. First, a UA's in-flight condition, location, flight parameters, and surrounding area are not assessed by a pilot who is on board the aircraft. Second, the need to transfer data between the UA pilot-in-command (control station) and the aircraft itself gives rise to problems previously unknown in manned aviation as communications may be limited or lost, resulting in the inability to control a UA. There is also the issue of delays between the moment a pilot makes a decision or maneuver and its execution by the aircraft. Third, collision avoidance and vehicle separation solutions used in manned aviation have a limited application in unmanned aviation – it is therefore necessary to develop new solutions in this field. Fourth, the lack of a crew means that no additional measures can be taken to ensure the safety of a crew or passengers in the event of an emergency. Some studies have even suggested the possibility of controlled destruction of a malfunctioning UA in a manner that would pose the smallest threat possible to third parties[133].

131 Unmanned Aircraft System Handbook and Accident Investigation Guidelines, ISASI, 2015, p. 9.

132 Ibidem.

133 K. Dalmagkidis et al. p. 163.

The differences indicated above require that special attention be paid to the following elements of a UAS. These can be considered crucial for the further development of this technology and its safe and widespread use.

The first is the necessity to **ensure communications between the pilot-in-command (control station) and the aircraft when it is airborne**. When a crew is on board an aircraft, the issue of maintaining control over it comes down to ensuring, through rigorous certification requirements, that the pilot(s) maintain(s) full control over the aircraft using the devices available to them in the cabin. By using the yoke, pedals, flap settings, and other controls, they are able to ensure that a specific and intended aircraft control configuration is fully achieved. Of course, in the case of more advanced aircraft (especially passenger aircraft), control system processes are automated to a certain degree through e.g. a fly-by-wire control system or autopilot, and use of redundancy. If there is no crew on board, aircraft control is maintained through a control station, with the UA operated by a pilot-in-command located elsewhere (usually on the ground). Such a situation creates an entirely separate issue of ensuring communications continuity in terms of transmission of the signal from the flight control station to UA in the air (the so-called command and control link, C2-link). The most common method of providing UA control is through radio waves emitted from control stations. However, radio control has its substantial limitations. Its main downside is limited range and the fact that the communications continuity is dependent on the presence of obstacles (e.g. bad weather, mountains) in the way. Moreover, there is the second issue of having a limited number of radio frequencies that can be used for this very purpose. Therefore, radio communications is mainly used for UA flying within a pilot's field of view. Of course, other remote data transmission technologies are being developed. The most advanced military UA use satellite technology. However, when it comes to civilian applications, the possibility of using ICT networks to transfer data, especially in cities, is gaining more and more endorsement. This method relies on Wi-Fi or cellular networks to transfer information. The main challenge in this regard is that the technologies in question were not created for purposes other than data transmission between users of terrestrial devices, such as computers or mobile phones. Regardless of the technology used in a given case, one issue remains – there are no industry or even regulatory standards in this field. This leaves questions on quite important matters, such as the availability, quality, or continuity of communications between a control station and a UA, as well as the possible latency in a devices' response to input commands (which is of crucial importance in critical flight phases) unanswered. There is also the issue of a possible deterioration in the quality or even a complete loss of communications. Therefore, a common requirement for UA in the event of a loss of communications is to be provided with emergency systems that can execute an emergency landing or flight (in automatic mode, i.e. following a pre-programmed route, a so-called fail-safe). This issue becomes even more complicated in the case of UA that are not remotely controlled, but are flying along a pre-programmed route (so-called automatic flights). In general, technology offers many possibilities for flying without human intervention, as in the case with autonomous operations, but also creates a number of new issues that need to be resolved.

The second of the aforementioned elements related to the lack of a crew on board is the **DAA system** (detect and avoid). In the case of manned aviation, the flight crew (pilot-in-command) is responsible for a flight's safety. A properly prepared and trained crew is only one of the elements of an entire safety system (so-called safety-nets) that is designed to organize and support the safety of aviation activities. This system, from a regulatory perspective, is a series of interrelated requirements on the organization of airspace, an aircraft and any ground equipment. The proper organization of airspace entails designating specific classes of airspace in which safety requirements and air traffic service volumes are sufficient to meet the traffic volume in each class. However, these requirements are based on the assumption that there is a crew on board, which monitors in real time both what is visible outside of the aircraft and their certified on-board instruments (systems) which indicate, for example, their current speed and position. Moreover, the crew is also provided with other crucial data by air traffic services and relies on certified anti-collision devices, which in some cases are a regulatory requirement (e.g. ACAS/TCAS or GPWS systems). In the case of an unmanned flight, we are faced with the question of how to provide similar situational awareness to the pilot-in-command. After all, a safe flight requires that any nearby traffic be detected as early as possible. Only then can appropriate action be taken to avoid a possible collision. There is also the issue of detecting and avoiding collisions with buildings or other infrastructure when flying at low altitudes. Designing appropriate technology to detect and avoid collisions is a necessary condition for the development of UA. Such technology should be, similar to devices used in manned aviation, subject to appropriate certification (or any other type of approval) based on developed and widely accepted standards.

A motion detection and collision avoidance system is downright a condition for allowing UA to fly outside of a pilot's field of vision. For this reason, as well as the lack of developed standards in the field of motion detection and collision avoidance systems, an essential manner of ensuring the safety of UA operations is the requirement to keep piloted aircraft within sight. A division into in- and out-of-sight operations is widely recognized.[134] Visual Line of Sight Operations (VLOS) are operations during which the pilot maintains visual contact with the aircraft they are piloting. This way, the pilot is able to determine the UA's position, allowing them to maintain a safe distance from other aircraft, obstacles, or people on the ground. VLOS operations are divided into day and night operations due to their effects on perception and the nature of night operations. So-called extended operations within the visual line of sight (extended-VLOS, E-VLOS) are another type of VLOS operation. During E-VLOS, a pilot does not have to keep the device in sight. However, an observer, i.e. another person, is obliged to maintain eye contact with the UA. In both cases, the aim is to ensure that the person controlling the UA has situational awareness similar to that of a manned aircraft pilot observing the area around his aircraft. Beyond Visual Line of Sight Operations (B-VLOS) are operations where visual contact is not required. However, in the case of B-VLOS operations, it is necessary to use motion recognition and collision avoidance systems, thanks to which a UA pilot is able to maintain situational awareness.

Both issues are conjoined with the need to clearly define UA pilots' roles and responsibilities. Here, regulations on the duties and powers of the pilot-in-command of a manned aircraft must be taken as a point of reference[135].

4. Differences between manned and unmanned aviation

Notwithstanding the abovementioned issues related to the lack of a crew on board UA, we must now take further differences between manned and unmanned aviation into account. These result from the operational capabilities of UA presently available on the market.[136]

4.1. Capability to operate at very low or very high altitudes

In principle, manned flights do not go below certain minimum altitudes. Of course, there are exceptions like take offs and landings at airports, but the general principle remains. Meanwhile, UA can operate at very low altitudes, even in urban areas. The current rules for the organization of airspace and air traffic do not provide for such situations, as these are based on the assumption that

134 For more see ICAO Doc. 10019, Section 9.5.

135 See e.g. the verdict of the Provincial Administrative Court in Warsaw of October 25th, 2017, file ref. no. VII SA / Wa 2771/16.

136 A. Masutti, F. Tomasello, op. cit., p. 13 in., K. Dalamagkidis et al., op. cit., p. 161.

aircraft, after taking off, gain altitude and proceed to fly above certain minimum altitudes. It seems difficult to even suggest a revision of these rules with regards to UA operating at low altitudes – therefore, rules for UA flights at low altitudes must be developed from the ground up. Moreover, it is worth noting that there are also UA capable of operating at very high altitudes, at which manned aviation practically does not operate.

4.2. Capability to operate over urban areas

In general, manned aircraft usually fly over sparsely populated areas[137]. This is due to rules of the air and air traffic organization, including noise abatement procedures, and limits in the number of flights over highly urbanized areas. Manned aviation operates on the assumption that certain phases of a flight follow one another. Take-offs and landings take place at airports, but the main part of any flight takes place along a specific route, which, as a rule, should not be directly above urban areas. Meanwhile, UA do not use airports by definition. Their characteristics allow for taking off and landing practically anywhere. Moreover, some UA applications assume that certain drones are specifically designed to be used in urban areas or over gatherings. This gives rise to questions on the safety of such operations.

4.3. Capability to transport people or goods

The main purpose of aviation is the transport of people and goods, primarily in international traffic. The use of UA for this purpose still seems like a distant solution. When it comes to passenger transport, the psychological barrier of getting into a pilotless aircraft seems to be the toughest wall to break, apart from numerous technological issues. For example, from the point of view of aircraft structure efficiency, the use of windows in passenger aircraft is not justifiable. However, they are still in use to cater to the human factor, and ideas to replace them with displays have not evolved beyond concepts[138]. Many have high hopes for the use of UA technology in the transport of goods – mainly as vehicles to ship smaller packages due to the operational limitations of UA. The range and safe working load of most UA is incomparably lower than that of manned aircraft. However, parcel delivery by UA is not that simple. First, it is justified only in operations beyond an operator's line of sight. Second, it must be justified

---

137 K. Dalamagkidis et al., op. cit., p. 163.

138 https://www.uk-cpi.com/windowless-plane [access February 28, 2020].

economically, which requires the enforcement of new regulations on flying at low altitudes. Third, it would take place over inhabited urban areas, which would require technical reliability at a level that ensures the safety of third parties on the ground. There are also a number of other issues that relate to such urban operations, such as noise pollution.

4.4. Multiple applications – unmanned aircraft as "flying platforms"

Apart from delivering parcels, UA offer a whole range of other applications. We can easily point out the most popular UA applications (even those classified as VLOS operations) in recent years: network infrastructure monitoring (e.g. power line condition inspections), monitoring and dusting of crops, search and rescue operations, support for fire-fighting operations, or security[139]. UA used for these purposes require the installation of additional systems necessary for these types of operations. This includes various types of cameras, sensors, or systems for transmitting or securing data. In the case of manned aviation, such situations occur sporadically e.g. when providing specialized services. The installation of such instrumentation on a manned aircraft requires certification of the new updated configuration. Figuratively speaking, a manned aircraft is adapted to be used for a purpose other than simply performing a flight itself, e.g. by installing thermal camera systems. However, any such changes require a check of how the updated configuration affects the safety of an aircraft's structure prior to carrying out a flight. In the case of UA, it is the purpose of using the aircraft that determines its design solutions. Therefore, in the case of unmanned aviation, the specific application of a vehicle determines its design solutions on a much greater scale than in manned aviation.

4.5. Universality and availability

Drones are commonly used in areas where the use of manned aviation would be practically impossible or very expensive. For example, they are used by state services, which normally have access to state aviation aircraft (e.g. police helicopters) but the purpose of their use is limited both by their technical characteristics and cost effectiveness. Among others, these are some of the reasons why government services use drones in areas such as maintaining public order or fighting crime. The costs of purchasing and using UA are incomparable to the cost of purchasing

---

139 For more, see SESAR Drone Outlook Study, 2016.

and using even the lightest or the smallest manned aircraft. Staff training is another pro for UA. The end result is the greater availability of UA[140]. All statistics prove this. For example, between 2013 and 2019 in Poland, the total number of certified UA operators (over 15,000) exceeded the total number of "traditional" aviation license holders (about 12,000). According to FAA data, at the beginning of 2019, the total number of UA considered models exceeded 1.25 million, and the total number of other UA (used for non-recreational purposes) reached nearly 300,000. Meanwhile, the total number of manned aircraft found in the FAA register is approximately 320,000.[141]

4.6. UA supervision

This topic is related to the issue of exercising supervision over the safety of UA operations and the enforcement of safety regulations. This is one of the major challenges that has been indicated in numerous studies, including those featured in legislative work. The current system of supervision over manned aviation seems to be inadequate for the challenges posed by unmanned aviation. The universality and availability of drones necessitates the development of a new supervision model, one that would define roles of services other than aviation supervision authorities, e.g. the police or the Boarder Guard. This new model should also consider the powers of state services, as well as criminal laws sanctioning certain requirements. It should primarily be based on new solutions, such as user registration, that allow for the remote identification of a UA and its owner. There are also other issues – for example, the concept of an interception of a manned aircraft. This is when air traffic regulation procedures are used by state-owned aircraft against civil aircraft that cannot be identified or which follow a route that is not in accordance with their submitted flight plan, do not have permission to cross a state border, or enter prohibited, dangerous, or restricted zones. The purpose of an interception is to identify the intercepted aircraft. Navigational guidance of the intercepted aircraft, including an order to land at a specific airport, can be carried out if necessary[142]. One of the basic responsibilities of any flight crew is to be familiar with these procedures. In the case of unmanned aviation, it is difficult to imagine applying these procedures,

---

140 A. Masutti, F. Tomasello, op. cit, p. 16.

141 See https://www.faa.gov/licenses_certificates/aircraft_certification/aircraft_registry/ua (accessed on February 4, 2023)

142 See more, e.g. the verdict of the Constitutional Tribunal of September 30th, 2008, file ref. no. K 44/07.

which, after all, were developed with manned aircraft in mind. Therefore, it is necessary to develop new regulations that take into account the nature of unmanned aviation. However, new issues emerge again. For example, should state services be authorized to take control of a UA by interfering with its control system? If so, what requirements should be met so that the seizure does not pose a greater risk to the public than allowing the operation to continue? Is it permissible to destroy an UA? Obviously, a detailed analysis of these issues goes beyond the scope of topics related to operational safety regulations, as it concerns not only aviation safety, but the much broader topic of public safety too. However, in the context of UA destruction, it is worth mentioning one other issue – in the case of manned aviation, one of the fundamental concerns of flight safety is to prevent the loss of an aircraft's ability to remain airborne. The consequences of any defect or damage that may result in the loss of lift are catastrophic for people on board. For this reason, the highest safety standards are applied when it comes to airworthiness – from design through production, to maintenance. In the case of unmanned aviation, the loss of lift will be tantamount to destruction or damage to the vehicle itself. However, if a crash landing is to take place in a controlled manner, with the safety of third parties and property in mind, such situations may constitute the basis for the creation of emergency systems installed as part of unmanned aircraft control systems[143].

4.7. Air Traffic Management

Recognizing UA as aircraft stems from their nature, i.e. the ability to remain airborne. Thus, UA development is strictly dependent on the principles of airspace, air traffic and air traffic service organization – an air traffic management system (ATM). The generally declared principle of the universal availability of airspace for its users requires rethinking, taking into account at least two aspects related to UA development. The first – enabling UA operations at low altitudes, as these are practically unused by manned aviation. The second – ensuring safe integration between manned and unmanned aviation. This is an issue that must be worked on supranationally due of its nature. The rules of airspace organization and air traffic are the subject of detailed international regulations (ICAO), implemented in Europe through EU legislature. The so-called Single European Sky initiative is crucial here, which aims to reduce the defragmentation of European airspace and increase its capacity and cost efficiency through the introduction of

143 K. Dalamagkidis et al. op. cit., p. 161.

modern requirements related to safety, airspace management, system interoperability, and the financing of air navigation services[144].

From the very beginning, the rules of airspace organization, including air traffic as well as air navigation service provision, have been based on the assumption that there is a crew on board an aircraft. Manned aircraft themselves take off and land at airports, and their routes are planned in advance, usually over long distances. Airspace is organized in such a way as to minimize the risks of collisions by, for example, dividing it into controlled airspace (with air traffic control services) and uncontrolled airspace. There are specific requirements and rules to follow depending on the designated class of controlled airspace. The greater the volume of traffic in a given area, the more stringent the rules. For example, in A-class airspace, only flights following Instrument Flight Rules (so-called IFR) are allowed, which means that it is essential to adhere to specific flight procedures and to cooperate with air traffic control, which is there to prevent collisions. However, IFR flights require both additional qualifications from their crews (authorization to perform IFR flights) and the necessary equipment, such as devices that allow for the identification of the position of an aircraft by air traffic services, e.g. transponders of a certain class, thanks to which it is possible to continuously monitor an aircraft's position with radar technology. A detailed presentation of the rules and regulations related to the organization of airspace, air traffic, or air navigation services would require a separate study just like the analysis of these regulations in the context of their applicability to UA flights. There is no doubt, however, that the revision of these rules in terms of UA operations is a key issue, for several reasons.

First of all, the existing air traffic management system was developed for the safety of passenger air traffic. Its dynamic development has resulted in its continuous modernization, sometimes by the introduction of new technologies (e.g. anti-collision systems, satellite positioning systems, improvements in communications between crews and air traffic services). One of the main constraints of this development is the issue of using technology based on radio waves (radio communications or radar positioning technologies). Therefore, it is unlikely that the fundamental assumptions of this system will change to enable its integration with unmanned aviation. All factors indicate, quite uniformly, that if UA were to fly in the same airspace as passenger planes, they would have to follow all the requirements that apply to a given airspace. Only the most advanced UA

144 For more see A. Cook (ed.), European Air Traffic management. Principles, Practice and Research, 2007.

systems are able to meet these requirements. In the near future, only research and development flights[145], reconnaissance flights with the most advanced military systems, or cargo flights of large transport aircraft flying in accordance with the same rules that apply to commercial transport flights will be permitted. Therefore, designating zones for UA flights will remain the general rule for these flights to take place in the public area. However, it is difficult to imagine that these zones would be designated for each individual UA flight every time one has to be conducted, as the procedures for doing so were created for entirely different needs (e.g. test flights, military exercises, etc.).

Taking into account the potential and characteristics of the majority of currently used UA, a new concept for unmanned traffic management (UTM) is being developed. Also, more and more operational concepts and strategic documents concerning the development of UTM are being published, in addition to numerous ongoing research and development programs in this field. Both conceptual and research work show that such a system should primarily focus on managing UA traffic at low altitudes, which, as a rule, is not used by manned aviation. The system should prevent collisions between UA themselves, collisions with terrain and obstacles (buildings), as well as between manned and unmanned aircraft. To achieve this, a far-reaching automation system, which would manage the exchange of data between airspace users, seems necessary. It is said that the design of such systems should be based on data transmission technologies developed for ICT systems, especially wireless data transmission networks. The fundamental condition for the development of the UTM concept is ensuring the possibility for electronic UA identification, as well as the development of traffic detection and collision avoidance systems. It will also be necessary to resolve issues related to UA location systems.

In manned aviation, conducting ongoing flight navigation (and thus being aware of an aircraft's location in a given airspace) is one of the basic responsibilities of the crew. Of course, traditional methods of air navigation (maps, calculations, and observations) and air radio navigation (terrestrial radio devices) have become replaced by advanced devices that rely on satellite technology. However, the introduction of these devices as a navigational standard in manned aviation has been a lengthy process. Before this was possible, it was necessary to identify and explain numerous issues related to, for example, the availability, quality, and

145 See e.g. flight in a controlled space, part of the CLAIRE project (SESAR program) https://www.sesarju.eu/node/1510 [accessed on February 28, 2020].

accuracy of data provided by satellite navigation systems[146]. Additionally, there is an entire system of air navigation services, including air traffic control and surveillance services, that helps – at least in certain parts of an airspace – air traffic control services locate any aircraft at any time. In the case of UA, a reliable location method is the primary element that provides its operator with information about a UA's exact location. It is of key importance for BVLOS operations, but knowing a UA's exact location is also important for VLOS operations, for example, to determine if at all it is possible to carry out a flight within a given airspace. Most of the location systems installed on UA presently available on the market are based on the same principles as "consumer" receivers, e.g. those found in mobile phones. Once again, the development of UA location standards similar to those developed for manned aviation requires further research and development. Issues with using satellite technology in air navigation has been ongoing for many years, and many remain unresolved. One of them, for example, is the use of satellite technology not just for navigation, but also for determining aircraft position for air traffic management, which is possible using so-called ADS-B (Automatic Dependent Surveillance-Broadcast) technology that will gradually be introduced to complement or replace traditional radar technology[147].

146 See R. Morales-Ferre et al. A Survey on Coping With Intentional Interference in Satellite Navigation for Manned and Unmanned Aircraft. IEEE Communications Surveys & Tutorials, Vol. 22, No. 1, 2020.

147 In the US, the transition to the ADS-B technology as the main source for establishing position in aviation is part of the Airspace Modernization Program (Next Gen). In the EU, the discussion is part of the Single European Sky program. See e.g. the SESAR report on ADS-B in Europe https://ec.europa.eu/transport/sites/transport/files/20180515-sesar-ads-b-report.pdf [accessed on February 28, 2020].

Chapter 3 The development of international standards in the field of safety of unmanned aviation

1. Introduction

As mentioned earlier, recognizing UA as aircraft is the starting point for creating and developing regulations concerning their operations. The presence of a crew on board an aircraft is the main assumption made in earlier aviation safety regulations. This system consists of a number of detailed regulations, unified at an international level with regards to the Chicago Convention, which constitutes the basis for shaping and unifying regulations regarding aviation safety. ICAO and the entire global system of standards and recommendations based on the aforementioned convention focuses its activity on international air navigation, which is understood as the transport of people and goods between states. Meanwhile, the use of UA for this purpose has been and still remains rather a distant vision than a real-life possibility. Considering the current state of development of UA technology, its widespread use should, as a rule, be considered local. Of course, cross-border flights are possible, but these are related to providing special types of services (e.g. sub-orbital flights of solar-powered UA used as data transfer platforms) rather than transporting people or cargo. On the other hand, enabling UA flights at a local level will always raise questions about the relationship between unmanned and manned aviation – most of all, in the context of passenger flight safety. Therefore, although the first regulations that concerned UA and their flights were in fact national, works on integrating manned and unmanned aviation are being carried out at international and supra-local levels. This chapter presents the state of these works at an international level (ICAO). Moreover, due to the close connection of these efforts with the unification of technical standards in aviation, this chapter will also present the works conducted by various organizations involved in the development of unified manned and unmanned standards. The US approach to UA regulations is also presented as a point of reference for shaping EU regulations.

2. International Civil Aviation Organization

2.1. The Chicago Convention

The Convention on International Civil Aviation[148], signed over 75 years ago, stipulated that "*no aircraft capable of being flown without a pilot shall be flown over the territory of a contracting State without special authorization by that State and in accordance with the terms of such authorization*" (first sentence of Art. 8). The following sentence states that "*each contracting State undertakes to ensure* [sic] *that the flight of such aircraft without a pilot in regions open to civil aircraft shall be so controlled as to obviate danger to civil aircraft*". The very wording of Art. 8 leads to the conclusion that while UA are recognized as aircraft, they are still clearly separated from what is considered "civil aircraft". First, international UA operations are to be subject to special authorization by the state in which they are to be carried out in. Therefore, they are not subject to the principles that the Convention defines as "freedoms of the air", which form the basis of international air transport. Second, UA flights performed within a country should never pose a threat to civil aviation safety. This gives rise to one fundamental question – are unmanned aircraft flights a special type of aviation activity which cannot be classified in accordance with the traditional division into civil and state aviation that is rooted into the Chicago Convention? Either way, Art. 8 of the Convention must be taken into account when drafting regulations on UA; not only because it requires that such flights be subject to special authorization, but also because it obliges states that allow for these operations to maintain control over them so that they do not pose a risk to civil aircraft.

Art. 8 of the Convention specifies "*pilotless aircraft*" as "*aircraft capable of being flown without a pilot*". However, this can be interpreted in various ways. If we take on a more literal approach, then this provision should only apply to aircraft that are capable of flying without a pilot's intervention.[149] In such a case, this provision would not apply to remotely piloted aircraft controlled via a control station, only applying to those UA in which human involvement is limited to setting the device in motion or programming an autonomous UA flight path. It seems wrong to agree with such an interpretation, since the same article obliges state authorities to maintain control over the operations of "*aircraft capable of flying without a pilot*". We should not forget the context of the Chicago

148 Convention on International Civil Aviation signed on December 7, 1944 in Chicago, ratified by Poland, Journal of Laws of 1959, No. 35, item 212 as amended.

149 Aleš Završnik (ed.), Drones and Unmanned Aerial Systems, 2016, p. 192.

Convention – back then, legislators were already aware of radio wave-controlled UA used for military purposes. Therefore, it is difficult to assume that such devices were intentionally omitted from the Convention, with attention aimed at autonomous UA flights, a solution then unknown[150]. This becomes even more difficult when we realize that the term used in Art. 8 was borrowed from an even older document entitled the Convention Relating to the Regulation of Aerial Navigation signed in Paris in 1919[151]. In practice, a much broader interpretation prevailed. According to ICAO, the concept of pilotless aircraft used in the Chicago Convention should be interpreted more broadly, so as to cover both flights of remotely piloted aircraft and flights of autonomous aircraft[152]. A position promoting a broad understanding of unmanned aviation within the meaning of Art. 8 of the Chicago Convention was first explicitly adopted at the 11th ICAO Air Navigation Conference and then confirmed at the 35th ICAO General Assembly[153]. This started ICAO's works in this field. The adopted approach determined the direction of these works. Recognizing UA primarily as aircraft necessitates the application of other provisions of the Chicago Convention to regulations governing their operations. The most important ones include[154]:

1. Art. 12, which states that "every aircraft flying over or maneuvering within a certain territory shall comply with the rules and regulations relating to the flight and maneuver of aircraft there in force. Under this provision, each contracting State undertakes to ensure the prosecution of all persons violating the regulations applicable".
2. Art. 31, which states that "every aircraft engaged in international navigation shall be provided with a certificate of airworthiness issued or rendered valid by the State in which it is registered".
3. Art. 29, which states that "every aircraft of a contracting State engaged in international navigation shall carry with it necessary documentation including a certificate of registration, a certificate of airworthiness, or appropriate licenses for each member of the crew".

---

150 Ibidem.

151 M. Huttunen, Unmanned, Remotely Piloted, or Something Else? Analyzing the Terminological Dogfight, 42. Air & Space Law, Vol. 3, 2017, p. 357.

152 B. Scott (ed.), The Law of Unmanned Aircraft System, 2016, p. 32.

153 ICAO Doc. 10019, comments 1.2.5–1.2.6.

154 See B. Scott, The Law of …, p. 34 et al. A. Masutti, F. Tomasello, op. cit., p. 41, ICAO Cir 328, p. 11 et seq.

Additionally, recognizing UA as aircraft means that standards and recommendations adopted in the form of annexes to the Convention should apply to them as well[155]. Consequently, it is possible and expedient to work out appropriate changes to these annexes so that they take into account the nature of unmanned aviation operations. ICAO adopted this very approach.

2.2. ICAO's work

ICAO began its work in this field in 2005. This involved consultations on the current state of unmanned aviation and prospects for the development of this field, actions taken by states to minimize threats to civil aviation in the case of flights performed by state-owned UA, and procedures and regulations that may be used to issue special permits referred to in Art. 8 of the Chicago Convention. Next, a Working Group (*UAS Study Group*) was established. The result of their work was an ICAO circular published in 2011 entitled "*Unmanned Aircraft System* (UAS)" (ICAO Cir 328). This circular, an informative publication, introduced a means of classification and standardization of concepts and terminology. It presented, *inter alia*, definitions of unmanned aircraft and unmanned aircraft system, which included both remotely piloted UA (and UAS) and autonomous UA. It also proposed separating the concept of a UA operator (as an entity responsible for operations) from the concept of a pilot of a remotely piloted UA (as the person in control of a flight, designated for this purpose by the UA operator), as in the case of manned aviation. The circular also indicated numerous challenges related to the development of UA technology and legal regulations in this area. The development of regulations in this field is a very time-consuming task, and understanding the similarities and differences between manned and unmanned aviation is of crucial importance[156], as well being up-to-date with the present state of development of new UA technology. Suffice it to mention that in the foreseeable future, in ICAO's opinion, unmanned aircraft:

1. will not be used for the commercial transport of passengers,
2. will not be allowed to perform autonomous operations, i.e. operations without the participation of a pilot remotely controlling the aircraft (except for operations that take place in designated airspace zones),
3. the pilot of a remotely controlled UA will be responsible for the safety of its operations just like a pilot-in-command is responsible for the safety of a

155 A. Masutti, F. Tomasello, op. cit., p. 42.
156 ICAO Cir 328, Note 2.9.

manned aircraft's operations – this will be a critical element in the safe integration of manned and unmanned aviation.

Among the more important guidelines that ICAO put in its 2011 circular, we can indicate some that require a detailed analysis when working on integrating unmanned and manned aviation:

1. the lack of a pilot on board requires that key issues related to ensuring safety should be addressed primarily through the development of technologies related to, for example, collision detection and avoidance (DAA);
2. a UA's capability to operate and respond to commands should be the same as for manned aircraft. This particularly concerns the issue of ensuring a UA's flight control and steering (C2link) via data transmission, i.e. signal quality or the time needed to "translate" transmitted data into specific actions;
3. the pilot of a remotely controlled UA should have the same situational awareness as a pilot of a manned aircraft – the basic assumption of air traffic regulations is that a pilot is able to observe the space around an aircraft and, consequently, maintain a safe distance from any obstacles. In the case of unmanned aircraft, this requires the development of traffic detection and collision avoidance systems that would identify other aircraft, terrain, objects, or difficult weather conditions in time;
4. the pilot of a remotely controlled UA should have the ability and competences to execute instructions given by air traffic services. This would require, for example, maintaining communications between the pilot and these services; air traffic service procedures must also take into account the distinctive nature of unmanned aviation;
5. the airworthiness of a UAS is not just based on the airworthiness of the aircraft itself – a UA system consists of at least an aircraft and its control station. We must also consider the way data is transmitted between the aircraft with its control station; if this takes place via radio waves, then the issue of available frequencies and their security must also be considered;
6. issues related to UA airworthiness must account for the fact that the technology relies on different technical and technological solutions than manned aviation. For example, multi-rotor propulsion that enables vertical take-off and landing, or electric energy as the source of power for UA propulsion;
7. we must promote an approach that is based on UA operation safety management for both states and operators. At a state level, this approach boils down to monitoring the effectiveness of implemented solutions. At an operator level, the requirement to manage the safety of operations necessitates a systematic approach to operational risk assessment (which should take all

risk-related factors into account, both in the air and on the ground), as well as measures that would reduce the risks of given operations to an acceptable level, e.g. technological or organizational solutions.

In 2014, ICAO established a permanent UA panel (*Remotely Piloted Aircraft Systems Panel*), the main task of which was to create a UA regulatory framework in cooperation with other organizations and to propose amendments to individual annexes of the Chicago Convention. The panel features seven groups of experts which focus on: (1) airworthiness, (2) C2link, (3) DAA, (4) personnel licensing, (5) operations, (6) ATM integration, and (7) human factor issues. Their work resulted in the creation of a *Manual on Remotely Piloted Aircraft Systems* (Doc. 10019) published in 2015. Here, it should be clarified that ICAO publishes manuals as explanations or non-binding recommendations to the Chicago Convention annexes. However, this published manual was one step ahead of any UA-related changes that were to be made to the Convention's annexes. This was an exceptional situation since usually, it is the annexes that are amended first and only then does ICAO publish any manuals. However, such an unconventional move was necessary due to the rapid development of the UA sector and the increasing number of regulations concerning UA operations adopted at a state level[157]. The basic assumptions of the manual can be summarized in two points[158]. First, a UA operator should play a key role in ensuring the safety of UA operations, especially since their safety can only be assessed individually for each operation. Different UA operate in different ways – a small UA flying within an operator's line of sight (e.g. filming) operates differently to a medium-sized UA that relies on radio communication (e.g. short-distance package delivery) and flies beyond an operator's line of sight, or a large UA that performs cross-border flights. Second, the integration of unmanned and manned aviation in the same airspace requires that the former be included in the entire civil aviation safety regulation system.

It should also be added that the ICAO manual indicates protection of the public against the effects of airborne collisions and collisions with the ground as the main goal of UA operation safety regulations. It mentions that the integration of both types of aviation cannot take place at the expense of safety or efficiency (e.g. airspace occupancy). In situations where complete integration is not possible, the manual advises to gradually enable unmanned aviation operations, e.g.

157 A. Masutti, F. Tomasello, op. cit., p. 45.
158 Ibidem, p. 47.

by designating separate airspace zones or allowing only those operations that are carried out within a pilot's line of sight.

The most extensive parts of the 2015 manual cover the following issues:

1. airworthiness certification of UA and other elements of a UA system such as control station. It is worth mentioning that a UA's control and command system (communications between the station and the UA) is not recognized as a product and therefore cannot be certified;
2. ensuring continued UA airworthiness. This includes regular maintenance of individual elements of a UA system;
3. considering UA operators as entities (a person, organization, enterprise) using or offering UA for use to other entities – such services must be properly organized in order to conform to the requirements in the fields of technical airworthiness, licensing, personnel competences, and operational requirements;
4. a UA operator safety management system as a requirement for ensuring continuous operational safety;
5. requirements for training, licensing, and maintaining UA pilot competences,
6. operational tasks, including emergency situations (e.g. loss of communications);
7. traffic recognition and collision avoidance systems (DAA);
8. control systems (C2link) and the ability to communicate with UA via third parties, so-called services providers;
9. air traffic management and air traffic service issues in the context of UA operations, including tracking of UA.

As part of further work, ICAO published a working document entitled "*RPAS Concept of Operation*" in 2017. This can be considered as an "operational concept", which indicates the issues that require further analysis in the process of working on the integration of unmanned and manned aviation[159]. The concept describes UA operations, UA systems, operational environments, control methods, as well as the relationship between unmanned and manned aviation, air traffic services, and air traffic management. Importantly, the concept applies only to certified UA that are to operate internationally in the same space as manned aviation (limited to controlled airspace), which is not expected to happen before 2031.

159 https://www.icao.int/safety/UA/Documents/ICAO%20RPAS%20CONOPS.pdf

This timeline is related to the objectives adopted in ICAO's *Global Air Navigation Plan*[160], which lists the following timeframes for the integration of UA in civil aviation:

1. adopting preliminary procedures for UA operating outside of designated air zones (2019),
2. developing detailed UA procedures, taking into account scenarios like loss of control (communications and control) and advanced systems for traffic detection and collision avoidance, including the possibility of using UA location data based on ADS-B technology (2025),
3. developing regulations that would enable the certification of UA operating in the same airspace as manned aviation, including airports (2031).

As highlighted in the 2017 concept, ICAO's work focuses on incorporating UA capable of carrying out international operations into the aviation safety regulation system. It is assumed that these operations will be conducted in accordance with IFR-based air regulations. There is simply no commercial justification for carrying out international VFR flights. As a consequence, the direction of ICAO work adopted in the 2017 concept does not apply to the following types of UA operations:

1. local (national) operations,
2. operations within line of sight (VLOS),
3. operations at very low altitudes (below 150 m)
4. operations at very high altitudes (above FL 600)
5. transport of people,
6. fully autonomous operations.

ICAO has also made an attempt to develop model regulations for those operations that have attracted the greatest interest of the UA sector in recent years. These model regulations are based on those developed in such countries as the USA, Canada, and Australia. These refer to the classification of operations developed under JARUS and later adopted in EU regulations which is based on assessing the risk related to conducting a given operation. At the beginning of 2020, a draft of these model regulations was published for the purpose of consultation[161].

160 https://www4.icao.int/ganpportal/

161 https://www.icao.int/safety/UA/Pages/ICAO-Model-UAS-Regulations.aspx [access: July 3, 2020]

The proposed regulations are to consist of so-called parts, supplemented by *advisory circulars.*

Part 101 concerns UA with a total mass of up to 25 kg, used within so-called Standard UA Operating Conditions. These conditions assume that the operation takes place within the operator's line of sight, no higher than 120 m above the ground, and maintains a safe distance from other people.

Part 102, which applies to other types of UA operations. According to this, each operation will have to be authorized individually by an aviation authority. It also provides for the option to obtain a UA operator certificate.

Part 149 concerns the possibility of delegating some of the aviation authority's tasks related to monitoring UA to so-called Approved Aviation Organizations.

It is worth adding that ICAO is involved in works on the development of concepts related to UA traffic management – a so-called UTM (*Unmanned Aircraft Systems Traffic Management*)[162].

2.3. Amendments to the Annexes to the Chicago Convention

ICAO's approach to the integration of unmanned and manned aviation means that amendments made to the Chicago Convention annexes have been rather modest.

The first amendment concerned Annex 13 on aircraft accident and incident investigation and was actually limited to extending the definition of accident to UA. The second amendment concerned Annex 7, which focuses on aircraft registration marks, and consisted of defining the division of aircraft into manned and unmanned, and a reduction in the size of registration marks for smaller aircraft. The third amendment concerned Annex 2 on rules of the air. The new appendix to Annex 2[163] specified the requirements related to the possible granting of a special permit for UA operations required by Art. 8 of the Convention. It also states that UA operations should be conducted in such a way as to minimize the risks they pose to people, property, and other aircraft, in accordance with the conditions detailed therein. These amendments were adopted between 2011 and 2012.

ICAO's further work concerned changes to Annex 1 on personnel licensing. Amendment 175 to Annex 1 was adopted in 2018[164]. Amendment 178 to Annex

162 https://www.icao.int/safety/UA/Documents/UTM-Framework%20Edition%202.pdf [access: July 3, 2020]

163 Appendix 4, Remotely Piloted Aircraft Systems.

164 AN12/1.1.23-18/11.

1 – Personnel Licensing of the Chicago Convention introduces new provisions for the use of electronic pilot licenses, which are increasingly being used by ICAO Member States. It sets out a new common format to provide for simplified license verification by other States. And entered into force in November 2022.[165] It provides for the introduction of a new type of license, i.e. a *remote pilot license*. This license is required for international UA flights and IFR operations. The license is issued by the state in which the operator is established (traditionally it is the state of registration of a manned aircraft). By assisting in the wider adoption of e-licenses, the amendment will also reduce the number of printed licenses in circulation and realize cost reduction and environmental benefits.[166]

Advanced work was also underway on further amendments to the already mentioned Annex 2 (rules of the air) and on a comprehensive amendment to Annex 6 on aircraft operation. The former three parts of Annex 6 concerned: international commercial air transport by airplanes (part I), international general aviation (part II), and international commercial air transport by helicopters (part III). The need to regulate UA operations in a manner that is proportional to the risk they involve is the main assumption of the new part IV to Annex 6. The classification of operations into low-risk operations (requiring no authorization), medium-risk operations (requiring authorization), and high-risk operations (requiring certification, as in the case of manned aviation), adopted by JARUS and in EU regulations is the model for these risk-proportional regulations. Annex 6 part IV is intended to deal with the latter type of operations, which are primarily performed beyond line of sight. High-risk operations require developing certification rules based on manned aviation regulations, i.e. operator and equipment certification.[167] The proposed flight operations SARPs for Annex 6 (Operation of Aircraft), Part IV, which are now out for State review and comment..

ICAO's further works assume appropriate amendments being made to the following Chicago Convention annexes[168]:

1. Annex 8 (airworthiness), amendments to the extent necessary for the certification of UA and flight control stations; expected year of publication – 2021;

---

165 https://www.icao.int/Newsroom/Pages/ICAO-Council-adopts-amendments-supporting-electronic-pilot-licenses-flight-operations-continuing-airworthiness-responsibili.aspx (access: February 4, 2023)

166 Ibidem.

167 A. Masutti, F. Tomasello, op. cit., p. 48.

168 Ibidem.

2. Annex 10 (aeronautical telecommunications), amendments to the extent necessary to regulate requirements of communications and control systems (C2link) and traffic detection and collision avoidance systems; expected year of publication – 2022;
3. Annex 11 (air traffic services), amendments to the extent necessary for UA integration; expected year of publication – 2023;
4. Annex 2 (rules of the air); expected year of publication – 2023;
5. Annex 19 (safety management); expected year of publication – 2022.

3. A national approach based on example regulatory activity in the USA

3.1. Introduction

Due to a lack of standards developed at an international level, as well as ICAO's focus on regulations for advanced RPAS capable of performing international flights, national and regional regulations hold fundamental importance. The further part of this publication presents the state of national (Polish) regulations, as well as other regional regulations developed at an EU level, in more detail. However, it is also worth presenting the state of works on UA integration in the United States as a reference point for EU regulations. The scale of the American UA market is definitely a key factor here, as evidenced by data mentioned in the introduction. Moreover, similar to the EU's situation, federal UA regulations are part of a wider strategy for the gradual future integration of manned and unmanned aviation.

3.2. FAA Modernization and Reauthorization Act 2012

The first regulations on the use of drones in the United States were related to military and public safety tasks. These were adapted and developed over time[169]. Among others, they included procedures to enable the first civilian operations subject to prior approval (UAS-Policy-05-01). The FAA took on a relatively conservative approach to this topic, reflecting its belief in the over early development of drone technology – especially in light of issues related to traffic and collision detection systems and communications[170]. In 2006, the FAA established the

169 For more see J. Rupprecht, Drones: Their Many Civilian Uses and the US Laws Surrounding Them, 2015, p. 43.

170 K. Dalamagkidis (ed.), op. cit., p. 60.

Unmanned Aircraft Program Office, the aim of which was to intensify works on UA regulations. In 2007, the Federal Aviation Administration published its overall UA policy[171]. UA operation procedures were then revised in 2008 (UAS-Policy-08-01). However, these rules were still quite restrictive, and it became necessary to start allowing for R&D flights. This way, the first test centers operating under the supervision of the FAA were established. It is worth noting that as a result of the Government Accountability Office's (GAO) 2008 post-audit recommendations, the US intensified the collection of UA-related data as well as works on UA integration[172]. Ultimately, issues relating to the integration of unmanned aviation into the *National Airspace System* (NAS) were included as part of a comprehensive FAA reform.

The reform had been worked on for several years. It mostly concerned systematic issues related to financing and organizing the air transport system. Eventually, some of the provisions of the *FAA Modernization and Reform Act*[173] of February 14, 2012, were devoted to UA. Among others, the document obliged the FAA to develop a plan for unmanned aviation integration, which was supposed to define a detailed method for achieving gradual integration. It was assumed that this integration should take place by the end of September 2015. The plan was published in 2013[174]. In parallel, a fairly comprehensive roadmap outlining a way to implement the integration plan was published as well[175]. Unfortunately, these ambitious assumptions, which were developed with active support from the drone industry, were given a reality check[176]. At the end of 2014, authorities accomplished only 9 out of 17 tasks defined in the Act of 2012. The reasons for this were unresolved technological, regulatory, and privacy issues as well as requirements for cooperation between a too high number of state agencies[177]. Apart from the systematic issues, it is worth pointing to certain provisions of the Act of 2012 which directly regulated issues related to the use of UAS:

---

171 https://www.faa.gov/uas/resources/policy_library/media/frnotice_uas.pdf [access: July 3, 2020]

172 https://www.gao.gov/products/GAO-08-511 [access: July 3, 2020].

173 FAA Modernization and Reform Act of 2012, Pub. L. No. 112-95, 126 Stat. 11 (2012).

174 https://www.faa.gov/about/plans_reports/congress/media/UAS_Comprehensive_Plan.pdf [access: July 3, 2020].

175 https://www.faa.gov/uas/resources/policy_library/media/uas_roadmap_2013.pdf [access: July 3, 2020]

176 B. Carey, Enter the Drones. The FAA and UAVs in America, 2016, p. 55.

177 Ibidem.

1. the FAA's obligation to issue regulations for so-called small drones (less than 25 kg) used in commercial operations. These regulations were to be published within 18 months;
2. the Act introduced statutory provisions for so-called models defined as UA weighing less than 25 kg used for hobby or recreational purposes (section 336).
3. the Act provided for the possibility of granting individual exemptions from general aviation regulations, including implementing provisions to be adopted for so-called small drones (Section 333);
4. the FAA's obligation to review the regulations for state UA operations carried out on the basis of granted permits;
5. the Act obliged the FAA to create UA test centers;
6. the FAA was also obliged to create a special area over Arctic Ocean waters around Alaska where it would be possible to conduct tests and commercial operations without major restrictions, subject to prior authorization.

3.3. First commercial operations

The 2012 Act did not regulate airworthiness requirements for UA in any way. Therefore, if a certain UA did not fall within the model category or the small aircraft category and was not a state aircraft, it had to be certified in advance and in accordance with the general requirements. In the absence of certification standards, obtaining an appropriate airworthiness certificate was only possible on the basis of regulations for issuing a so-called Special Airworthiness Certificate (SAC). Previously, these provisions were the basis for issuing airworthiness certificates for experimental aircraft. However, after the 2012 Act was passed, the FAA issued the first SAC for UA used for commercial purposes limited only to parts of the Arctic Ocean around Alaska (where the Act provided for the creation of a test area). Notwithstanding the acquisition of an SAC for the UA itself, it was also necessary to obtain a permit for the operator. The first two SACs were issued for UA intended for use in the oil industry. Certification of these UA was also possible because they were previously authorized for use by the military[178]. After obtaining an SAC for the UA itself, it was also necessary to obtain operating authorization.

The first commercial operation took place on August 12, 2013. The UA was called *Scan Eagle* and the manufacturer – *Insitu* – was its operator. The flight was

178 https://www.faa.gov/news/updates/?newsId=73118 [access: July 3, 2020].

carried out over Arctic waters, after taking off from a sea ship. *Scan Eagle* flights were carried out on behalf of *ConocoPhillips*, an oil company, and involved monitoring the state of the environment in search for new oil fields in the Arctic Ocean. *Scan Eagle*'s second commercial flight experienced an engine failure and led to a water landing[179].

The second SAC was issued for an aircraft called *Puma* operated by manufacturer *AeroVironment*. The flights were carried out on behalf of the BP fuel company, also over Arctic waters and on the basis of a COA permit issued under the 2012 Act. A year later, an official exemption from the general regulations allowed for commercial flights to take place over land (also over Alaska)[180].

3.4. Implementing regulations for small drones (Part 107)

The 2012 Act required that the FAA adopt implementing regulations concerning so-called small drones. These regulations were to be adopted within 18 months, i.e. by August 2013. However, a draft legislation was published in February 2015 and only then subjected to public consultation (the project received more than 4,600 comments). These provisions – called Part 107 – were published on June 29, 2016 and entered into force on August 29, 2016.[181]

The regulations included in Part 107 are quite detailed. Their basic premise is the recognition of UA as aircraft. Consequently, these requirements concern aircraft operations, pilots, and airspace. Meeting the requirements of Part 107 is equivalent to authorization to perform UA operation, regardless of their purpose. Part 107 therefore made it possible to carry out commercial operations without the need for additional permits.

First, Part 107 requires that a UA pilot has a *remote pilot certificate* issued by the FAA. In order to obtain such a certificate, one must be at least 16 years of age, have the necessary authorization from the TSA (*Transportation Security Administration*), and pass the FAA's theoretical exam. From those who already hold a different pilot's license, the authorities require passing a different FAA test on-line. The license is valid for 2 years and needs to be renewed by passing an exam. These regulations do not require the holder to pass specific aero-medical examinations. However, the pilot is obliged to self-assess his own state of health

---

179 For more see B. Carey, op. cit., p. 9 et seq.

180 https://www.faa.gov/news/press_releases/news_story.cfm?newsId=16354 [access: July 3, 2020].

181 https://www.federalregister.gov/documents/2016/06/28/2016-15079/operation-and-certification-of-small-unmanned-aircraft-systems [access: July 3, 2020].

in order to avoid dangerous situations during a flight. The UA pilot shall carry out a pre-take off inspection before each flight, which includes checking the device itself and the control station to ensure that operations can be executed safely. Apart from this general obligation, there are no specific requirements regarding UA airworthiness. Part 107 imposes a special obligation on pilots to report incidents which result in serious bodily injury or damage to property valued at over $500 to the FAA. Part 107 regulations apply only to UA with a total weight of less than 55 pounds (25 kg) and allow only VLOS-type operations. The law permits carrying out VLOS operations with the assistance of non-pilot observers. However, these must meet certain requirements related to space observation and communications. The pilots themselves remain responsible for giving way to other aircraft. Flying over people is forbidden, except for those directly involved in the UA's operation. Night flights or flights of more than one UA operated by the same pilot simultaneously are also prohibited. Part 107 contains fairly detailed operational requirements – it allows for a maximum flight speed of 100 mph and a maximum flight ceiling of 400 feet above the ground or structures. Minimum visibility from a control station is 3 miles.

Flights in controlled airspace are only possible with prior authorization from air traffic control services. Permits for flying within a certain altitude (at low altitudes) are issued on the basis of publicly available maps (so-called FAA UAS Facility Maps)[182]. In 2018, the US introduced an electronic system for applying for such permits, allowing for obtaining permits to fly in controlled airspace around 500 airports, up to an altitude of 400 feet (LAANC, *Low Altitude Authentication and Notification Capability*)[183].

Part 107 also provides for the possibility of issuing exemptions from certain requirements that it contains[184]. In order to be granted such exemptions, a UA operator must submit a request describing their planned operation(s) and demonstrating that these does not pose a threat to safety. The Aviation Administration may impose additional obligations when issuing a *certificate of waiver*. As a result of the GAO's recommendations on the FAA's safety management of UA

182 https://www.faa.gov/uas/commercial_operators/uas_facility_maps/ [access: July 3, 2020].

183 https://www.faa.gov/uas/programs_partnerships/data_exchange/ [access: July 3, 2020].

184 https://www.faa.gov/uas/commercial_operators/part_107_waivers/ [access: July 3, 2020].

operations, all issued certificates of waiver have been made publicly available[185]. According to cyclically updated AUVSI[187] reports, the FAA has issued 4,144 certificates to date, the vast majority of which involved nighttime operations (almost 3,813). Flights over people are next in line (125). It is worth noting that only 53 BVLOS operations have been approved.

It should also be mentioned that Part 107 does not apply to UA, which, according to the 2012 Act, are defined as model aircraft. That is to say, aircraft used exclusively for hobby or recreational purposes, with a mass of less than 55 pounds (25kg). Provisions concerning aircraft models are fairly general (Section 336) and they exempt models from the FAA's jurisdiction. In 2015, the Administration introduced legislation requiring all UA to be registered. Then, in 2017 the FAA's right to regulate models, including the imposition of registration obligations, was challenged in the Taylor vs. Huerta[188] court case. However, the FAA's competences to regulate all issues related to UA, including models, was confirmed with a dedicated law[189].

As already mentioned, the FAA introduced legislation at the end of 2015 requiring the registration of models and UA that carry out operations defined in Part 107[190]. These provisions require (from December 21, 2015) owners to register their UA as well as corresponding UA markings. Registering and marking a UA is a condition for performing operations in accordance with Part 107 (or model regulations). The register is dedicated to owners of UA weighing up to 25 kg. UA weighing less than 250 g are excluded from registration. The register was created in electronic form, with a mandatory fee of $5. UA with a mass of over 25 kg must be registered in the traditional aircraft registration system. According to FAA statistics at the end of 2018[191], the register for so-called small UA (weighing up to 25 kg) included:

---

185 https://www.faa.gov/uas/commercial_operators/part_107_waivers/waivers_issued/ [access: July 3, 2020].

186 "Small UAS. FAA should improve Its Management of Safety Risks" https://www.gao.gov/products/GAO-18-110 [access: July 3, 2020].

187 https://www.auvsi.org/our-impact/waivers-under-Part 107-updated-interactive-report [access: July 3, 2020].

188 https://law.justia.com/cases/federal/appellate-courts/cadc/15-1495/15-1495-2017-05-19.html [access: July 3, 2020].

189 R.J. Wallace, J.M. Loffi, (2017). Evolution of UAS Policy in the Wake of Taylor v. Huerta. International Journal of Aviation, Aeronautics, and Aerospace, Vol. 4, Issue 3.

190 https://www.federalregister.gov/documents/2015/12/16/2015-31750/registration-and-marking-requirements-for-small-unmanned-aircraft [access: July 3, 2020].

191 FAA Aerospace Forecast 2019–2039.

1. 900,000 model aircraft owners (recreational or hobby use); registration is obligatory for owners only, not aircraft. However, it is estimated that the number of model UA amounts to about 1.25 million;
2. 277,000 UA other than models. Registration in this case is obligatory for both the owner and the aircraft.
3. It is worth noting that FAA forecasts predict that the number of model aircraft will increase slightly (to approx. 1.37 million) by 2021, while the number of non-model UA will increase by over 250% (to 711,000).

3.4.1. FAA Reauthorization Act 2018

Six years after the adoption of the FAA Modernization and Reform Act of 2012, a new law on the modernization of the air transport system was passed in October 2018. The *FAA Reauthorization Act of 2018*, signed on October 5[192], replaced the previous 2012 Act. It ensured additional funding for the FAA and included plans for various modernization programs for the aviation sector. A significant part of the Act focused on development policies for the UA sector and its further integration with unmanned aviation. The most important of these provisions are as follows[193]:

1. the FAA was obliged to present plans for UA integration to Congress, taking into account the need to develop a UA traffic management system (UTM), fight illegal UA operations, and implement pilot programs aimed at testing new technologies;
2. the FAA's right to require registration of all UA, including models, was confirmed;
3. the FAA was mandated to develop regulations requiring electronic identification of all UA (including models). At the same time, the FAA was mandated to launch pilot programs on electronic identification;
4. the FAA and NASA were obliged to continue working on the development of a UA traffic management concept (UTM);

192 FAA Reauthorization Act of 2018, Pub. L. No. 115–254.

193 For more, see M.A. Swanson, Comprehensive "FAA Reauthorization Act of 2018" Charts ambitious course forward on drones, article presented at ICUAS 2019; J. Poss, The "Why's" of the 2018 FAA Reauthorization, https://insideunmannedsystems.com/the-whys-of-the-2018-faa-reauthorization-act/ [access: July 3, 2020].

5. the FAA was obliged to work on operational regulations aimed at ensuring the safety of aviation and critical infrastructure. These regulations should be deeply rooted in a *risk-based approach*;
6. the FAA was obliged to develop an action plan to enable the operational use of detection and neutralization systems on unauthorized UA operations, mainly around airports (C-UAS, *Counter-UAS*). The plan provided for the development of draft regulations for the certification of such systems, as well as test (pilot) programs. It was decided that these systems would not be subject to the general provisions that prohibited intercepting someone else's signal / device;
7. the FAA was obliged to develop guidelines for activities conducted by agencies responsible for public safety in relation to monitoring UA operations. In parallel, the authorities took steps to review regulations on the competences of individual federal and state agencies regarding UA supervision;
8. funding was extended for testing programs for new UA technologies. These programs created new testing facilities. Currently, there are seven such "proving grounds"[194]. It is worth mentioning that three of them are used by the ASSURE (*Alliance for System Safety of UAS through Research Excellence*) consortium of companies and scientific institutions, which uses 340 UA for research and development purposes[195];
9. the FAA was obliged to develop regulations on small package transportation and support testing of various solutions in this field within the *Integration Pilot Program*[196].

The most important works undertaken in the implementation of the 2018 Act included:

1. revision of the regulations on the use of UAS. In 2019, a series of detailed questions and assumptions related to ensuring safety of so-called small UA operations[197] was subject to public consultations;

194 https://www.faa.gov/uas/programs_partnerships/test_sites/ [access: July 3, 2020].

195 https://www.assureuas.org/about.php [access: July 3, 2020].

196 https://www.faa.gov/uas/programs_partnerships/integration_pilot_program/ [access: July 3, 2020].

197 https://www.federalregister.gov/documents/2019/02/13/2019-00758/safe-and-secure-operations-of-small-unmanned-aircraft-systems [access: July 3, 2020].

2. presentation of draft changes to the provisions of Part 107, which were to enable small UA operations at night and flights over people. The public consultation process was carried out in 2019;[198]
3. introduction of implementing provisions regarding markings on so-called small UA. These provisions required that small UA be marked with the number obtained during registration by their owner, which should be visible on each UA's exterior[199];
4. a draft regulation on remote UA (*e-remote*) identification published in December 2019[200]. Public consultations on the project lasted until March 2020. Over 53,000 comments were submitted. According to the draft, drone operators will be required to provide data that enables identifying the location of a UA, its flight path, and the location of its operator. As a rule, this data transmission will take place through the use a radio device installed on the UA. In the case of VLOS flights, the operator can transmit this data via the Internet. In May 2020, the FAA also established a consortium of companies to support the development and implementation of this electronic identification system[201];
5. the development of a support program for agencies responsible for public safety, especially in the event of incidents involving UAS (LEAP, *Law Enforcement Assistance Program*)[202];
6. activities related to the development and certification of systems detecting UA activity around airports[203];
7. the continuation of the FAA and NASA's cooperation in the development of a UA traffic management concept (UTM, *UAS Traffic Management*)[204].

198 https://www.federalregister.gov/documents/2019/02/13/2019-00732/operation-of-small-unmanned-aircraft-systems-over-people [access: July 3, 2020].

199 https://www.federalregister.gov/documents/2019/02/13/2019-00765/external-marking-requirement-for-small-unmanned-aircraft [access: July 3, 2020].

200 https://www.regulations.gov/document?D=FAA-2019-1100-0001 [access: July 3, 2020].

201 https://www.faa.gov/news/press_releases/news_story.cfm?newsId=24956 [access: July 3, 2020].

202 https://www.faa.gov/about/office_org/headquarters_offices/ash/ash_programs/investigations/leap/ [access: July 3, 2020].

203 https://www.faa.gov/airports/airport_safety/media/Updated-Information-UAS-Detection-Countermeasures-Technology-Airports-20190507.pdf [access: July 3, 2020].

204 https://www.faa.gov/uas/research_development/traffic_management/ [access: July 3, 2020].

In March 2020, a new version of the UTM Operational Concept was published[205]. The purpose of the UTM system is to enable UA activity (flights) and BVLOS operations to be performed at low altitudes where a "traditional" air traffic control service is usually not provided. This system is to serve as a place where drone operators and system managers can exchange necessary data. Contrary to a "traditional" air traffic management system, where communications are based on radio correspondence between pilots and air traffic controllers, data exchange in a UTM will take place based on a network of automated systems. In 2019, as part of the UTM Pilot Program[206], US authorities began testing a UTM for UA equipped with remote identification systems.

3.5. State regulations

It should be mentioned that many local regulations regarding UA have been passed at the level of individual states. Most of them concern the use of UA by public services, which is related to the constitutional principle of protecting the privacy of US citizens, i.e. the possibility of obtaining data by state services only on the basis of a court order[207]. However, state legislature often covered issues related to UA operations or to the organization of airspace (e.g. flights in cities). In the opinion of the FAA, regulations regarding airspace and the operational use of drones are reserved to the competences of the federal legislator[208].

4. Standardization among specialist organizations

4.1. Introduction

The development of legal regulations regarding UA is closely related to the development of technical standards for most of the elements that make up a UAS. Standards developed by specialist organizations dealing with the standardization

205 https://www.faa.gov/uas/research_development/traffic_management/media/UTM_ConOps_v2.pdf [access: July 3, 2020].

206 https://www.faa.gov/uas/research_development/traffic_management/utm_pilot_program/ [access: July 3, 2020].

207 Dawn M. K. Zoldi, Gregory R. Speirs, Josie Lewber, Unmanned Aircraft System Legislative Trends in the United States at the State Level, 2013–2016: A Comprehensive Review. https://doi.org/10.1007/978-3-319-32193-6_160-1 [access: July 3, 2020].

208 https://www.faa.gov/uas/resources/policy_library/media/UAS_Fact_Sheet_Final.pdf [access: July 3, 2020].

of technical requirements in aviation are often used in the certification of manned aircraft. Therefore, the involvement of these organizations in works on drafting regulations concerning UA seemed like an obvious step to take. Below is a brief presentation of these organizations, as well as others that have a direct impact on the development of UA policies and regulations.

4.2. Organizations engaged in standardization activity in aviation

As already mentioned, aviation authorities (regulators) often rely on standards developed by specialized technical organizations. In the USA, it is the RTCA (established in 1935 as the *Radio Technical Committee for Aeronautics*) which develops detailed technical standards used in the FAA's certification of aviation equipment. The work of the RTCA is organized within special committees that deal with specific topics. For example, there are committees that deal with standards for anti-collision devices or satellite technology in air navigation. In May 2013, a new Committee (SC-228) was established to develop minimum performance standards for unmanned aircraft systems[209]. The work of this committee focused on the development of standards for traffic detection and collision avoidance (DAA) systems and UA control systems (C2link).

The European counterpart of the RTCA is the EUROCAE organization, established in 1963 (the *European Organization for Civil Aviation Equipment*). The EUROCAE's WG-105 working group deals with the development of standards and advisory materials related to the safe use of UAS[210]. WG-105's scope of work concerns the following areas:

1. UA traffic management (UTM),
2. control and communications systems (C2, C3 link),
3. traffic detection and collision avoidance (DAA) systems,
4. UA design and production standards,
5. risk analysis of UA operations in the specific category (SORA), and
6. automation of UA operations.

The works of the RTCA and EUROCAE are coordinated with the works of ICAO. Both organizations engage aviation industry experts in their work.

209 https://www.rtca.org/content/sc-228

210 https://www.eurocae.net/about-us/working-groups/

Among these experts, we can find representatives of the aviation industry and aviation authorities.

The aforementioned organizations mainly deal with the development of standards related to devices and technical systems.

As the UA market grew, these organizations began working on developing international UA standards. And so in 2003, within ASTM International, a committee dealing with this issue was established[211]. The ISO organization also established a Committee dealing with UA standards in 2014[212].

Moreover, the AW-Drones project was also launched as part of the SESAR JU program. The aim of the project was to come up with standards and good practices regarding the use of UA by 2021[213].

4.3. JARUS (Joint Authorities for Rulemaking on Unmanned Systems)

JARUS is an association of aviation authorities. Its objective is to develop regulatory standards related to ensuring the safety of UA operations, particularly on technical and operational issues. JARUS was established in 2007 out of a need for a body that would take on a practical approach to solving the issues at hand. The association was formed as a result of the coordination of supervision activities of an EU country with other supervision bodies and was directly related to the first applications for UA certification. Back then, UA certification was beyond EASA's competences[214]. JARUS aims to develop standards that can serve as an exit point for adopting national regulations. Today, JARUS consists of aviation authorities from over 60 countries and EASA[215]. There are seven Working Groups within JARUS. Each of them deals with a different issue:

- WG 1 – Flight Crew Licensing
- WG 2 – Operations
- WG 3 – Airworthiness
- WG 4 – Detect and Avoid
- WG 5 – Command and Control
- WG 6 – Safety and Risk Management

211 https://www.astm.org/COMMITTEE/F38.htm [access: July 3, 2020].
212 https://www.iso.org/committee/5336224.html [access: July 3, 2020].
213 https://www.aw-drones.eu/ [access: July 3, 2020].
214 K. Dalamagkidis (ed.), op. cit., p. 78.
215 http://jarus-rpas.org/ [access: July 3, 2020].

- WG 7 – Concepts of Operations

JARUS works in parallel with EASA. Therefore, EU regulations proposed by EASA and JARUS documents are largely convergent. For example, JAR-Doc-09 *UAS Operational Categorization* recommends introducing risk-based regulations and dividing UA operations into open, specific, and certified categories. The document is divided into the abovementioned categories depending on the degree of risk that a given operation entails. Risks in the open category are minimized with specific operational requirements. Risks in the specific category require risk analyses and approvals from aviation authorities. In the certified category, it is necessary to adopt requirements for the certification of equipment (a UA system), pilots (licenses), and operators. Similarly, the document JAR-Doc-06 on the methodology for *Specific Operation Risk Assessment* (SORA) was practically directly copied by EASA and implemented into its guidelines adopted in 2019 for EU legislation on specific category operations. However, EASA also took into account airworthiness guidelines developed by JARUS (along with its participation) when it was developing relevant requirements.

4.4. European Organization for the Safety of Air Navigation – Eurocontrol

Eurocontrol (the *European Organization for the Safety of Air Navigation)* is a regional, specialized international organization established in 1961. Its main goal is to support and coordinate cooperation between EU Member States in order to ensure the safety of air navigation and civil and military cooperation in this field. Eurocontrol works with Member States and air navigation service providers. It also supports the EU in implementing the Single European Sky program. Although some competences (mainly in the field of preparation of specialized air navigation safety requirements) were taken over by EASA, Eurocontrol actively participates in works related to the integration of unmanned aviation and cooperates with EASA. The documents developed by Eurocontrol in the field of unmanned aviation integration include:

1. a document for the assessment of airspace occupancy (the assessment is part of a risk analysis of UA operations in the specific category)[216];

216 https://www.eurocontrol.int/publication/uas-atm-airspace-assessment [access: July 3, 2020].

2. a document on rules of the air recommending changes to the EU's rules of the air[217];
3. a document on the need to ensure that UA use the same altitude determination methods as those used in manned aviation[218];
4. an operational concept for the integration of UAS with existing air traffic management systems[219] assuming, among others, the need to create new rules of the air for VLL operations (Very Low Level, less than 500 ft.), as well as VHL operations (Very High Level, above 600FL);
5. a report on the implementation of services related to the U-space concept (UAS traffic management) in EU countries[220].

Furthermore, Eurocontrol participates in various SESAR JU projects related to the development of U-space services. It was also involved in the PODIUM project, within which UAS Traffic Management systems were tested in several selected locations in various EU countries[221]. There's also the CORUS project, within which a detailed operational concept for European UAS Traffic Management was prepared[222].

A project implemented by Eurocontrol and the Latvian Civil Aviation Agency is also worth mentioning. The project included the assessment of the performance of UA operations in controlled airspace at Riga Airport[223]. It included continuous monitoring of UA operations and showed that the vast majority of UA flights conducted in this area were performed above the maximum altitude permitted by national regulations for UA flights in controlled airspace.

Eurocontrol also participates in activities related to the development of a European policy in the field of detection and neutralization systems for illegal UA operations around airports (C-UAS)[224].

---

217 https://www.eurocontrol.int/publication/uas-atm-flight-rules [access: July 3, 2020].

218 https://www.eurocontrol.int/publication/uas-atm-common-altitude-reference-system-cars [access: July 3, 2020].

219 https://www.eurocontrol.int/publication/unmanned-aircraft-systems-uas-atm-integration [access: July 3, 2020].

220 https://www.eurocontrol.int/publication/u-space-services-implementation-monitoring-report [access: July 3, 2020].

221 https://www.sesarju.eu/projects/podium [access: July 3, 2020].

222 https://www.sesarju.eu/projects/corus [access: July 3, 2020].

223 https://www.eurocontrol.int/publication/riga-airspace-assessment [access: July 3, 2020].

224 https://www.eurocontrol.int/event/high-level-workshop-drone-detection-2019 [access: July 3, 2020].

4.5. Organizations representing the UA industry

The industry itself and users of UA have great influence on shaping policies related to the integration of unmanned aviation. The largest organization representing what can be broadly defined as the UA industry is AUVSI (*The Association for Unmanned Vehicle Systems International*), established in the USA in 1973. Other organizations established for a similar purpose are the *Small UAV Coalition* (USA)[225] and *Drone Alliance Europe*[226]. The GUTMA organization (*Global UTM Association*)[227] was also established as a forum for exchanging experiences related to the development of a UTM. National and regional organizations such as the UAV Dach [228] (German-speaking countries) or ARPAS (UK) are also important[229]. Of course, the largest producers of UA systems and companies developing such technologies also present their position during legislative works and inform about the results of their own research. Among European companies is the AIRBUS consortium, which established *Airbus Urban Mobility*[230] in May 2018 which deals with the development of flying vehicles for urban transport (e.g. City Airbus) and also the development of a UTM system[231].

4.6. Other aviation organizations

As the number of operations involving drones increases, so does the number of incidents. This has resulted in manned aviation organizations taking positions on the matter more frequently. Unambiguous views related to shaping policies for unmanned aviation integration were expressed by, among others:

1. The International Air Transportation Association (IATA)[232],
2. The Aircraft Owners and Pilots Association (AOPA)[233],
3. The Airports Council International (ACI)[234],

---

225 http://smalluavcoalition.org/ [access: July 3, 2020].
226 http://dronealliance.eu/ [access: July 3, 2020].
227 https://gutma.org/ [access: July 3, 2020].
228 https://www.uavdach.org/ [access: July 3, 2020].
229 https://www.arpas.uk/ [access: July 3, 2020].
230 https://www.airbus.com/newsroom/stories/urban-air-mobility-the-sky-is-yours.html [access: July 3, 2020].
231 For example, the UTM Concept has been published https://www.airbusutm.com/uam-resources-airbus-blueprint [access: July 3, 2020].
232 https://www.iata.org/en/programs/safety/drones/ [access: July 3, 2020].
233 https://www.aopa.org/go-fly/aircraft-and-ownership/drones [access: July 3, 2020].
234 https://aci.aero/about-aci/priorities/safety/drones/ [access: July 3, 2020].

4. The International Federation of Air Line Pilots' Associations and European Cockpit Association (IFALPA[235], ECA[236]).

It is worth noting that these aforementioned organizations, along with a dozen others, sent a joint letter to the European Commission in May 2020 demanding a revision of EASA's proposal regarding the introduction of a U-space concept.[237]

235 https://www.ifalpa.org/news/global-pilots-industry-partners-call-for-new-guidance-on-drone-operations/ [access: July 3, 2020].

236 https://www.eurocockpit.be/campaign/integrating-drones-safely [access: July 3, 2020].

237 https://www.iata.org/contentassets/8c2566421a524258896e89aceb739333/we-are-all-one-in-the-sky-open-letter-to-the-european-commission.pdf [access: July 3, 2020].

Chapter 4 Public law regulations in the EU and their impact on national regulations

1. Legal regulations in the EU as an element of Europe's strategy for the integration of unmanned aviation

1.1. Introduction

The EU started creating a system of unified safety regulations in civil aviation at the end of the 1990s. Up until this point, European cooperation in this field took place through the JAA (*Joint Aviation Authorities*), which aimed to create common regulatory standards for safety and procedures in commercial aviation. However, the JAA system had its imperfections, which eventually sparked a discussion on the necessity to take action at an EU level[238]. Establishing the European Aviation Safety Agency (EASA) was first proposed in the year 2000. The Agency was supposed to assist the European Commission in drafting and supervising EU aviation safety regulations[239]. On July 15, 2002, Regulation (EC) 1592/2002 of the European Parliament and of the Council of 15 July 2002 on common rules in the field of civil aviation and establishing the European Aviation Safety Agency saw the light of day[240]. The principal objective of this regulation was to establish and maintain a high level of uniformity in civil aviation safety across Europe. Additional goals also included promoting profitability in regulatory and certification processes, avoiding duplication of efforts at a national and European level, and assisting Member States in fulfilling obligations that stemmed from the Chicago Convention.

Regulation 1592/2002 authorized the European Commission to regulate tasks related to the design, production, and maintenance of aircraft and their parts, as

238 P. Fastnacht-Stupnicki, P. Kasprzyk, Od JAA do EASA – ewolucja europejskiego systemu prawnego w zakresie bezpieczeństwa w lotnictwie cywilnym (w) „Internacjonalizacja i europeizacja prawa lotniczego: księga pamiątkowa ku czci profesora Marka Żylicza" – collective work edited by A. Konert, Warsaw, 2015.

239 Commission Working Document "In view of the discussions within the Council on the creation of the European Aviation Safety Authority in the Community framework", COM (2000) 144 final.

240 OJEU of September 7, 2002, L 240.

well as the activities of organizations and personnel involved in this (i.e. through initial and continued airworthiness). Later, Regulation 1592/2002 was replaced by Regulation (EC) 216/2008 of the European Parliament and of the Council of February 20, 2008[241]. It extended the EU's competences to include licensing of aircrew personnel and air operations, as well as assessing operational safety of third-country aircraft entering into the European Union. Regulation (EC) 1108/2009[242] of the Parliament and the Council amended regulation 216/2008, extending the EU's competences once again to also cover tasks related to the safety of public airports, air traffic management, and air navigation services. Pursuant to the delegation in the basic regulation, the European Commission – at the request of EASA – has been adopting new implementing regulations since 2003, which regulate in detail individual issues related to the safety of civil aviation. These regulations are listed in Chapter 1 of this publication.

However, these regulations did not apply to unmanned aircraft. Both Regulation 1592/2002 and Regulation 216/2008 did not include "unmanned aerial vehicles weighing less than 150 kg" in the EU's competences. This meant that it was up to each Member State to regulate all issues related to UA weighing less than 150 kg, while the EU's competences were limited only to those UA weighing above 150 kg. This classification quickly led to a situation in which the newly established EASA, which was supposed to handle matters related to civil aviation safety, had no power over one of the most rapidly developing sectors of the UA market. This state lasted for over 15 years. However, it should be pointed out that EASA's founding and the development of a system based on regional (not national) organization were truly major and positive changes. The system assumed transferring lawmaking competences in the field of aviation safety from a national to an EU-wide level – this required the unifying of the rules of work of national supervisory bodies, each of which had different resources and potential[243].

241 Regulation (EC) No 216/2008 of the European Parliament and of the Council of 20 February 2008 on common rules in the field of civil aviation and establishing a European Aviation Safety Agency, and repealing Council Directive 91/670/EEC, Regulation (EC) No 1592/2002 and Directive 2004/36/EC, OJEU L079.

242 Regulation (EC) No 1108/2009 of the European Parliament and of the Council of 21 October 2009 amending Regulation (EC) No 216/2008 in the field of aerodromes, air traffic management, and air navigation services and repealing Directive 2006/23/EC, OJEU L 309.

243 For more see M. Ratajczyk, Regional Aviation Safety Organizations: Enhancing Air Transport Safety Through Regional Cooperation, 2015.

The lack of EU competences to establish regulations on UA weighing less than 150 kg resulted in a situation where national regulations were of crucial importance. The need to coordinate operational and legislative activities gave us the JARUS organization. At some point, EASA worked closely with this organization, later basing its own legislative projects on JARUS' work and the outcomes of this cooperation.

It should also be mentioned that EASA had taken measures to develop legal regulations on UA operations in previous years (2005–2014). These, however, were limited to two issues. The first was to start a discussion on UA requiring mandatory EASA certification (UA weighing over 150 kg). EASA published its initial regulation proposal on this in a document entitled A-NPA 16/2005,[244] which was actually based on recommendations made in a joint report by the JAA and EUROCONTROL back in 2004. This report, based on works started at the beginning of the new millennium, proposed creating European-wide regulations for civilian UA operations[245] and included recommendations on creating national rules for UA weighing less than 150 kg which were to operate within line of sight of their operators. In the following years, EASA also developed what it called "special conditions", which were to be the basis for applying for UA certification (over 150 kg). The second issue was that EASA had twice proposed amending implementing regulations on air traffic (EC Regulation 923/2012)[246]. The purpose of these amendments was to transpose Annex 2 of the Chicago Convention, which concerned issuing authorization for UA flights, into the EU's regulations. Ultimately, this work was abandoned and a decision was made to focus on developing a comprehensive approach to UA regulations, which included reviewing the basic regulation. However, further works were significantly influenced by decisions taken at the level of the European Commission.

244 Advance-Notice of Proposed Amendment (NPA) No 16/2005 Policy for Unmanned Aerial Vehicle (UAV) certification.

245 UAV Task-Force Final Report. A Concept for European Regulation for Civil Unmanned Aerial Vehicles.

246 NPA 2012-10 and NPA 2014-09.

1.2. Shaping EU policies and regulations on unmanned aviation operations

1.2.1. UA Panel (2012)

Recognizing the potential of UA, the EC conducted a series of consultations at the turn of 2011/2012 with key stakeholders including EASA, EUROCONTROL, ICAO, JARUS, national authorities, representatives of military and police agencies, and representatives of the aviation and drone industries. These consultations, carried out under the name "*UAS Panel Process*", resulted in a working document entitled "*Towards a European strategy for the development of civil applications of Remotely Piloted Aircraft Systems (RPAS)*"[247] published on September 4, 2012. This document emphasized the need to coordinate work on the harmonization of UA regulations – started by JARUS – with work on regulations for UA weighing above 150 kg – started by EASA. Moreover, it stressed the necessity for further works in the field of radio frequency availability, protection of privacy, and civil liability. It was also recommended to conduct further research and development activities. The document additionally asked the European Commission to start working on a roadmap for the integration of unmanned aviation (*RPAS Roadmap*). This is how the "*European Steering Group*" came to be.

1.2.2. Roadmap for UA integration (2013)

In July of 2013, the European Steering Group published the results of its works in the form of a Roadmap for the integration of civil Remotely Piloted Aircraft Systems into the European Aviation System[248]. This report contained three annexes that dealt with the regulatory approach, research and development works, and social issues. It indicated that the integration of unmanned aviation requires the development of dedicated regulations related to UA airworthiness, their operations, and personnel licensing. Its authors declare that due to the complexity of these issues, gradual integration would take about 15 years and that close

247 Commission staff working document " is a European strategy for the development of civil applications of Remotely Piloted Aircraft Systems (RPAS). SWD (2012) 259 final.

248 Roadmap for the integration of civil Remotely-Piloted Aircraft Systems into the European Aviation System. http://ec.europa.eu/DocsRoom/documents/10484/attachments/1/translations/en/renditions/native

coordination of regulatory and R&D works was crucial for it to succeed. These works were to cover at least six areas:

1. integration with air traffic management systems and organization of airspace,
2. collection, verification, and confirmation of data,
3. UA control and management systems, including the issue of radio frequency availability,
4. traffic detection and collision avoidance systems,
5. issues related to counteracting unauthorized attacks,
6. operational issues, including those related to contingency procedures.

Furthermore, the report also recommended abandoning the division of competences related to UA safety regulations and extending EU competences in this area.

1.2.3. Communication from the EC – "A New Era for Aviation" (2014)

A Communication from the European Commission published in April 2014 extended the recommendations contained in the 2013 Roadmap. It concerned opening the aviation market up to the civil use of UA in a safe and sustainable manner. The Commission named this Communication, "*A New Era for Aviation*"[249]. The EC initialized a series of actions at an EU level, including legislative action, and also indicated that a number of different categories of UA, varying in size and capabilities, would come into use by 2050. Some of these would even be fully automated. It also pointed to the industry's potential for generating employment, driving innovation, and fostering economic growth, while indicating challenges related to safety, protection, and respect for citizens' rights. The lack of unified regulations as well as the need for further research and development were the main obstacles to be encountered. The Communication made the following recommendation, among others:

1. creating uniform legal regulations for all civilian UA at an EU level, ensuring a level of safety equivalent to that in manned aviation. The new regulatory framework should apply proportionately to the potential risk of a given operation. These regulations are to be gradually implemented and would first focus on areas where technologies are best developed;

249 COM (2014) 207 final. See also M. Bujnowski, Integracja bezzałogowych statków powietrznych z unijnym systemem lotnictwa załogowego. IKAR 2017, nr 2(6).

2. conducting research and development activities on solutions and technologies enabling the gradual and safe integration of UA, primarily within the SESAR project. These R&D activities would particularly focus on technologies related to control in UA systems, collision avoidance, protection against unauthorized control takeover, or contingency procedures;
3. developing solutions to prevent acts of unlawful interference or unlawful use of UA;

1.2.4. Riga Declaration (2015)

4. In March 2015, after the publication of the aforementioned Communication, a High Level Conference on RPAS was held in Riga. The conference ended with the signing of a declaration[250] which set out five key principles for the EU to follow in its future actions[251]:
1. UA need to be treated as new types of aircraft, with proportionate rules applied based on the risk of each operation;
2. EU rules for the safe provision of drone services need to be developed in order to foster industry growth and encourage investments;
3. technologies and standards need to be developed to allow for the full integration of drones in European airspace;
4. public acceptance is key to the growth of drone services;
5. the operator of a drone is responsible for its use.

Implementing the provisions of the Riga Declaration, EASA started intensive work on the premises for future UA regulations to be implemented throughout the EU. It decided to depart from the standard legislative processes and introduced numerous solutions to accelerate and intensify work on the new regulations. EASA's approach resulted from quite clearly defined expectations of the European Commission and the European Parliament[252]. And so:

---

250 The declaration is available at https://ec.europa.eu/transport/modes/air/sign-up_en [access: July 10, 2017]

251 For more, see V. Correia, N. Rouissi, The European Union and Civil Drones: The Riga Declaration and the Future of the European RPAS Industry, w: B. Scott, The Law of Unmanned Aircraft Systems. op.cit., p. 123 et seq.

252 European Parliament resolution of 29 October 2015 on safe use of remotely piloted aircraft systems (RPAS), commonly known as unmanned aerial vehicles (UAVs), in the field of civil aviation (2014/2243(INI)).

1. in May 2015, EASA published a document defining the concept of drone operations entitled "Concept of Operations for Drones. A Risk Based Approach to Regulation of Unmanned Aircraft"[253]
2. in July 2015, it published the premises for future regulations, the so-called A-NPA (Advance of Proposed Amendments) entitled "A-NPA-10 Introduction of a Regulatory Framework for the Operation of Drones"[254];
3. in December 2015, after the A-NPA-10 consultations, EASA published a so-called technical opinion under the same name "Introduction of a Regulatory Framework for the Operation of Drones"[255];

The proposed approach was based on an assessment of the risk posed by a given UA operation. It recommended adopting different solutions in three UA categories: open, specific, and certified. According to the document, open category operations would not require permits but would be subject to many restrictions, e.g. in terms of weight (up to 25 kg), type of operation (only within line of sight), operational restrictions, or requirements relating to the UA itself (e.g. compliance with product safety requirements). Specific category operations were to require a permit from the aviation authority, preceded by detailed operational risk analyses. Certified category operations were to be subject to the same regulations that are in force in manned aviation, but after their appropriate modification.

It should be emphasized that EASA's work on the premises for future regulations was carried out in parallel with preparations for the commencement of legislative work, aimed at extending the EU's competences to all issues related to UA safety. The legislative process focused on reviewing the so-called basic regulation, which extended the EU's competences to cover all UA-related topics, and officially began together with the establishment of the European Civil Aviation Strategy.

1.2.5. European Civil Aviation Strategy (2015)

By publishing the *European Civil Aviation Strategy* in December 2015, the European Commission indicated a number of actions that needed to be taken to strengthen the competitiveness and sustainability of European aviation. In

253 https://www.easa.europa.eu/document-library/general-publications/concept-operations-drones

254 https://www.easa.europa.eu/document-library/notices-of-proposed-amendment/npa-2015-10

255 https://www.easa.europa.eu/document-library/opinions/opinion-technical-nature

addition to issues related to access to the aviation market or the Single European Sky, it also undertook work to review the aviation safety regulation system. The assumed direction in which aviation was to develop required measures that would maintain the current level of safety, and regulatory framework should be well prepared to identify and reduce risks effectively. To do so, the Commission promoted incorporating a *risk-based approach* rather than a *performance-based* approach, as the former is focused on legislative recipients achieving whatever goals have been assumed by the legislator. Therefore, the Commission proposed to amend the currently applicable Basic Regulation 216/2008 and to adopt a new regulation on common rules for aviation safety. The Strategy proposed "a basic legal framework for the safe development of drone operations in the EU, as part of the new basic aviation safety Regulation replacing Regulation 216/2008" and tasked "*the European Aviation Safety Agency with preparing more detailed rules which will allow drone operations and the development of industry standards.*"

When the Strategy was published, the Commission formally submitted a draft of a new basic regulation on common rules in the field of civil aviation[256]. It also presented a detailed impact assessment of the regulation, also in terms of UA regulations[257], and potential approaches in this regard. Option 1 was to apply manned aviation regulations to UA, considering necessary modifications have been made. Option 2 was a risk-based approach. The modification of manned aviation regulations was proposed only for those UA operations that showed a level of risk similar to that of manned aviation operations, and included the certification of equipment and UA operators, and personnel licensing. All remaining operations would take advantage of solutions proportionate to their associated risks. Option 2 also provided for using product safety regulations as a regulatory mechanism for ensuring a minimum level of safety for small UA. Ultimately, it was this option that was recommended.

Regardless of the regulatory actions taken, it was emphasized to conduct research and development works on technologies necessary for the further integration of UA. Steps taken within the SESAR program identified key areas of interest (collision avoidance and detection systems, command and control links, etc.).

256 COM(2015) 613 final.
257 SWD(2015).

1.2.6. *EASA's further legislative work (2016–2018)*

In September 2016 – in parallel with the ongoing work on the new basic regulation – EASA published a draft of future regulations for the open and specific categories, a so-called "*Prototype' Commission Regulation on Unmanned Aircraft Operations*"[258].

In May 2017, EASA presented another NPA 2017-05 (A) and (B) (NPA – Notice of Proposed Amendment)[259] containing draft rules for the open and specific categories. Draft EASA guidelines for these rules and a regulatory impact assessment were also published. The publication of NPA 2017-05 started the process of formal consultations. According to the internal legislative procedure[260], EASA should refer to comments submitted to the provisions proposed as an NPA in the form of a CRD (Common Response Document). However, the CRD for NPA 2017-05 was not published[261] despite the fact that it was announced in the first quarter of 2018. Only general information was revealed, including the fact that more than 3,700 comments were submitted.

In February 2018, Opinion 01/2018, which was already a formal draft of the new implementing regulations, was submitted to the European Commission for further processing[262]. The Opinion was published without waiting for the formal adoption of the basic regulation, which was to be the legal basis for issuing new regulations. In the Opinion, we read that its publication was justified by a consensus reached in December 2017 between the European Commission, Parliament, and Council on the new basic regulation.

1.2.7. *The new basic regulation (2018)*

Work on the new basic regulation ended with the adoption of Regulation (EU) 2018/1139 of the European Parliament and of the Council of 4 July 2018 on

258 https://www.easa.europa.eu/system/files/dfu/UAS%20Prototype%20Regulation%20final.pdf and
https://www.easa.europa.eu/system/files/dfu/Explanatory%20Note%20for%20the%20UAS%20Prototype%20regulation%20final.pdf [access: July 11, 2020].

259 https://www.easa.europa.eu/document-library/notices-of-proposed-amendment/npa-2017-05 [access: July 11, 2020].

260 EASA Management Board Decision 18-2015 (Rulemaking Procedure).

261 https://www.easa.europa.eu/document-library/comment-response-documents [access: July 11, 2020].

262 https://www.easa.europa.eu/document-library/opinions/opinion-012018 [access: July 11, 2020].

common rules in the field of civil aviation and establishing a European Union Aviation Safety Agency[263], which entered into force on September 11 of 2018. At the same time, the previous basic regulation 216/2008 was repealed, while the implementing regulations (Art. 139) issued on its basis were retained, with a transitional period of 5 years for their adaptation.

As indicated in the preamble to Regulation 2018/1139, its scope covers UA regardless of their operating mass. It was also indicated that technologies for UA make a wide range of operations possible and these should be subject to rules that are proportionate to the risks involved in each particular operation or type of operation. Therefore, it was found that subjecting some types of UA to the mechanisms provided for in-product safety legislations would be sufficient in ensuring higher levels of safety. However, the certification of organizations involved in UA design, production, maintenance, and operations should still be the basic methods for ensuring safety. Reserving competences related to regulating operational safety to the EU legislator, it was decided that Member States have the right to introduce local regulations, bans or additional requirements for reasons other than operational safety, such as public safety, protection of privacy, or protection of personal data. The legislator also provided for the obligation to register UA and UA operators at a national level. These registers must allow for the exchange of data throughout the EU. The most important parts of Regulation 2018/1139 are reflected in the following provisions:

1. Art. 2 sec. 1 (b), which explicitly stipulates that the scope of the Regulation also covers UA;
2. Art. 55 covers essential requirements for the design, production, maintenance, and operation of UA (and UAS, where necessary), as well as for personnel, including remote pilots, and organizations. Essential requirements dedicated to UA are set out in Annex IX and the remaining requirements for all aircraft are set out in Annexes II (Airworthiness), IV (Personnel licensing), and V (Operations). The dividing line between UA subject to the requirements of Annex IX and UA subject to the same requirements as other aircraft is to be defined in the implementing acts issued under Art. 57 and 58;
3. Annex IX provides so-called essential requirements for UA. These essential requirements are guidelines that are binding for the European Commission when issuing implementing regulations and provide a number of quite generally indicated obligations and requirements related to, for example, UA

263 OJEU of August 22, 2002, L 212.

airworthiness, UA operations, personnel, or organizations involved in design, production, maintenance, operations, or training;
4. Art. 56 indicates mechanisms for ensuring compliance with the requirements that can be introduced in implementing regulations. These mechanisms feature certification (sec. 1–4), declaration (sec. 5), or applying so-called product legislation (sec. 6). Moreover, the bill indicates the obligations of Member States in terms of UA registration (sec. 7) and the right to introduce national laws related to public safety, protection of privacy, or personal data (sec. 8);
5. Art. 57 forms the basis for issuing executory provisions (in the form of the European Commission's implementing regulations) regulating UA operations, persons, and organizations involved in these operations, including UA pilots;
6. Art. 58 is the basis for issuing executory provisions (in the form of commission-delegated regulations) concerning the design, production, and maintenance of UA, including their parts, as well as people and organizations involved in such activities.

It should be clarified that the aviation safety regulation system provided for the possibility of issuing a delegated regulation for the first time. All the previous regulations issued on the basis of the basic regulation were executive regulations. The main difference between an implementing regulation and a delegated regulation lies in the issuance procedure – an implementing regulation is subject to so-called comitology, while a delegated regulation requires opinions of expert groups. The latter may also be subject to reservations from the European Parliament or the Council. Moreover, in the case of delegated acts, the Commission has "significant discretion", meaning the right to amend non-essential elements of the basic regulation[264].

1.2.8. Implementing regulations (2019)

On June 11, 2019, the European Commission published[265] two regulations, issued pursuant to Art. 58 and 57 of the Basic Regulation, respectively:

1. Commission Delegated Regulation (EU) 2019/945 of 12 March 2019 on unmanned aircraft systems and on third-country operators of unmanned aircraft systems and

264 For more, see J. Barcz, Traktat z Lizbony. Wybrane aspekty prawne działań implementacyjnych, Warsaw, 2012, Chapter 5.
265 OJEU of June 11, 2019, L 152.

2. Commission Implementing Regulation (EU) 2019/947 of 24 May 2019 on the rules and procedures for the operation of unmanned aircraft.

Regulation 2019/945 regulates in detail the requirements for the design and production of those UA that are intended for use in the open category. In place of the classic equipment certification procedures, the regulation provides for the use of a so-called product safety harmonization legislation. Meanwhile, Regulation 2019/947 regulates issues related to operations performed within the open and specific categories, including requirements for pilots and UA operators.

It should be mentioned that EASA supplemented Regulation 2019/947 with so-called guidance and advisory materials in the form of a an EASA Executive Director Decision. The relevant Decision (2019/021/R) was published on October 9, 2019[266]. The guidelines, known as *Acceptable Means of Compliance* (AMC), are non-binding standards. In the opinion of EASA, meeting these standards is equivalent to demonstrating compliance with the provisions of the Implementing Regulation. Additionally, the *Guidance Materials* (GM) serve as non-binding examples or explanations for a better understanding of the provisions of the Implementing Regulation.

Also in 2019, EASA published Opinion 05/2019 proposing changes to both Regulations. This proposal included the introduction of provisions on so-called standard scenarios to the specific category, which allowed for the performance of operations based on previously submitted declarations (in place of required authorization) in the case of:

1. operations by UA weighing up to 25 kg within sight, up to an altitude of 120 m, in an area where people may be present (STS-01),
2. operations by UA weighing up to 25 kg, out of sight, up to an altitude of 120 m, at a distance of not more than 2 km from the pilot, provided observers are involved (STS-02).

As a result of these proposals, Commission Implementing Regulation (EU) 2020/639 of 12 May 2020 amending Implementing Regulation (EU) 2019/947 as regards standard scenarios for operations executed in or beyond the visual line of sight was adopted[267]. It is said that the Delegated Regulation (EU) 2019/945 will also be amended and that there will be new requirements for those UA that

---

266 https://www.easa.europa.eu/document-library/agency-decisions/ed-decision-2019021r [access: July 22, 2020].

267 OJEU of May 13, 2020, L 152.

will be allowed to perform operations defined under the two abovementioned standard scenarios.

New delegated regulations have changed the understanding of the operations and unified those across Europe. EASA has developed this common requirement in order to ensure the free movement of drones and UAS operators and pilots within the European Union. Common regulatory framework was aimed to facilitate obtaining the flight authorization from respective authorities for tourists using drones as well as business owners. When creating the unified requirements EASA has taken into account different aspects – obligations of drone manufacturers contained in Commission Delegated Regulation (EU) 2019/945 of 12 March 2019 on unmanned aircraft systems and on third-country operators of unmanned aircraft systems, as well as the respect for privacy, environment, noise, and safety issues.

The Implementing Regulations of the EC provided for a year-long *vacatio legis* for UA users and Member States as a period necessary to prepare for their application. These Regulations were to apply from July 1, 2020. Due to the COVID-19 pandemic, this period has been extended. The new EU Regulations entered into force on December 31, 2020.[268]

1.3. General assumptions of EU regulations

Discussing the solutions adopted in the Implementing Regulations requires a prior presentation of the general assumptions made by EU legislators. Some of them have already been mentioned. However, it is worth going over these principles for a better understanding of the quite detailed Implementing Regulations.

Although EU regulations mainly concern issues related to the safety of UA operations, they also cover other issues considered important from the point of view of UA operations and their widespread social acceptance. This relates to such matters as protection of privacy, personal data, and noise pollution. Requirements for operator registration or UAV identification are not only intended to achieve an appropriate level of safety, but also help solve other problems.

When it comes to safety, there are two basic risks associated with UA operations – so-called *air risks* and *ground risks*. Air risks are related to collisions with other aircraft, both manned and unmanned. Ground risks are related to

268 Commission Implementing Regulation (EU) 2020/746 of 4 June 2020 amending Implementing Regulation (EU) 2019/947 as regards postponing dates of application of certain measures in the context of the COVID-19 pandemic, OJEU of June 5, 2020, L 176.

collisions with people or anything considered critical infrastructure. These risks are different for different categories of UA operations; therefore they can be "addressed" in different ways. Regulations should be *operation centric*. Instead of focusing on the whos, whys, wheres, and whats of a given operation, we should focus on the operation itself and the risks it carries, both in the air and on the ground. To do so, it is necessary to move away from the traditional approach, which considers aircraft as the starting point of any safety regulations, and focus more on the operations to be performed. This will allow for individual risk identification and assessment for each operation. The greater the risk, the higher the requirements necessary to reduce that risk. Thus, regulations should be proportional to the level of risk (*risk based*). For example, the fact that someone is performing a commercial operation should not prejudge the necessity to require an operator's permit or certification. This should be determined by the risk associated with a given operation. Moreover, where possible, regulations should identify and set specific goals or indicators, the achievement of which is equal to ensuring the desired level of safety. And it is the addressee of these provisions who should determine how these requirements are met. *Performance-based* regulations should therefore supplement (or even replace) traditional methods of regulating safety requirements, which would define an ever-growing number of detailed requirements to be met by their addressees. These new rules for drafting safety regulations for UA are promoted throughout the entire aviation safety regulation system. Their introduction was part of a revision of the entire system and was reflected in the general part of the new Basic Regulation 2018/1139[269].

While implementing the abovementioned rules, three categories of operations and their associated risks were identified. The **open category** concerns operations that pose no or very little risk to third parties (on the ground and in the air). Operations in the open category should be carried out according to strictly defined rules that pilots should be familiar with. Moreover, the vast majority of risks should be included in the technical requirements and operational limitations of open category UA. This will be implemented by various product compliance mechanisms, and UA intended for use in the open category will simply have to meet these requirements, which will be confirmed by appropriate marking on the product itself (a CE mark).

The **specific category** includes operations that pose a greater risk than open category operations or operations that are impossible to perform within the operational limitations for that category. Such operations will require authorization

269 See Art. 12 and Art. 4 sec. 1 and 2.

(permission) from the competent authority (designated by a Member State). An individual will have to supplement a request for authorization by demonstrating that operational safety is maintained at an acceptable level. In other words, the risk associated with an operation in the specific category should be identified, mitigated, and assessed through a risk analysis process used in aviation safety management systems. Nevertheless, authorization from the competent authority will be the final confirmation of this process's proper execution.

Risks in the **certified category** are similar to those in manned aviation. Therefore, this category will rely on solutions used in ensuring the safety of manned aviation operations, such as the certification of products, operators, and licensing of personnel.

The Basic Regulation and the EC regulations issued on its basis share the same definitions. The basic ones concern:

1. *unmanned aircraft*, i.e. any aircraft operating or designed to operate autonomously or to be piloted remotely without a pilot on board[270];
2. *unmanned aircraft system*[271] meaning an unmanned aircraft and the *equipment to control it remotely*[272];
3. *remote pilot* meaning a natural person responsible for safely conducting the flight of a UA by operating its flight controls, either manually or, when the UA flies automatically, by monitoring its course and remaining able to intervene and change its course at any time[273];
4. *UAS operator* meaning any legal or natural person operating or intending to operate one or more UAS[274]. This term is based on the definition of an aircraft operator[275];

Before moving on, the concept of operator and the relationship between the operator and the pilot require further discussion. The use of any aircraft (manned or unmanned) usually means that that aircraft carries out a flight. From the point of view of civil law, the decision to operate an aircraft is based on having the necessary rights to do so. Such rights may result from ownership or have an obligatory

270 Art. 3 p. 30 of Regulation 2018/1139, Art. 3 p. 1 of Regulation 2019/945.
271 Art. 2 p. 1 of Regulation 2019/947, Art. 3 p. 1 of Regulation 2019/945.
272 Art. 3 p. 32 of Regulation 2018/1139, Art. 2 p. 1 of Regulation 2019/947, Art. 3 p. 2 of Regulation 2019/945.
273 Art. 3 p. 31 of Regulation 2018/1139, Art. 3 p. 27 of Regulation 2019/945.
274 Art.2 p. 2 of Regulation 2019/947, Art. 3 p. 4 of Regulation 2019/945.
275 Art. 3 p. 13 of Regulation 2018/1139.

nature (e.g. leasing, tenancy, rent) – either way, they allow for the exploitation of an aircraft in accordance with civil law. Therefore, it seems that operating an aircraft within the meaning of administrative regulations is the same as "using" an aircraft within the meaning of civil law. Thus, it is tantamount that an aircraft is "used" in the sense it has under the Civil Code[276]. Therefore, it can be stated that the basic rule for identifying an aircraft's operator is based on the criterion of "using" aircraft for one's own purposes within the meaning of civil law. The right to use an aircraft as transportable property in itself presupposes full control over the movement of that aircraft, in person or through a designated crew. EASA confirms this notion and indicates that the entity that owns or leases a drone is considered that drone's operator. It should be mentioned that one person can be an operator and a drone pilot at the same time. A good example is a situation in which a company providing drone services owns a UA and the pilot is its own employee. Another situation is when an individual buys a drone for recreational flights. In such case, they are both an operator and a pilot.[277]

1.4. Registration of UA and their operators

To comply with the requirements included in Basic Regulation 2018/1139, Regulation 2019/947 introduced (Art. 14) the obligation to register UA and their operators.

Mandatory UA registration concerns certified category UA. This is the same obligation that manned aircraft have to meet under the Chicago Convention and national regulations. However, national UA registration systems are required to be digital, harmonized, and interoperable.

The registration of UA operators is required in the case of both the open and specific categories. Only operators of certain open category UA are exempt from registration – this includes operators of UA with a mass of less than 250 g (or those which, in the event of a collision with a human, do not transfer energy above 80 J) unless they are equipped with a "personal data collection sensor", and also those UA which have been manufactured and designated as toys in accordance with Directive 2009/48/EC of the European Parliament and of the Council

276 In the provision of Art. 140 of the Civil Code specifying the scope of the owner's rights, it admittedly uses the term "using a thing", but in the provisions on using and in the provisions regulating contracts for the use of things, the legislator consistently uses the term of "using the thing" in other light, see Art. 252, 659, 693, 709 p. 1 or Art. 710 of the Civil Code.

277 https://www.easa.europa.eu/the-agency/faqs/drones-uas [access: July 22, 2020].

of 18 June 2009 on the safety of toys. Registration takes place in the Member State where the operator is domiciled (natural person) or headquartered (legal person). Member States shall establish and maintain accurate digital registration systems while maintaining interoperability and the possibility of exchanging data with registers kept in other States. These registration systems are to store the following data:

1. data identifying the UA operator as a natural or legal person,
2. operator's address, e-mail address, and phone number,
3. insurance policy number, if required,
4. a statement that the UA will be operated only by pilots with an appropriate level of competency, in the case of operators who are legal persons, and
5. authorizations or certificates issued (for the specific category).

In addition, the State running the register will be required to assign a registration number to the operator. The operator, on the other hand, will be obliged to affix this number to each aircraft they operate.

The EASA Guidelines (AMC) clarify that if a UA operator uses a UA owned by another person, the registration obligation lies with the operator and the UA in use should carry the operator's registration number.

Creating a registration system for UA operators is an obligation of Member States[278]. This is undoubtedly one of the most important obligations imposed on the competent authority of a Member State.

After December 2020, the Civil Aviation Authority of Poland has ceased issuing the certificated of competency on basis of National law and started to register drone operators and pilots in accordance with the Regulation 2019/947. According to article 14 of the Regulation UAS operators shall register themselves: (a) when operating within the 'open' category any of the following unmanned aircraft: (i) with a MTOM of 250 g or more, or, which in the case of an impact can transfer to a human kinetic energy above 80 Joules; (ii) that is equipped with a sensor able to capture personal data, unless it complies with Directive 2009/48/EC. (b) when operating within the 'specific' category an unmanned aircraft of any mass.

The possibility to have the UAVO certificate issued by the Civil Aviation Authority CAA of Poland (CAA of Poland) on the basis of the training and dedicated exam resulted in increasing number of operators who were allowed to fly drones commercially. The overall number of Unmanned Aerial Vehicle Operator

278 Art. 14 sec. 1, art. 18 letter m of Regulation 2019/947.

(UAVO) certificate holders are greater than glider pilot and private pilot licenses combined in Poland. Until the change from the Polish to European regulation, the number of operators holding the certificates had been increasing rapidly, from 1979 in 2015 reaching 22 962 in 2020. However the current statistics of registration under the EU regulations showed that the theoretical number of operators (those flying recreationally) were even higher than expected. In 3rd quarter of 2021 the number of registered UAS operators reached 86 272.

Since December 31, 2020, Civil Aviation Authority has also started the conversion process.. VLOS competency certificates are being converted into respective levels of competency exempting from the obligation to undergo online e-learning and online test to reach A1/A3 level of competency and exemption of e-learning, online test, self-practical training, and additional theoretical exam at appointed training center to obtain A2 competency. VLOS ratings depending on the weight and type of unmanned aircraft (multirotor – MR, aircraft – A, helicopter – H) also allows UAS pilots to obtain competences for selected and published National Standard Scenarios (NSTS) and European Scenarios. In Poland there are 9 Standard Scenarios and 2 EU Scenarios available[279]. Polish certificates (BVLOS) are no longer valid directly. However, holders of the rating have a possibility to convert the rating in a similar way to VLOS rating and obtain A1/A3, A2 level of competency to fly in open category and authorization to use selected National and European Standard Scenarios to fly in specific category[280].

Many of the European countries have not published the National Standard Scenarios. Standard scenarios however are one of the possibilities to fly in accordance with specific category. In case of Poland there are few NSTS which allow flying VLOS and BVLOS on short distances up to 2 km. The most advanced is NSTS which is issued on the basis of previously obtained authorization issued by CAA of Poland and allows to fly on larger distances. In accordance with regulation 2019/947 European scenarios are scheduled to be applicable on 3 December 2023. National Scenarios could be used after filling the declaration to use selected scenario. The UAS operators can send the declaration up to 2 December 2023. The National Standard Scenarios will be applicable up to 2 December 2025.

---

279 https://www.ulc.gov.pl/pl/drony/czesto-zadawane-pytania-faq/493-kategoria-szczegolna/5546-jakie-sa-dostepne-krajowe-scenariusze-standardowe-nsts

280 https://www.ulc.gov.pl/pl/drony/konwersja-swiadectw-kwalifikacji

1.5. Open category operations

According to Art. 4 of Regulation 2019/947, an operation is classified as an open category operation if it meets the following requirements. First, the maximum weight of the UA does not exceed 25 kg and the UA itself meets the requirements of the class in accordance with Regulation 2019/945, which is confirmed by the CE mark. Second, a safe distance must be maintained from people when carrying out such operations. Third, it is imperative to keep the UA in sight (VLOS). Fourth, flight altitude should be less than 120 m above ground level (or an obstacle). And finally, it is forbidden to drop any items from the UA or to transport hazardous materials. If any of these requirements are not met, the operation is assigned to the specific category. Open category operations are further divided into three subcategories:

1. Subcategory A1 – flights over people (but not over assemblies of people) are allowed, UA cannot exceed weight of 250 g;
2. Subcategory A2 – flights over people are allowed with a maximum distance of 30 m (5 m if the UA has a low-speed flight mode), UA cannot exceed weight of 4 kg;
3. Subcategory A3 – operations are preformed away from people and at least 150 m from residential, industrial, or recreational sites.

If the requirements of a given subcategory are not met, the operation is not included in the open category and is treated as a specific category operation.

Apart from operational constraints, the basic way to ensure operational safety in the open category is to subject the UA performing such operations to the requirements specified in the provisions of Regulation 2019/945. These regulations define specific UA classes and their respective operations. Each class has minimum requirements, and meeting these lies with the manufacturers (Art. 6). Confirmation of compliance takes place through a mechanism of conformity assessment, which is confirmed by drawing up a declaration of conformity and affixing the CE marking to the UA. The manufacturer is also responsible for appropriately marking the UA, as well as attaching the operating manual and any relevant information. Regulation 2019/945 also imposes certain obligations on UA importers (Art. 8) and distributors (Art. 9). Regulation 2019/945 describes in detail the conformity assessment mechanisms as well as the market surveillance system.

The Annex to Regulation 2019/945 sets out detailed requirements for five UA classes that can be used in the open category.

Class C0 involves UA with a mass of less than 250 g, a maximum speed of 19 m/s, which have a secure mechanism that does not let the UA depart more than 120 m from the control station. Class C0 UA can perform operations in any of the operational subcategories.

Class C1 involves UA with a mass of less than 900 g, a maximum speed of 19 m/s, constructed in such a way that they will not transfer more than 80 J of energy in the event of a collision with the head of a human. These UA are designed and constructed in such a way as to minimize injuries in the event of a collision with a human. Class C0 UA can perform operations in any of the operational subcategories.

Class C2 involves UA with a mass of less than 4 kg, designed and manufactured in such a way as to minimize injuries in the event of a collision with a human. Class C2 UA can perform operations in subcategories A2 (near people) and A3 (away from people).

Class C3 involves UA weighing less than 25 kg which are also equipped with an automatic flight control system. Class C4, in turn, involves UA weighing less than 25 kg which are not equipped with such a system, apart from the automated flight stabilization support. Class C3 and C4 UA are approved for operations in A3 subcategory (away from humans) only.

Each class has requirements that are related to noise pollution, altitude limitations, UA construction and mechanics, control systems, emergency systems (in case of loss of communication), or lighting. Moreover, with the exception of the C0 class, it is required to equip each UA with:

1. a *remote identification* system to ensure continuous broadcasting of an open transmission protocol so that data including the operator's registration number, the UA's serial number, and the UA and operator's location can be read. The regulations do not specify the emission range of such data;
2. a *geo-awareness* system, providing the ability to update data on airspace restrictions, alerting the pilot of a potential violation of these restrictions.

The subcategories and UA which is used are presented in the form of a table below.

UAS		Operation		Drone Operator/pilot		
Class	MTOM	Subcategory	Operational restrictions	Drone Operator registration	Remote pilot competence	Remote pilot minimum age
Privately built	< 250 g	A1 (can also fly in subcategory A3)	- may fly over uninvolved people (should be avoided when possible) - no fly over assemblies of people	No, unless camera / sensor on board **and** a drone is not a toy	- no training needed	No minimum age
0					- read user's manual	16*, no minimum age if drone is a toy
Legacy drones (art. 20)						16*
1	< 900 g		- No expected fly over uninvolved people (if happens, should be reduced) - no fly over assemblies of people	Yes	- read user's manual - complete online training - pass online theoretical exam	16*
2	< 4 kg	A2 (can also fly in subcategory A3)	- no fly over uninvolved people - keep horizontal distance of 30 m from uninvolved people (it can be reduced to 5 m if low speed function is activated)	Yes	- read user's manual - complete online training - pass online theoretical exam - conduct and declare a self-practical training - pass a written exam at the CAA (or at recognized entity)	16*
3 4 Privately built Legacy drones (art. 20)	< 25 kg	A3	- fly away from people - fly outside of urban area (150 m distance)	Yes	- read user's manual - complete online training - pass online theoretical exam	16*

Table 4.1. Requirements under the subcategories A1/A2/A3 of the 'open' category[281]

A two-year transition period has been set to allow manufacturers to adapt to these requirements. After this, meeting the requirements of Regulation 2019/945 will be a condition to introduce a UA model in the open category. The possibility of using UA available on the market before the end of this transitional period is envisaged only in subcategory A3 (away from people), and in the case of UA weighing less than 250 g in subcategory A1 (Art. 20 of Regulation 2019/947).

Manufacturers are also obliged to provide an EASA information leaflet (along with the UA) which will describe the rights and obligations of the operator and pilot related to a given UA class.

It should be mentioned that in addition to the operational limitations related to a given subcategory, which apply to pilots, the provisions of Regulation 2019/947 impose certain obligations on operators as well[282]. First of all, the operator

281 https://www.easa.europa.eu/faq/116452 [access: November 20, 2021].
282 UAS.OPEN.050.

assigns a pilot for each UA operation – in doing so, they must ensure that the pilot and other personnel are familiar with the UA operating manual and have appropriate competences.

There are also specific obligations for pilots related to conducting a flight and the necessary preparation beforehand[283]. For example, it is the pilot's responsibility to follow the UA operating manual as well as any exploitation procedures. The pilot is also obliged to keep the UA within visual range and to observe the surrounding airspace in order to avoid colliding with manned aircraft. The pilot is further obliged to stop the flight should the operation pose a threat to other aircraft, people, animals, the environment, or property.

The minimum age for a pilot in the open category is 16 years, which may be reduced by the Member State to 12 years (the age restriction does not apply to Class C0 UA). Passing a theory test in order to confirm a pilot's knowledge is another condition for performing operations in individual subcategories of the open category. Both trainings and exams should be held on-line and may be organized by a designated authority of a Member State or by an organization authorized for that purpose by the aviation authority of a Member State. Training completion is confirmed with an appropriate certificate, which may be issued in electronic form.

Open category operations can be performed outside the operator's country of registration without any additional requirements presupposing they respect local conditions and airspace restrictions.

1.6. Specific category operations

If an operation cannot be performed within the requirements and limitations provided for in the open category, then it will be classified as a specific category operation (provided that the related risks do not require the operation to be considered a certified category operation). Three elements – indicated in Regulation 947/2019 – are essential for recognizing an operation as a specific category operation:

1. Art. 5 sec. 1 – failure to meet any of the requirements or limitations provided for in the open category and its related subcategories (e.g. BVLOS operations, UA with a mass greater than 25 kg, flights near humans with a UA heavier than 4 kg);

283 UAS.OPEN.060.

2. Art. 6 sec. 1 – failure to meet the minimum conditions specified in the regulations as conditions for the certified category;
3. Art. 6 sec. 2 – the results of a risk assessment confirm that there are no grounds to consider that the potential risk that the operation carries would require it to be considered a certified category operation.

Certified category operations are divided into three types. The first – operations over assemblies of people, understood as gatherings where persons are unable to move away due to the density of the crowd they are in in the event of a possible collision with a UA over which control has been lost[284]. Second – operations related to the transport of hazardous materials. Third – operations related to the transport of hazardous materials.

The basic rule for special category operations is that they must be authorized by the authorities in the Member State in which the operator is registered (Art. 5 sec. 1). When applying for operational authorization, the operator shall back their request with a risk assessment for a given operation (Art. 5 sec. 2). Regulation 2019/947 specifies both the requirements for the risk analysis itself (Art. 11) and the authorization to perform the operation (Art. 12).

The operational risk assessment should include:

(a) a description and characteristics of the operation, including the operational environment (ground and air), in accordance with Art. 11 sec. 2
(b) operational safety objectives, which should specify a safety level equivalent to that in manned aviation, in accordance with Art. 11 sec. 3
(c) identification of an operation's risks on the ground and in the air, detailed in Art. 11 sec. 4, taking into account whether the operation is performed within or out of the operator's line of sight, the population density of overflown areas, UA characteristics, airspace class and occupancy, impact on other air traffic,
(d) risk mitigation measures, in particular risk mitigation measures for people on the ground (e.g. rescue parachute systems, emergency response programs), operational restrictions (e.g. limiting the geographical or temporal scope of the operation), actions based on airspace management regulations (e.g. zone designation), organizational activities (internal procedures of the

284 Art. 2 sec. 3 of Regulation 2019/947. The GM EASA clearly indicates the freedom to be able to move around and out of the way to avoid a possible collision with a UA. For example, sports, cultural, religious, or political events, beaches or parks on clear days, ski resorts.

operator), activities related to ensuring personnel competence, and activities related to the UA's equipment and construction (anti-collision systems, location system, etc.).

Member State's authorities then verify the risk analysis, which includes assessing the effectiveness of its risk mitigation measures. The verification is successful when it is confirmed that:

1. the safety objectives take into account the risks associated with the operation,
2. the competence of personnel and the technical characteristics of the UA are sufficient to ensure the safety of the operation in the context of the identified risks, both on the ground and in the air,
3. the operator states that the planned operation complies with all applicable regulations, including provisions on the protection of privacy, personal data, the environment, and insurance.

Positive verification of the above by the competent authority provides the basis for issuing *operational authorization*, which indicates:

1. the scope of authorization
2. special conditions that apply to the operation, personnel, and the UA,
3. information on the operator, UA, operational risk analysis, risk mitigation measures, and the place of operation.

The issuing authority determines the period of validity of the authorization, and its validity depends on meeting the requirements specified in the regulations, as well as in the permit itself[285]. This means that it may be revoked in the event that these requirements are not met. It must be noted that the provisions of the regulation do not clearly specify the grounds for revocation, but only indicate the possibility of doing so (Art. 18 let. d).

According to Art. 13 of Regulation 2019/247, it is possible to fly in one EU Member State based on operational authorization issued by another. However, the operator is obliged to update the risk analysis, including adapting the risk mitigation measures to local conditions. The condition for commencing such operations is to obtain confirmation from the competent authority of the state of operation that any additional actions taken to adapt to local conditions are sufficient.

---

285 SPEC.UAS.080.

Operational risk assessment is of key importance when it comes to specific category operations. It should be carried out before applying for authorization. The provision of Art. 11 of Regulation 2019/947 has been quite detailed in providing so-called Acceptable Means of Compliance (AMC) published by EASA. AMC1 recommends using the risk assessment methodology developed by JARUS (called SORA – *Specific Operations Risk Assessment*), with some modifications. SORA focuses on two main types of risks. Risks on the ground – in the case of specific category operations, these should not be greater than the risks posed by UA in the certified category (this concerns flights over assemblies of people in particular). Risks in the air – these should not be greater than those in the case of manned aviation operations and concern collisions with manned aircrafts (an extension to SORA to include risks of collision with other UA is planned). SORA is a structured assessment process, by which the operator (and a member State's competent authority) should be able to determine if the intended operation is sufficiently safe. It consists of successive interdependent actions:

1. a detailed description and characteristics of the intended operation (*concept of operation*),
2. an assessment of the risk posed by the operation on the ground (*ground risk class*),
3. an assessment of the measures taken to minimize the risk on the ground,
4. an assessment of the risk posed by the operation in the air (*air risk class*),
5. an assessment of strategic measures taken to minimize the risk in the air (operational restrictions or restrictions related to the organization of airspace),
6. an assessment of the tactical measures taken to minimize the risk in the air (e.g. use of collision detection and avoidance systems for BVLOS operations),
7. a combined assessment of the ground and air risks and the measures taken to minimize them (*specific assurance and integrity level*) to determine the extent to which control of the operation can be maintained,
8. establishing *operational safety objectives*,
9. additional *adjacent area/airspace* requirements in case of loss of control over the operation.

An analysis of EASA guidelines and JARUS materials leads to the conclusion that the application of the SORA methodology requires operators to be familiar with all the issues related to their intended operations, including having fairly detailed knowledge on regulations related to the organization of airspace and the basic principles of risk management (conducting risk analyses)[286]. Such requirements also apply to employees (inspectors) of a Member State's authorities responsible for verifying risk assessment processes.

In the case of the most popular operations in the specific category, the risk assessment and SORA methodology was carried out by EASA. The Agency also based its actions on the experiences of those Member States where so-called standard scenarios had been allowed to take place. In Opinion 05/2019, EASA presented the possible implementation of a significant part of SORA for the following so-called standard scenarios (*STS*), i.e. operations performed with UA weighing less than 25 kg:

1. VLOS operations performed up to 120 m above ground level in areas where people may be present (e.g. in cities) – STS-01;
2. BVLOS operations performed up to 120 m within a 2 km radius of the pilot, provided that observers are present – STS-02

As a result of the analyses, EASA proposed the introduction of relevant requirements for each of these scenarios in Opinion 05/2019 to Regulation 2019/947. According to the standard scenarios, a relevant statement (declaration) submitted by the operator to the competent authority is the basis for performing a specific category operation (Art. 5 sec. 5 in conjunction with Art. 12 sec. 5). Submitting this declaration is tantamount to confirming that the operation meets the relevant requirements provided for in the regulations. These requirements were set out as a result of proposals contained in Opinion 05/2019 and resulted in changes being made to Regulation 2019/947[287], which added an annex detailing the requirements for each STS as well as additional pilot competences. Operators who have submitted their declarations are subject to supervision (audits and controls) by the authorities.

Art. 5 sec. 6 of Regulation 2019/947 provides for two additional exceptions to operations in the specific category requiring operational authorization.

First, this does not apply to UAS operators holding an operator's certificate (LUC) with appropriate privileges. The possibility of applying for a certificate

---

286 For more on the application of SORA in practice, see M. Huttunen, Drone Operations in the Specific Category: A Unique Approach to Aviation Safety. The Aviation and Space Journal, No. 2, 2019.

287 Commission Implementing Regulation (EU) 2020/639 of 12 May 2020 amending Implementing Regulation (EU) 2019/947 as regards standard scenarios for operations executed in or beyond the visual line of sight, OJEU of 13 May 2020, L 150/1.

is reserved only to operators who are legal persons. To obtain such a certificate, it is necessary to create an operational supervision system, receive approval of a manual describing internal procedures, and implement a safety management system adequate to the scale and type of the operator's activity, among other requirements. Upon its issue, the certificate will define an operator's capacities, including (if necessary) the areas or zones designated for operations and any restrictions or conditions. The operator is also granted the right to approve their own operations without submitting declarations (STS) or asking for operational authorization. The certificate is valid for an indefinite period of time, provided that the requirements of Regulation 2019/947, as well as the requirements established by the issuing Member State, are met constantly. The issuing body is responsible for auditing and controlling operators. The regulations also provide for the possibility of withdrawing a certificate; however they do not specify what the exact reasons for such withdrawal may be.

Second, it is possible to issue a general authorization to perform operations for model aircraft clubs and associations, in accordance with Art. 16 of Regulation 2019/947. Operations performed under such a permit are not subject to the requirement to obtain individual operational authorization. A club or association must meet the following requirements to obtain a general permit – meet national requirements, prove that its management system and internal procedures guarantee that remote pilots are informed about the conditions and limitations specified in the permit, and that the entity assists them in minimum competency required to operate UAS safely.

Summing up, specific category operations require operational authorization preceded by a risk assessment process. Operations performed according to a standard scenario are an exception, since they require submitting a declaration and complying with the requirements specified in the regulations. Authorization is also not required for UA operators holding an LUC with appropriate privileges. Certified operators are free to approve their own operations, and this approval has to be based on a safety management system. They are to remain under the supervision of a Member State's aviation authorities. There are also special arrangements for model aircraft organizations and associations. In each case, risk assessment procedures still hold utmost importance. Should operational authorization be required, the operator carries out a risk assessment which is later reviewed by the competent authority. In the case of so-called standard scenarios, such assessments have been carried out at a regulatory level and their results are explicitly specified in the regulations. In the case of certified UA operators, such analyses are to be performed as an element of the operator's safety management system. The risk assessment process is to demonstrate and confirm that a specific category operation does not pose a risk that would require the operation to be considered eligible for the certified category.

During the risk assessment process, the operator should determine – with approval from the competent authority in the form of authorization – what activities related to the operation, their competences, and the UA's technical requirements are necessary. Art. 8 sec. 2 of Regulation 2019/947 requires remote pilots performing operations in the specific category to meet competency requirements set out in the operational authorization, in the standard scenario, or as defined in the operator's certificate. Similarly, Art. 40 sec. 3 of Regulation 2019/945 provides that a UAS used in the specific category should meet the technical requirements specified in the operational authorization or standard scenario, or in the operator's certificate. As for the operation itself, provisions of Regulation 2019/947 state that the requirements for an operation are specified in the authorization (Art. 12 sec. 4 in conjunction with Art. 7 sec. 2), STS requirements (Art. 7 sec. 2), or in the operator's LUC (UAS.LUC.050). Additionally, the provisions of Regulation 2019/947 define the obligations of the operator and the remote pilot.

UAS.SPEC.050 specifies the obligations of the operator, whose responsibilities include:

- ensuring that operational procedures adapted to the operation type and the risk involved are established, including operational procedures to ensure safety, measures to protect against unlawful interference and unauthorized access, as well as guidelines for pilots to minimize noise pollution;
- designating the pilot for each operation and ensuring that they have the required competences;
- making sure that personnel are competent to perform their tasks and familiar with UA operator procedures;
- executing the operation within its limits, conditions, and measures specified in the declaration (STS), or in the operational authorization;
- using UA that are designed in such a way so as their potential failure will not lead to a situation in which the UA will fly beyond its area of operations or result in fatalities;
- keeping the UA in an appropriate condition that guarantees safe operations by defining a maintenance program and employing appropriate personnel.

UAS.SPEC.060 also specifies the duties of the remote pilot, which include:

- having appropriate competences;
- an assessment of their ability to perform their duties;

- obtaining up-to-date information on UA restrictions before each flight;
- ensuring that the environment (area, airspace) in which an operation is to be performed complies with the conditions and requirements specified in the authorization or declaration;
- ensuring that the UAS is in a proper condition, including proper functioning of the remote identification system;
- providing air traffic services or other airspace users with relevant information as required by the authorization or site requirements;
- complying with applicable conditions or restrictions, as well as procedures established by the operator;
- avoiding collisions with manned aircraft, which may include stopping the flight if its continuation were to endanger other aircraft, people, animals, the environment, or property.

In the case of autonomous operations, some of the pilot's responsibilities rest with the UA operator. This results from the fact that autonomous operations are understood as operations during which it is not possible for the pilot to intervene (Art. 2 para. 17 of Regulation 2019/947). It should be emphasized that autonomous operations are allowed only in the specific and certified categories. Of course, risk assessment remains the decisive factor for their authorization[288].

1.7. Certified category operations

As already mentioned, Art. 55 of the Basic Regulation 2018/1139 introduced a general mechanism that allowed implementing (delegated) regulations to define the division between those UA whose production and operations are subject to certification requirements and other UA which are subject to more flexible rules. The certified category is to be subject to the same essential requirements that apply to all aircraft (airworthiness, crew, operations) as set out respectively in Annexes II, IV, and V of the Basic Regulation. Remaining UA categories may be subject to essential requirements set out in Annex IX of this Regulation. Thus, there are two directions in the development of UA regulations. Certified category UA and their operations need to be included in the executive provisions that regulate aviation safety in its entirety, meaning that some EC implementing regulations in the field of aviation safety require gradual revision. Remaining UA and their related operations are subject to completely new rules. We have already discussed regulations for the open and specific categories. It should be

288 GM1 UAS.SPEC.050(1)(b).

emphasized that these regulations set the "dividing line" between the certified category and the two others.

And so, according to Art. 6 sec. 1 of Regulation 2019/947, an operation must meet two conditions in order for it to be recognized as a certified category operation.

First of all, the UA itself is subject to certification, in accordance with Art. 40 sec. 1 of Regulation 2019/945. This can happen if the UA has been designed to:

(a) perform operations over assemblies of people spanning at least 3 meters in diameter;
(b) transport people; and
(c) transport hazardous materials.

Regardless of UA certification, a certified category operation is classified as such if:

(a) it is performed over gatherings of people, i.e. situations where persons are unable to move away due to the density of the crowd they are in in the event of a possible collision with a UA over which control has been lost[289],
(b) it is to be expected that the UA will be used to transport people,
(c) it is to be expected that the UA will be used to transport hazardous materials.

The wording of Art. 6 sec. 1 of Regulation 2019/945 leads to the conclusion that it will be possible to operate within the specific category with the use of UA that has been subjected to certification[290]. However, it is necessary to distinguish between two situations. The first – when the specific category operation presupposes the use of a certified UA. The second – when the risk assessment shows that the only way to reduce the risk is to subject the UA to a certification process. According to Art. 40 sec. 1 letter d) of Regulation 2019/945, the UA may also be subject to certification if the operational authorization issued by the competent authority considers that the risk of the operation cannot be adequately mitigated without the certification of the UAS. Although the UA itself is subject to certification, the rules for performing an operation or personnel requirements are still subject to the regulations governing the specific category (i.e. operational

289 Art. 2 sec. 3 of Regulation 2019/947. The GM EASA clearly indicates that it is about being able to move around in order to avoid a possible collision with a UA, the control over which has been lost. For example, sports, cultural, religious, or political events, beaches or parks on clear days, ski resorts.

290 This is confirmed by UAS.SPEC.100 and the GM to this provision.

requirements defined as a result of risk assessment procedures and approved in the operational authorization by the competent authority).

The certified category itself is subject to the same implementing regulations as manned aviation. This results from the general rule provided in Art. 55 of the Basic Regulation (by referencing the same essential requirements) and the provisions of the implementing regulations concerning UA. According to Art. 3 letter (c) of Regulation 2019/947, UA operations in the certified category require not only UA certification, but also operator certification and the certification of the remote pilot, where necessary. This principle was specified in:

1. Art. 40 sec. 2 of Regulation 2019/945, which requires applying the provisions of the regulations concerning initial and continuing airworthiness (EC Regulations 748/2012 and 1321/2014) to the UA subject to certification.
2. Art. 7 sec. 3 of Regulation 2019/947, which subjects certified category operations to the provisions of the Air Operations Regulation (EC Regulation 965/2012);

When it comes to the certified category, the obligation to certify UA is only one element that requires the revision of airworthiness regulations. Nevertheless, it is necessary to draw up rules on UA operations (including operator certification), pilot competency (licensing), and amendments to the regulations on air traffic rules and air traffic services. According to the European Plan for Aviation Safety 2020–2024[291], EASA has begun working on executive regulations for the certified category. The work features a holistic approach to requirements related not only to UA certification (airworthiness) but also to pilot licensing, UA operations, air traffic regulations, as well as ATM/ATS regulations and airports. Therefore, the approach to certified category regulations assumes not so much the development of completely new rules, but a gradual revision of all the implementing regulations on aviation safety issued so far by the EC. One of the first tasks here is to develop provisions (amendments to the existing aviation safety regulations) for those UA that are able to perform IFR operations from airports in controlled airspace (e.g. cargo flights). Draft regulations (amendments) are expected by the end of 2020 and these are to be adopted (amendments to the Implementing Regulations) by the end of 2022.

New UA certification requirements (CS, *Certification Specification* – CS-UAS) are also expected by 2021. These shall be published in the form of a decision

291 https://www.easa.europa.eu/document-library/general-publications/european-plan-aviation-safety-2020-2024

of the EASA Executive Director and will constitute the basis for the aircraft certification process, based on the provisions of Regulation EC 748/2012 of 3 August 2012. The absence of these requirements generally prevents the certification process from taking place. However, Regulation 748/2012 provides for the possibility of issuing certification for aviation equipment under certain conditions – so-called *special conditions* – which also take the form of decisions of the Executive Director of EASA. In July of 2020, EASA published a draft of special conditions for UA[292] that:

1. have a takeoff mass of less than 600 kg,
2. are not designed to transport people,
3. will be used within the certified category,
4. will be used within the specific category, if the risk analysis indicates the need for UA certification.

This project identified issues related to the design and construction of various components of a UAS, propulsion equipment, systems[293], control stations, and UA communications and control systems (C2link). The main objective of the proposed special conditions is to move away from traditional methods of issuing lengthy lists of detailed requirements, replacing these with clearly defined safety objectives. These objectives are defined, among others, by the probability of a fatal accident for a third party on the ground. This requires taking data such as population density of the overflown area into account, technical data (potential for harm) of the UA, or the number of hours that the UA model has performed without a component failure or its involvement in a dangerous situation. Putting matters simply, it can be assumed that the probability of a fatal accident must be equal to (or lower) than in manned aviation. This concerns incidents that may result from a technical issue related to the design of the aircraft, and not incidents caused by other external factors (improper handling, pilot error, weather conditions, collisions, etc.). The draft of the special conditions is therefore based on the need to achieve (and demonstrate) a set of safety objectives (structure reliability) rather than on detailed definitions and requirements related to the design of a UA itself. This *performance-based* approach has been used for some

---

292 https://www.easa.europa.eu/document-library/product-certification-consultations/proposed-special-condition-light-uas

293 However, the project does not include collision detection and avoidance systems, as these depend on the requirements related to air traffic and airspace. Nevertheless, the required systems will be assessed against the safety objectives related to reliability.

time now in certain areas of "traditional" manned aviation (e.g. general aviation aircraft[294]). Both EASA and JARUS have recommended this approach in their earlier documents on UA airworthiness[295]. As often indicated in various sources, this approach seems most appropriate when it comes to the development of unmanned aviation[296]. However, it should be stressed that it has evolved since the first EASA documents on unmanned aviation certification, which were quite conservative, i.e. they were based on the same rules as in the case of manned aviation[297].

In EASA's opinion, special conditions for UA are the first step toward developing desirable certification requirements for certified category UA. Although, it should be noted that the development of UA certification requirements alone will not solely enable carrying out operations in this category. Indeed, it is crucial to draw up the necessary amendments to the remaining implementing regulations which would concern, for example, the certification of operators or the licensing of remote pilots. This should be gradually put in motion starting 2022. However, the adoption of special conditions for UA is also necessary for another reason.

As already mentioned, in accordance with Art. 40 sec. 1 part 4 of Regulation 2019/945, specific category UA are also subject to certification if the risk assessment indicates certification as a risk mitigation measure. Therefore, the adoption of special conditions for UA weighing below 600 kg will allow UA certification for certain operations in the specific category.

It is worth mentioning that EASA proposed (in AMC and GM) amendments to Regulation 2019/947 in April 2020, the purpose of which was to increase the number of specific category operations requiring the use of certified UA. The reason for the proposed amendment (NPA 2020-07)[298] was an incident that took place on May 2019, when a drone that was being tested by the Swiss Post had its emergency systems activated, including deployment of a parachute, but due to a system's failure the aircraft fell to the ground near a local preschool. In consequence, EASA proposed amendments to the SORA methodology (applicable as

294 See e.g. changes to CS-23 (EASA) and PART-23 (FAA), more at https://www.easa.europa.eu/new-cs-23-%E2%80%93-smart-and-flexible-rules-support-innovation [access: July 22, 2020].

295 See e.g. EASA SC-RPAS.1309 and JARUS AMC.RPAS.1309.

296 K. Dalmagkidis et al. op. cit., p. 92 et seq., A. Masutti, F. Tomasello, op. cit., p. 130.

297 A. Masutti,, F. Tomasello, op. cit., p. 120.

298 https://www.easa.europa.eu/document-library/notices-of-proposed-amendment/npa-2020-07

AMC guideline to Art. 11 of Regulation 2019/947) and as a result, standards for determining *ground risk class* will be elevated. The proposed amendments assume that UA intended for BVLOS operations over populated areas and having a mass of more than 4 kg will require using certified UA (which have achieved so-called restricted type certification).

1.8. Air traffic regulations

The enacted UA regulations do not interfere with the regulations on air traffic management. This means that when performing UA operations accordingly to EU regulations, the pilot is obliged to comply with the applicable regulations on airspace organization and air traffic rules. There are certain mechanisms in place to ensure that UA operations comply with these rules.

In the open category, operations can only be carried out within the operator's line of sight. Being familiar with the principles of airspace organization is one of the basic requirements for pilots in this category (Regulation 2019/947 lists this as part of the theoretical exam). Moreover, Regulation 2019/945 introduced the obligation to have a *geo-awareness system* as a technical requirement for the majority of UA classes in the open category. This solution allows for:

- the option to upload and update data on airspace restrictions and UA location,
- the option to warn a pilot about a potential violation of these restrictions,
- the option to inform a pilot about improper operation of the system.

In the case of specific category operations, issues related to airspace organization and the applicable air traffic rules are an important element of the risk assessment process preceding the acquisition of operational authorization.

Interestingly, EU legislators directly referred the detailed requirements resulting from the provisions on air traffic (EC Regulation 923/2012) in the case of the specific and certified categories (Art. 7 sec. 2 and 3 of Regulation 2019/947). The aforementioned EC Regulation 923/2012 previously excluded "model aircraft and toy aircraft" (Art. 1 sec. 4) from the scope of its application, and defines an "aircraft model" as "unmanned aircraft with a takeoff mass specified by the appropriate aviation authority, used solely for recreational or demonstration purposes" (Art. 2 para. 95 a).

It should also be mentioned that the violation of air traffic regulations in most countries is subject to criminal liability, which is rooted in Art. 12 of the Chicago Convention. Art. 212 paragraph. 1 letter (a) of Poland's Aviation Law sanctions any breach of air traffic regulations, including an inadvertent breach (paragraph 2). These regulations also apply to UA pilots[299].

Designating so-called geographical zones is another mechanism used to ensure that UA pilots comply with air traffic restrictions. Regulation 2019/947 defines them as portions of airspace established by the competent authority that facilitates, restricts, or excludes UAS operations. The premises for introducing these zones are very general and by no means limited to issues related to the safety of air traffic. Due to this premise, EU regulations do not regulate in detail issues related to, for example, UA operations taking place near airports. Such zones may be introduced for reasons related to aviation safety, public safety, protection of privacy and the environment (e.g. protection against noise pollution). Art. 15 sec. 1 of Regulation 2019/947 gives Member States the possibility of designating such geographical zones, giving Member States authority to:

(a) prohibit certain or all UA operations;
(b) request particular conditions for certain or all UA operations;
(c) request prior operational authorization for selected or all UA operations;
(d) subject UAS operations to specified environmental standards;
(e) allow access to the zone to certain UA classes only;
(f) allow access only to UA equipped with certain technical features, in particular remote identification systems or geo-awareness systems.

On the basis of a risk assessment carried out by the competent authority, Member States may designate certain geographical zones in which UA operations are exempt from one or more of the open category requirements specified in Regulation 2019/947.

When defining geographical zones, Member States are obliged to ensure that information on these zones, including their period of validity, is made publicly available in standardized digital format (so that this information can be uploaded to geo-awareness systems).

1.9. UA traffic management. The U-space concept

Integrating manned and unmanned aviation, including UA traffic management, has been discussed in virtually every document published over the course of work on the EU's UA regulations. Work on a UA traffic management concept and

299 See Statement of the President of the Civil Aviation Authority of March 25, 2014 on violations of the rules governing model and UA flights.

its integration with existing air traffic management systems were initially the domain of specialist organizations such as EUROCONTROL. Moreover, EC Communication of 2014 assigned these issues to research and development programs under the SESAR initiative. The first SESAR report on the UA market indicated that a concept for low-altitude operations and their management is crucial for the development of the UA sector as a whole[300]. The next SESAR document concerned the assumptions of this concept called U-space[301]. It presented a roadmap for development which was published in 2018[302]. U-space started being defined as a set of a new types of services and procedures designed to enable the safe and efficient movement of a large number of UA. These services must ensure a high level of automation and digitization. The purpose of the system is to ensure safe UA operations (avoiding collisions between different UA) and their safe integration with manned aviation and air traffic management (ATM) systems. The 2018 Amsterdam Declaration was a further impulse for the development of the U-space concept. It emphasized how important the concept was and indicated the need to draft and build new legal framework enabling its implementation[303]. The EU began working on the main assumptions of the concept, taking into account the EU's risk-based approach to UA regulations. These assumptions already took into account the division into open, specific, and certified categories. And so, the European Network of U-space Demonstrators[304] was born. As part of the SESAR program, and in cooperation with EUROCONTROL, the Concept of Operations for European UTM Systems[305] (the CORUS project) was developed. In March 2020, EASA published a draft of legal framework for the U-space concept (Opinion 01/2020[306]), which proposed a new EC implementing regulation which would concern the "general legal framework for U-space". The proposed legal framework is to be the first step in the development of U-space. It should enable the introduction of services supporting UA traffic management, which are

300 Drone Outlook Study, 2016

301 U-space Blueprint, SESAR, 2017

302 European ATM Master Plan. Roadmap for safe integration in Europe, SESAR, 2018.

303 https://ec.europa.eu/transport/modes/air/news/2018-11-28-drones_en [access: July 22, 2020].

304 https://ec.europa.eu/transport/modes/air/news/2018-10-19-network-u-space-demonstrators_en [access: July 22, 2020].

305 https://www.eurocontrol.int/project/concept-operations-european-utm-systems [access: July 22, 2020].

306 https://www.easa.europa.eu/document-library/opinions/opinion-012020 [access: July 22, 2020].

to be provided by certified organizations designated by Member States. Such organizations are to ensure the exchange of data and information between institutions providing traditional air traffic services and institutions providing U-space services (a so-called *common information service*, CIS). Mandatory services will include providing remote UA identification, providing information supporting "geo-awareness systems", authorization of UA operations in airspace, and providing information on air traffic. Additional services are related to tracking UA location, providing information on weather conditions, or monitoring the compliance of operations with their individual requirements. The main objective of the U-space concept at this stage is to create and ensure a uniform environment that allows for the exchange of data between airspace users. Leaving further details of EASA's idea aside, it should be noted that nearly all aviation organizations representing air carriers, air traffic service providers, airport management, and representatives of professional associations of pilots and air traffic controllers took on a negative approach to this proposal[307]. They pointed to significant reservations as to the proposed solutions, which were related but not limited to the need to maintain the current level of safety in civil aviation as well as a lack of solutions on financing these news services.

1.10. EU regulations and national law

When EC regulations enter into force, they will become directly applicable in the national legal order of Member States. The issue of the relationship of regulations issued on the basis of so-called EASA Basic Regulations and national law has already been the topic of various discussions. Suffice it to mention the opinion of the Legislative Council to the Prime Minister on the draft amendment to the Aviation Law Act of 2015[308]. It is worth recalling the basic principles that shape this relationship. First, since regulations have a general scope, are binding in their entirety, and are directly applicable in all Member States, countries should, as a rule, refrain from actions "implementing" the provisions of regulations into their national legal order. However, there are exceptions to this rule. The first is when the regulation itself assumes taking legislative action by a Member State. Such action may also mean postponing the application of EU regulations[309].

307 https://www.ifatca.org/2020/05/all-one-in-the-sky/ [access: July 22, 2020].

308 Opinion on the draft act amending the Polish Aviation Law Act and some other acts. Legislative Council at the Prime Minister, RL-0303-9 / 15 and the literature referred to there.

309 See ruling of the Supreme Administrative Court of October 5, 2018, I OSK 2708/16.

Moreover, countries may be obliged to adapt their national legislation to the regulation so that its application is not impeded. In any event, the national legislator should refrain from repeating the provisions of EU regulations in national law. We should mention that in the opinion of the Legislative Council, the issue of authorization for "Member States" or "the competent authority" to regulate or clarify certain issues is extremely important. If these issues concern generally applicable requirements, they should be regulated in compliance with the constitutional system of sources of law in force in Poland. These regulations should therefore have at least the rank of an ordinance of the minister responsible for transport.

Bearing in mind the above, we can deduce that it would be necessary to amend Poland's Aviation Law in order to adjust national law to EC regulations and to ensure their effective application. This is due to, for example, the necessity to repeal Art. 33 sec. 2 of the Aviation Law – which, in its present form, refers to a repealed EU regulation, i.e. the former Basic Regulation 216/2008. Other executive provisions based on Art. 33 sec. 2 of the Aviation Law Act concerning UA operations should be repealed as well (Annexes 6, 6a and 6b in particular). Unless Art. 126 is limited to UA used by state aviation, it should also be repealed. UA operations performed by or for the purposes of state aviation seem to be an issue that requires a statutory resolution. The EC's implementing regulations on UA, like all regulations issued on the basis of Regulation 2018/1139, do not apply to state aviation (including unmanned aircraft). This results directly from Art. 2 sec. 3 of Regulation 2018/1139. These are aircraft used for military, customs, police, border guards, coast protection, or firefighting flights by or on behalf of public authorities. However, Member States have the option, resulting from Art. 2 sec. 6 of the EU Regulation 2018/1139, to extend the scope of application of the EU's UA regulations to the abovementioned operations. Therefore, it is necessary to resolve the issue of UA operations carried out by or on behalf of state aviation when adapting national law to EU regulations. Two solutions are possible here – the first is to extend the scope of application of EU regulations to state aviation UA. The second is to create national regulations directly applicable to such operations. They could be based on solutions developed in the Implementing Regulation in Art. 33 sec. 2 (which apply directly to state-owned UA, in accordance with para. 1 section 2). In the latter case, however, it should be borne in mind that pursuant to Art. 2 sec. 3 of Regulation 2018/1139, a Member State is obliged under EU law to ensure that flights of state aviation aircraft are conducted with due respect for the safety of civil aviation operations. Where necessary, Member States should ensure that state aviation flights are separated from those of civil aircraft. Therefore, if a national legislator decides to subject state aviation (including flights performed on behalf of public authorities) to national regulations, it will be necessary to ensure that state UA operations will be performed in designated zones of public airspace in situations where regulations on the matter were to significantly deviate from EU regulations on "civil" UA flights.

Supervision over the application of EU provisions on UA is another issue. Member States are obliged to designate competent authorities to fulfill the tasks imposed by the provisions of the EC regulations. Pursuant to Art. 21 sec. 2a of the Polish Aviation Law, if there is no special provision, the President of the Civil Aviation Authority exercises the powers of a Member State or the competent authority provided for in the EU regulations.

Regardless of the decision whether certain powers should belong to the President of the Civil Aviation Authority, it is necessary to regulate the following issues, which EU regulations transfer directly to national regulations:

1. organizing and maintaining a supervision system for UA defined as products[310];
2. determining the age of UA pilots, if it is to be lower than EU regulations provide for[311];
3. creating and managing a registration system for UA and UA operators[312];
4. coming up with a method for designating geographical zones mentioned in Art. 15 of Regulation 2019/947 and a method for providing data on these zones. The issue of determining limitations and requirements for these zones also needs to be resolved, since the corresponding national regulations on air traffic declare that the minister responsible for transport can introduce such limitations. In very few cases, this role can be played by an institution providing air navigation services;
5. making it possible to define rules for using model UA by modeling associations[313],
6. defining sanctions for infringements of the provisions of the implementing regulations[314].

310 Art. 35 of Regulation 2019/945.
311 Art. 9 of Regulation 2019/947.
312 Art. 14 of Regulation 2019/947.
313 Art. 16 of Regulation 2019/947.
314 Art. 131 of the Basic Regulation 2018/1139.

Moreover, the following issues seem to require clarification in national legislation. Regulation 2019/947 puts them in the hands of the competent authority (Art. 17 and 18), but does not regulate them explicitly:

1. the method of conducting trainings and examinations for pilots in the open category, including determining which bodies are authorized to carry out such trainings[315];
2. procedures for issuing (as well as changing and withdrawing) operational authorization for operations in the specific category, including their related conditions and requirements[316],
3. procedures for authorizing operations in the specific category for operators holding operational authorization issued in another country[317],
4. procedures for issuing, as well as changing and withdrawing, UA operator certificates (in the specific category)[318].

1.11. Comments on solutions adopted in EU regulations

There is no doubt that the regulations adopted at an EU level constitute a new quality in regulating the UA sector. When creating the new regulations, the legislator used mechanisms developed in manned aviation, and basing legal solutions on risk assessment made the requirements scalable and proportionate. Focusing on achieving safety objectives (rather than providing highly detailed requirements) allows for greater flexibility on the operator's side. Coupled with introducing requirements based on the concept of proactive safety management, this move allowed for maintaining the necessary safety level of UA operations. Therefore, the development of legal regulations is based on mechanisms that have been discussed for years and gradually implemented in manned aviation. Such changes take place on a step-by-step basis in manned aviation due to the extensive scope of its safety regulation systems. However, it is possible to develop detailed requirements based on new mechanisms practically from scratch, the purpose of which was confirmed in Basic Regulation 2018/1139.

The development of these detailed solutions was largely based on the works of specialist organizations like JARUS – again, we can see the interdependence between EASA and JARUS. EASA was first to propose the original concept of

---

315 UAS.OPEN.020, UAS.OPEN.030 of Regulation 2019/947.

316 Art. 11 of Regulation 2019/947.

317 Art. 13 of Regulation 2019/947.

318 UAS.LUC.010 of Regulation 2019/947.

operation classification based on risk assessment. However, the concept was later developed mostly by JARUS. One can easily see that the new regulations were based on practical experience gained at national levels and that which came from years of research and development, such as that carried out under the SESAR program.

A more detailed assessment of the EU's UA regulations would go beyond the purpose of this publication. It would also be quite difficult considering the large volume of the new regulations and their advisory materials. Moreover, these provisions were adopted gradually, and often supplemented after precedent regulations had been adopted. EASA also has further amendment proposals, although these are not yet in force. A detailed assessment would be premature as well, since only their implementation in practice allows for a more complete assessment of any adopted solutions. However, it is necessary to make some general remarks related to these regulations, which were adopted at an EU level in the field of UA operational safety.

First, the intense pace of legislative work is very apparent. And while it took some time to find a compromise as to the general assumptions in the new basic regulation, works on implementing regulations were quite fast. This was due to the EC's political priorities, which were expressed in various high-level declarations (Riga, Warsaw, Amsterdam). When speaking at a high-level conference in Amsterdam, EASA's Executive Director emphasized that it took approximately 4 years to develop the EC's new regulations in the field of aviation safety (from draft to publication). Meanwhile, the EC's regulations on unmanned aircraft operations took approximately just 2 years. This was also due to the fact that the formal commencement of legislative work (2017 NPA) was preceded by a non-standard preparatory process, which involved publishing and consulting technical opinions or preliminary drafts of future regulations. This resulted from the EC's adopted approach, which assumed that works on implementing provisions would happen simultaneously to works on the new basic regulation.

Second, we should positively assess the adopted approach to developing these new solutions, which takes the specifics and risks of new UA-related technology into consideration. The alternative, which includes "adapting" already existing solutions found in manned aviation to unmanned aviation, seems justified only to a limited extent. The adopted classification of operations into open, specific, and certified narrows the application of this alternative to the certified category only. However, the certified category will require quite lengthy regulatory processes, even if the principles of UA certification are focused on achieving set safety goals. These processes require collection, validation, and assessment of data, which in turn allows for safety level assessments of the adopted solutions.

The basic assumption that risk should be assessed not so much in relation to individual aircraft but rather to operations themselves lets legislators focus less on detailed technical requirements and more on regulating applications that apply directly to the use of new UA technology, i.e. operations and their related risks. This method seems to be optimal when it comes to regulating the issue of safety of new technologies. The level of development of new UA technologies limits the will of regulators to introduce hard to define technical requirements in their regulations.

Third, it should be noted that the new approaches to safety regulations, combined with the adopted pace of work and the need to develop regulations that are applicable in all EU countries, also had their drawbacks. This is visible, for example, in the mechanism adopted in Art. 15 of Regulation 2019/947 which undermines the concept of adopting uniform, EU-wide regulations. Based on this article, Member States can introduce additional UA requirements limited to specific geographic zones (it is possible, however, to recognize the entire airspace above a given country as a "zone"). Additionally, there are no guidelines or advisory materials for this general provision, which means that its implementation at a national level will allow for its assessment. The EU legislator also left behind some "intentional" legal loopholes. For example, the requirement for electronic UA identification in the open category does not specify any technical requirements, e.g. the range of transmitting an open data signal. Similarly, the provision requires ensuring an appropriate level of operability of the control and command (C2) link system for UA in the open category, without specifying what an "appropriate level" is. Initial assumptions on introducing geofencing[319] systems, which would not allow a UA to enter specific zones, have also changed during the course of this work. In the end, the legislator decided that open category UA should be equipped with *geo-awareness* systems.

Fourth, it is clear that new UA safety regulations, although focusing precisely on issues related to safety, also consider many other aspects of new UA technology. These technical requirements could, for example, affect UA operations by indirectly enforcing certain solutions, such as those related to noise pollution. The mandatory operator register makes it easier to identify UA operators not only in the event of an accident, but also in the event of a breach of privacy. Therefore, it facilitates the pursuit of claims for damages resulting from UA operations. Similarly, mandatory electronic UA identification not only enables the development of the U-space concept, but also facilitates the supervision of UA

319 See A-NPA-2015-10.

operations. However, we should bear in mind that implementing the EC's regulations may not go beyond the scope of the delegations contained in the Basic Regulation. Nevertheless, it is clear that when regulating safety issues, it is possible to shape certain requirements in such a way so they also cover other aspects of the development of new UA technology.

Chapter 5 Key issues regarding the safety of UAS operations (including those related to investigating accidents)

1. Reporting and investigating occurrences involving UA

1.1. Introduction

A growing number of drone operations has resulted in a higher number of drone incidents and accidents – and these aren't just close encounters between manned and unmanned aircraft. These also include incidents that result in damage or destruction of UA, i.e. air accidents exclusively involving UA. Meanwhile, the principles that guide air accident investigations developed over the last few decades remain virtually unchanged. They are a manifestation of what may be called a reactive approach to aviation safety. Accidents and serious incidents are investigated in order to avoid similar situations taking place in the future. This is assured through detailed investigations, the determination of causes and, if necessary, the issuing of safety recommendations which must then be enforced. As aviation developed, it became necessary to supplement the traditional approach to safety with proactive solutions. This meant reporting and analyzing incidents that posed safety hazards so that conclusions could be drawn at earlier stages. This approach is related to the development of what are called *safety management systems* (SMS) in aviation organizations[320]. Reporting all occurrences that may affect aviation safety, not just accidents or serious incidents, is one of the pillars of an SMS. It enables identifying potential hazards at the earliest possible stage, which in turn allows for action to be taken before an accident or serious incident occurs[321]. This publication will later discuss the legal regulations that govern how aviation accidents, serious incidents, and other occurrences involving UA are reported and investigated[322]. From the perspective of safety, these issues

---

320 For more, see K. Łuczak (ed.), Zarządzanie bezpieczeństwem w lotnictwie cywilnym, 2016.

321 For more on the topic: P. Kasprzyk „Odpowiedzialność a bezpieczeństwo transportu lotniczego. Kilka uwag o Just Culture" (w) Ius Est Ars Boni Et Aequi, Księga pamiątkowa dedykowana Profesorowi Józefowi Frąckowiakowi, Wrocław 2018.

322 This part of this paper is further developed in A. Konert, P. Kasprzyk, Reporting UAS related incidents under aviation occurrence reporting legislation.

seem closely related; however they are subject to different legal regimes. While discussing these issues, a number of safety statistics will also be presented.

1.2. Regulations for reporting and investigating air accidents

1.2.1. International regulations

Regulations for investigating air accidents are an important element of wide-ranging aviation safety and apply to air accident investigation processes which are aimed at improving aviation safety[323]. Annex 13 to the Chicago Convention[324] includes international standards and recommendations for the investigation of aircraft accidents and serious incidents. The 13th edition of Annex 13, published in 2010, introduced the very first amendments that took UA into consideration in air accident reporting and investigation.

First and foremost, these recommendations recognized UA as aircraft. Consequently, the standards and recommendations of Annex 13 apply to accidents and serious incidents involving UA. Thus, the definition of an air accident – which is crucial for the assessment of whether or not an occurrence should be investigated – was clarified. It states that any event associated with the operation of an aircraft that takes place between the time any person boards the aircraft with the intention of flight and all such persons have disembarked, and in which any person suffers death or serious injury, or in which the aircraft is substantially damaged or goes missing, is an accident. In the case of UA, this definition required clarification that an accident is an event that happens from the moment a UA is ready to take off until it comes to a full stop and its primary propulsion system is switched off at the end of its flight. Moreover, the general definition of an air incident, i.e. an event other than an accident associated with the operation of an aircraft, which affects or could affect the safety of operations, remained unchanged. However, should the circumstances of an incident indicate that an

---

323 For more on the regulations concerning air accident investigation, see e.g. P. Kasprzyk, Postępowanie w sprawie badania wypadku lotniczego a postępowanie cywilne, Przegląd Sądowy, No. 4, 2009, J. Walulik, Badanie wypadków i incydentów statków powietrznych, Kontrola Państwowa, No. 2, 2011.

324 See announcement No. 2 of the President of the Civil Aviation Authority of February 5, 2018 on the publication of the text of Annex 13 to the Convention on International Civil Aviation (Journal of the CAA No. 2 of 2018).

accident nearly occurred, the incident is treated as serious and is subject to mandatory investigation[325].

Pursuant to Annex 13, if an air accident or serious incident occurs, it is subject to an investigation to be carried out by an independent state body. However, Annex 13 provides that the obligation to investigate accidents and serious incidents involving UA should only apply to UA with a design and/or operational approval[326].

Therefore, according to Annex 13, accidents and serious incidents involving UA should be investigated in situations where a UA operation caused or contributed to causing an air accident or a serious incident involving a manned aircraft. This could be, for example, a collision between a regular aircraft and a UA which resulted in the manned aircraft having an accident. Similarly, a serious incident involving a manned aircraft and a UA will be subject to mandatory investigation should the circumstances indicate that an accident could have happened.

On the other hand, if an accident involves only UA i.e. an unmanned flight causes death, serious injury, or serious damage to another UA, an investigation will only take place if the UA and the flight had been subject to previous authorization.

Since receiving authorization for an operation requires using a certified UA, then in practice the obligation to investigate accidents involving solely UA is limited, as ICAO says, to those UA operations that have been granted *operational approval*. However, determining the authorization requirements for each operation must be checked independently, based on laws applicable at the site of the accident. Despite the limitations concerning investigative activity included in Annex 13, it is recommended as good practice that countries investigate UA accidents regardless of UA certification requirements or prior operational authorization[327].

Ultimately, it is up to each Member State to determine the rules on investigating air accidents and serious incidents involving UA by implementing Annex 13's norms into their national legal systems.

Regardless of the regulatory framework, ICAO's advisory materials identify additional important issues that require further analysis necessary to support research on UA accidents[328]. Some of the most important issues involve ensuring

---

325 However, Annex 13 limits the obligation to investigate serious incidents to aircraft with a maximum takeoff mass above 2,250 kg (5.1.2.).

326 See comment 4 to 5.1 of Annex 13.

327 ICAO Cir. 328, 5.41.

328 Doc. ICAO 10019.

that: (1) UA operational data is registered (requirements in this field should be adapted to the type of UA and operation), (2) potential loss of communications with a UA does not cause loss of data, and (3) a UA is capable of transmitting its position within a radius of at least 6 NM in case of an accident or should the UA go missing.

It is also worth noting that, in 2015, the *International Society of Air Safety Investigators* published a handbook on the investigation of accidents and serious incidents involving UA which analyzes a number of practical issues[329]. It examines in detail the differences between manned and unmanned aviation, indicating how they translate into the process of investigating an air accident or serious incident involving UA.

1.2.2. EU regulations

The EU has implemented the standards and recommendations of Annex 13 in the provisions of EU Regulation 996/2010[330]. Here, we must add that Regulation 996/2010 uses the same definitions of air accident and serious incident as Annex 13 and they both concern UA[331]. "Accident" means an occurrence associated with the operation of an aircraft which, in the case of a manned aircraft, takes place between the time any person boards the aircraft with the intention of flight until such time as all such persons have disembarked, or in the case of an UA, takes place between the time the aircraft is ready to move with the purpose of flight until it comes to rest at the end of the flight and the primary propulsion system is shut down, in which a person is fatally or seriously injured, the aircraft sustains damage, or the aircraft is missing. The provisions of the Regulation also define a serious incident, following the provisions of Annex 13. "Serious incident" means an incident involving circumstances indicating that there was a high probability of an accident and is associated with the operation of an aircraft,

---

329 Unmanned Aircraft System Handbook and Accident/Incident Investigation Guidelines (International Society of Air Safety Investigators, 2015).

330 Regulation (EU) No 996/2010 of the European Parliament and of the Council of 20 October 2010 on the investigation and prevention of accidents and incidents in civil aviation, OJEU 295/35 of 12 November 2010 as amended. For more, see Aspekty prawne badania zdarzeń lotniczych w świetle Rozporządzenia 996/2010, ed. A. Konert, Warszawa, 2013 r.

331 Meanwhile, the definition of an air accident adopted at the national level (Art. 134 (2) of the Aviation Law) still does not cover unmanned aircraft. Due to the principle of primacy of EU law, this inconsistency is of little importance.

which, in the case of a manned aircraft, takes place between the time any person boards the aircraft with the intention of flight until such time as all such persons have disembarked, or in the case of an UA, takes place between the time the aircraft is ready to move with the purpose of flight until such time it comes to rest at the end of the flight and the primary propulsion system is shut down. A list of examples of serious incidents is set out in the Annex and it includes:

- near collisions in the air,
- near collisions with the ground,
- aircraft structural failures or engine disintegrations not classified as an accident.

Before 2018, the Regulation had limited applicability in the case of UA. Its scope was basically limited to the obligation to report accidents and serious incidents. However, only occurrences resulting in an accident or a serious incident of a manned aircraft were subject to mandatory investigation. The decision to undertake an investigation of an accident or a serious incident involving UA alone was left at the discretion of an air accident investigation committee. Such a situation was the result of the EU's lack of competences when it came to UA weighing less than 150 kg. Regulation 996/2010 is closely interrelated to the so-called Basic Regulation establishing uniform rules for civil aviation safety. Until 2018, the Basic Regulation provided that EU's competences cover UA weighing more than 150 kg, i.e. those that were practically not in use in the civilian sector. Therefore, as a general rule, Member States were not required to investigate air accidents which only involved UA lighter than 150 kg, even if such an accident resulted in death or serious injury[332]. It should be stressed here that Member States (accident investigation committees) had the option to undertake such investigations, which stems from Art. 5 sec. 4 of Regulation 996/2010. As the EU's competences were extended, it was necessary to amend the rules on reporting and investigating air accidents involving UA. It is worth mentioning the opinion of the European Network of Civil Aviation Safety Investigation Authorities (ENCASIA), which promoted far-reaching discretion of accident investigation committees in terms of deciding whether to investigate an accident involving UA. The opinion argued that such entities have limitations of an organizational nature

332 Support study to the evaluation of Regulation (EU). No 996/2010 on the Investigation and Prevention of Accidents and Incidents in Civil Aviation. Final Report Link https://ec.europa.eu/transport/modes/air/studies/support-study-evaluation-regulation-eu-no-9962010-investigation-and-prevention_

(the committees were focused on investigating manned aviation accidents, particularly in the commercial sector)[333]. Taking this into consideration, Regulation 2019/1139 amended Art. 5 of Regulation 996/2010 and currently the rules on reporting and investigating accidents and serious incidents involving UA look as follows.

Any accident or serious incident involving UA must be reported to the accident investigation committee of the country, on the territory of which the accident or serious incident took place and has been caused by so-called "persons involved", as defined in Art. 9 sec. 1 following Art. 2 sec. 11 of Regulation 996/2010. "Person involved" means the owner, a member of the crew, the operator of the aircraft involved in an accident or serious incident; any person involved in the maintenance, design, manufacture of that aircraft or in the training of its crew. The term also covers aviation authority personnel.

Reporting an accident or serious incident does not mean that the occurrence will be the subject of an investigation. Art. 5 sec. 5 narrows the obligation to report UA occurrences to the following situations:

1. the UA has been manufactured in accordance with certification or a declaration by the manufacturer, and in accordance with UA implementing regulations issued on the basis of the Basic Regulation, or
2. the occurrence resulted in death or serious injury.

In any other situation, the decision to investigate an accident or serious incident rests with the air accident investigation committee. The only factor that the committee has to take into account when making such a decision is whether they could have expected to reach any new conclusions that may help increase levels of safety.

Considering that Regulation 2019/945 neither provides for a certification system nor provides for the possibility of production based on a manufacturer's declaration, the obligation to investigate aircraft accidents involving UA in EU Member States presently applies to the following situations:

1. the UA operation results in death or serious injury,
2. the UA operation results in an accident of a manned aircraft, which results in death, serious injury, or serious damage to the manned aircraft,

333 See NCASIA opinion of 30 August 2015: https://ec.europa.eu/transport/modes/air/encasia/activities/opinions_en

3. the situation is recognized as a serious incident, meaning an occurrence the circumstances of which indicate a high probability of an air accident of a manned aircraft with a takeoff mass exceeding 2,250 kg.

Any other accident or serious incident involving UA (e.g. serious damage) may, however, become the subject of an investigation by the committee investigating air accidents, if the committee makes such a decision taking into account the expected lessons to be learned to improve aviation safety. This is left to the discretion of the air accident investigation committee. Usually, these will be *ad hoc* decisions at the stage of assessing the reported accident or serious incident. However, it is also possible to adopt a more systemic approach.

For example, the UK AAIB[334] has adopted a general rule that UA accidents and serious incidents are subject to investigation if they concern UA that have been authorized for flight by the aviation authority. In turn, authorization is required for:

1. UA with a mass of over 20 kg (authorization for flight requiring a UA's technical airworthiness assessment),
2. certain operations, e.g. BVLOS (authorization to perform an operation is required).

This approach is generally consistent with ICAO recommendations. Moreover, it allows for the investigation (and thus the analysis and lessons to be learned) of accidents and serious incidents of those UA that have been approved for flights on the basis of national regulations.

However, it should be borne in mind that the abovementioned criteria, which are based on national regulations, will lose their relevance as EU regulations on UA operations enter into force. Therefore, it is worth considering applying future principles of investigating accidents or serious incidents to those UA that will carry out operations within the specific category according to EU regulations, i.e. their operation will be based on operational authorization, or to BVLOS operations carried out on the basis of national regulations (state aviation), provided that they remain in force.

1.2.3. Investigating accidents involving UA

As already mentioned, some aviation accident investigation authorities have published reports on accidents or serious incidents involving UA. However,

334 Following AAIB Aviation Safety Report 2018.

when comparing the data available, one should remember that there are no unified rules as to when an UA accident investigation should be undertaken.

As far as the USA is concerned, available sources indicate that there were five investigations of accidents of this type between 2010 and 2017[335].

UK AAIB published the largest number of available UA accident investigation reports and a relevant summary, which was included in their AAIB Aviation Safety Report 2018[336]. The report shows that there were 36 accidents involving UA between 2015 and 2018. Most of these were caused by technical issues, mainly loss of control over the UA.

Findings in the UK AAIB's reports on UA accidents lead to the conclusion that investigating such occurrences does indeed increase the level of safety. The list of accident causes includes, but is not limited to, technical issues, software bugs, organizational issues, and preparation for flight, including the impact of weather conditions on UA operations. What is interesting is that 18 out of 59 reported accidents all involved the same one model.

Conclusions that follow can be used both in the process of acquiring or improving the skills of UA operators or remote pilots. They can also be used in the process of preparing safety analyses.

As the AAIB indicates in its 2018 annual report, investigation of UA accidents allows for acquiring knowledge about UA by AAIB experts, identifying trends that may affect regulation or operator training, informing manufacturers of potential design issues, creating safety recommendations, and raising awareness.

We also have reports on UA accidents from other countries. For example, a final report by the Belgian AAIU[337] describes the following case. A UA was supposed to fly in a designated zone. However, communications with the UA were lost after takeoff. Despite the activation of the automatic landing system, the UA interrupted the landing procedure, changed its course and flew another 110 miles. Eventually, it crashed on French territory. Importantly, the UA was equipped with a transponder which allowed air traffic services to separate air traffic, particularly when the UA flew through controlled airspace. A software error was the immediate cause of the accident. It enabled the device to stop the forced landing phase initiated after communications had been lost. The incident was classified as an accident due to the destruction of the UA.

335 J. Guzetti, op. cit.
336 AAIB Aviation Safety Report 2018.
337 AAIU-2016-AII-01.

A similar event also took place in Poland, although it concerned a military UA. The UA lost communications during an exercise at a military training ground and left the zone designated for the purpose of the exercise. The *fail-safe* system did not work in this case either, which meant that the drone continued its flight in a straight line for approx. 75 km before falling into the woods. Since the UA was used in a military operation, the accident itself was not investigated by the State Commission on Aircraft Accidents Investigation (SCAAI). However, the Polish Air Navigation Services Agency investigated the occurrence under the supervision of SCAAI and qualified it as an incident (376/16)[338]. Apart from determining the cause of the accident (loss of communications), the issue of how air traffic services should behave in such a situation also required its own analysis. Preventive recommendations were issued and indicated the need to develop procedures for air traffic personnel, which would define how to act in similar situations. It is likely that the above situation was classified as an incident due to the fact that, as indicated in the investigative report, it was possible to determine the direction in which the UA was moving and thus narrow down on the area where it could pose a potential threat to air traffic. However, this situation was more of a stroke of good luck. As a rule, loss of communications with an unmanned aircraft's control system usually entails the loss of the ability to track its flight parameters.

It is worth adding that it was on the basis of the available final reports on the investigation of UA accidents that EASA identified the basic issues related to UA safety. The annual report on the state of civil aviation safety for 2017 indicated[339]:

1. UA airworthiness, particularly related to loss of communications with UA,
2. risk of collision in the air, and
3. risk of collision with an obstacle on the ground.

It is key that both EASA and UK AAIB found that technical failures were the main cause of the accidents whose investigations were included in their reports.

Currently available research confirms the above conclusion. An analysis of over 150 publicly available reports on accidents and incidents involving civilian UA (data from the USA and Australia between 2006 and 2015) shows that 61% of incidents were caused by a technical failure of one of the components of the

338 https://www.gov.pl/documents/905843/1047987/20160376RK.pdf [access: January 31, 2020].

339 EASA Annual Safety Report 2017.

UAS (CFS, Component Failure System)[340]. However, the analysis also concluded that the available data on accidents and other incidents involving UA was highly heterogeneous.

As for the EU, reference data on reported accidents and serious incidents involving UA can be obtained from the ECCAIRS database, where occurrences are reported at a national level. According to data concerning the period between 2015 and 2018, the following occurrences were reported in the EU[341]:

- ✓ 104 accidents involving UA (only one occurrence of a collision between a UA and a manned aircraft),
- ✓ 90 serious incidents involving UA.

Meanwhile, practically all of serious incidents concerned situations where a manned aircraft passed a device that, in the crew's opinion, was or resembled a UA. Investigating such types of serious incidents consists primarily of conducting fairly detailed verification to determine whether the object observed was in fact a drone (or was it a so-called *false positive*)[342]. It seems that only if findings confirm that it was, or there is a high probability that it could have been, a UA, then the incident will be classified as a serious incident. It is also worth noting that each incident of this type also involves police activities such as initiating criminal proceedings in connection with a possible violation of air traffic rules.

1.2.4. Accident and serious incident reporting

As already mentioned, according to the ECCAIRS database, 104 accidents and 90 serious incidents involving UA were recorded in all EU countries in the period 2015–2018. According to the same statistics, there was no accident and only one serious incident involving UA in Poland recorded in the period 2010–2018. The incident, which took place in 2015 and was classified as a serious incident, consisted of the crew of a passenger plane notifying the authorities that a UA was being operated at Warsaw Chopin Airport when the plane was coming in for landing[343]. It seems unlikely that there was no single accident or serious incident

---

340 G. Wild et al., A Post-Accident Analysis of Civil Remotely-Piloted Aircraft System Accidents and Incidents. Journal of Aerospace Technology and Management, Vol. 9, No 2, 2017.

341 CAA document LBB-2/811-0006/19 of December 4, 2019.

342 J. Guzzetti, op. cit.

343 According to the crew, the drone was operating at an altitude of 2,500 feet and was spotted less than 100 meters from the plane. The final report on the investigation of this

involving UA in an 8-year period. For example, in 2017, media reported of a DJI-type drone colliding with a building (the last floor of the Sky Tower) and suffering serious damage[344]. A comparison of statistics on UA incidents reported in Poland and in all EU countries seems to confirm the discrepancy between the number of reported incidents and actual number of occurrences involving drones.

The reason for this may be low legal awareness among UA users as to whether and to whom they should report accidents and serious incidents involving UA. As a reminder, since 2010, EU Regulation 996/2010 provides for the obligation to report both accidents and serious incidents involving UA, even if the incident did not involve a manned aircraft. It seems that changing the existing state of affairs, i.e. the number of reported (or rather unreported) events involving UA in Poland requires at least two types of action.

First, the SCAAI should adopt a "policy" on accident and serious incident investigation. It can be argued that the accidents of UA performing BVLOS operations should be investigated. Some of the accidents and serious incidents could be investigated by UA operators under the supervision of the SCAAI (following similar rules present in sport aviation, for example).

Second, rules should be developed for informing users about the obligation to report accidents and serious incidents involving UA and the benefits of having them reported and investigated (i.e. accident prevention, updated database, safety management, increasing the level of safety, lessons learned, increasing SCAAI's competences on UA, raising competences on reporting and investigating occurrences among UA users).

Until awareness among UA users increases in this area, which can only be confirmed through collected data and statistics, it is difficult to assess the status of safety of UA operations in Poland. Available data on aviation incidents other than accidents and serious incidents involving UA, which are analyzed in a further part of this publication, can paint a certain picture of the current state of affairs.

---

serious incident has not been published (1425-1415). See http://avherald.com/h?article=48996163 [access]. February 15,2023 http://avherald.com/h?article=489f59be

344 https://wroclaw.wyborcza.pl/wroclaw/1,35771,21282088,dron-uderzyl-w-ostatnie-pieto-sky-tower.html [access: January 31, 2020].

1.2.5. Conclusions

Current accident and serious incident investigation regulations are (and always have been) focused on the safety of manned aviation. If UA are recognized as aircraft, then any accident or serious incident involving one should be recognized as reportable and, in certain situations, be subject to an investigation. However, determining which accidents involving UA should be subject to an investigation requires a balanced approach so as not to undergo costly and time-consuming investigation procedures (developed for manned aviation) that may turn out to be unnecessary. Therefore, aviation accident investigation authorities focus their resources and attention on investigating those accidents and serious incidents in which a manned aircraft has collided with or closely encountered an UA. Particular attention should be paid to those incidents in which pilots report potential collisions with UA, but a detailed examination can in turn reveal that what they thought was a UA was actually something else. The rapidly progressing development of the UA sector means that more and more attention is paid to accidents exclusively involving UA. ICAO indicates that it is necessary to investigate those incidents which involve UA that require certification or authorization for use. Since UA certification requirements have not yet been developed, this in practice points to UA operations that require authorization at a national level. Due to aviation accident investigation authorities' limited resources and the costs of conducting investigation activities, investigations focus mainly on UA with a relatively high takeoff mass and incidents involving death or serious injury. In other cases, it is up to the accident investigation committee to make the decision whether to launch an investigation or not.

Investigating accidents and serious incidents involving UA requires being acquainted with new UA technology and regulations that govern their use. Obviously, investigating accidents allows for a better understanding of their possible causes. However, it seems necessary to introduce changes to regulations so that it is possible to, for example, locate a UA that has lost communications, or access secure flight parameter data or the working parameters of a ground station.

UA users' awareness on reporting accidents remains a separate issue. Available statistics suggest that a significant number of accidents and serious incidents involving UA are never reported. This seems to be due to relatively low legal awareness among drone users. For example, the general rule in EU countries is to report any incident involving a UA, regardless of its mass or type of operation. Meanwhile, data for 2015–2018 show that people reported between 30 and 40 accidents in all EU countries altogether. This means that accidents involving UA were not reported at all in some countries, and such incidents do not appear in official statistics despite media coverage indicating the contrary. Changing this state of affairs requires, similar to the case of manned aviation, the gradual building of trust between authorities responsible for aviation safety and UA operators, as well as spreading legal awareness among the latter.

It should be emphasized that the available studies on accidents and serious incidents involving UA indicate that **the level of technical advancement of UA technology is much lower than that of manned aviation**. For this reason alone, it seems crucial to ask the question how much this difference can alter the integration of unmanned and manned aviation operations. One of the key assumptions of the integration process is that it should not reduce the current level of safety of manned aviation. As already mentioned, the available studies indicate that more than half of all accidents caused by UA devices are the result of technical issues, mostly related to the unreliability of individual elements of an entire UA system. However, debating the safety of UA operations requires much more data of a much higher quality. For this reason alone, it seems justified to take action aimed at increasing UA users' awareness on the need to report accidents and serious incidents involving UA, and to involve UA users in investigation processes.

1.3. Occurrences involving UA other than accidents and serious incidents

As mentioned in the introduction, the evolution of the approach to aviation safety brought about new safety regulations. Regardless of the obligation to report and investigate air accidents, we have seen recommendations made at both organizational and national levels to proactively manage the issue of safety. The development of safety management systems necessitates ensuring that any event that has a potential impact on safety is reported and analyzed.

1.3.1. Incident reporting regulations in the EU

At an EU level, the rules for reporting civil aviation occurrences have been harmonized and apply to both organizations which are required to have a safety management system, and other organizations that employ licensed aviation personnel. These rules are settled in the provisions of EU Regulation 376/2014[345],

345 Regulation (EU) No 376/2014 of the European Parliament and of the Council of 3 April 2014 on the reporting, analysis, and follow-up of occurrences in civil aviation, OJEU L 122/18 of 24 April 2014.

which has been in force since November 2015. Its most important assumptions are as follows:

1. persons performing operational tasks in aviation (these persons usually hold a required license, e.g. pilots, controllers, mechanics) are required to inform about aviation incidents related to aviation safety,
2. an aviation incident is a very broad term. It covers both accidents and serious incidents (subject to investigation by independent commissions), as well as much less serious (but much more frequent) incidents and so-called other events that affect or may affect the safety of aerial operations. These types of events have been indicated in some detail in the provisions of Regulation 376/2014[346],
3. organizations employing such personnel are required to create an internal system for reporting and analyzing such events. Moreover, they are also required to create a voluntary system for reporting events other than those that are mandatory to report,
4. after an event has been reported within an organization, it is also forwarded to the competent authority (e.g. the SCAAI in Poland),
5. if an organization has decided to take corrective action as a result of an incident analysis, the competent authority should be notified of the implemented action,
6. persons reporting incidents are subject to legal protection, which means that the organization that employs them, as well as the competent authority or aviation authority, may not take any negative action against them (or persons participating in the event), unless the incident was caused intentionally or through negligence,
7. based on data on aviation incidents, entities take corrective action following a particular incident or group of incidents, and also carry out analyses and undertake action at an organizational, Member State, or EU level;
8. the obligation to report incidents through this system is independent and complementary to the obligation to report accidents and serious incidents to an air accident investigation committee. In Poland, since the SCAAI is the competent authority to collect information on all occurrences, it is up to the SCAAI itself to assess whether an occurrence qualifies as an accident or

346 Commission Implementing Regulation (EU) 2015/1018 of 29 June 2015 laying down a list classifying occurrences in civil aviation to be mandatorily reported according to Regulation (EU) No 376/2014 of the European Parliament and of the Council, OJEU L 163/1 of 30 June 2015.

a serious incident (and thus is subject to the provisions of Regulation 996/2010) or another type of event (subject only to Regulation 376/2014).

EU Regulation 376/2014 combines the obligation to report incidents that may affect the safety of aerial operations involving those aircraft for which EU competences arise from the so-called New Basic Regulation. This is a similar mechanism as in the case of EU Regulation 996/2010. This rule, mentioned in Art. 3 sec. 2 of EU Regulation 376/2014, was specified when the New Basic Regulation, i.e. EU Regulation 2018/1139, was adopted. Extending the EU's competences to UA would provoke the necessity to report all UA safety-related events. This is why the applicable subjective scope of Regulation 376/2014 has been limited when it comes to UA-related events.

Primarily, the focus here are complex UAS that are either manufactured within a certification system or are part of a system of declarations submitted by the producer. They are a category provided for in the New Basic Regulation but not regulated in the executory order. EC Regulation 2019/945 published in 2019 orders production of open category UA to comply with CE compliance regulations and refers production of specific category UA to technical requirements specified in the process of issuing operational authorizations.

When it comes to other UA (other than complex ones), the obligation to report an event involving UA is interrelated with two situations:

1. an incident involving an UA results in death or serious injury,
2. a manned aircraft took part in an incident involving an UA.

1.3.2. EU Statistics (ECCAIRS)

One of the first sets of statistics on UA incidents at an EU level was published in EASA's Annual Safety Report for 2016. These were based solely on data from ECCAIRS. According to this data, approx. 400 drone incidents were noted in 2015. Due of reasons further unknown, the data was not published in the following ASR EASA editions. The ECCAIRS data on incidents involving UA between 2015 and 2017 was presented in the CAA's Safety Report for 2017. This data indicated that the total number of notifications regarding RPAS (excluding incidents classified as "undefined") looks as follows: approx. 100 (2014), approx. 400 (2015), approx. 800 (2016), approx. 1 150 (2017). A rapid increase in the number of reported incidents year after year is fairly clear (increases of several hundred percent). However, it should be noted that the vast majority of these incidents (reported in ECCAIRS) have been classified as incidents or events that are not incidents.

It should be borne in mind that data from the ECCAIRS database are subject to some systemic imperfections. Since data for the ECCAIRS database are reported at a Member State level, sometimes events get re-classified after being reported (in light of new information). Some notifications are also recorded multiple times under different labels (e.g. if submitted by an organization established in two different countries).

It is possible to provide the total number of UA-related incidents that were reported to the ECCAIRS database via reporting systems at a national level between 2015 and 2018. This data was obtained at the end of 2019 from the Polish CAA as a response to a motion submitted on the basis of Regulation 376/2014[347].

At an EU level between 2015 and 2018, there were:

- ✓ 104 accidents involving UA (only one event involving a collision between a UA and a manned aircraft),
- ✓ 91 serious incidents,
- ✓ 3 301 incidents,
- ✓ 424 occurrences, and
- ✓ 594 other reports (so-called not determined).

The vast majority of reported serious incidents and incidents was related to incidents involving both unmanned aircraft and manned aircraft. This is due to, as mentioned earlier, the specifics of the incident reporting system, which imposes the obligation on manned aviation personnel to report such incidents.

Anyhow, it can be assumed that the number of official reports in this database does not correspond to the number of all reported incidents involving UAS. These discrepancies are illustrated by other EASA statistics.

1.3.3. National Statistics (Poland)

Existing reports on UA operations in Poland do not mention statistical data on the safety of UA operations. Similarly, none of the explanatory memorandums to subsequent draft laws regulating the use of UA provide any information on statistics or analyses relating to the issue. The only publicly available data on the safety of UA operations can be found in the following documents on the safety of civil aviation drafted by the CAA:

1. Civil Aviation Safety Review for 2017,
2. National Aviation Safety Plan (since 2017).

---

347 CAA document LBB-2/811-0006/19 of December 4, 2019.

It stands to reason that more recent statistics are more reliable, based on which it can be concluded that, in total, 1 serious incident, 40 incidents, and 5 events involving UA were reported in Poland between 2015 and 2017.

There are, however, several reasons why this statistical data is not sufficient for performing an analysis of the safety of UA operations in Poland – either separately or in relation to manned aviation, and they are as follows:

- ever-changing legislation on reporting aviation occurrences, including drone-related events;
- difficulty in classifying events reported as UA-related due to the inability to confirm whether they actually involved a UA and not another flying object;
- lack of awareness among UA operators with regards to the obligation to report specific types of UA-related events as aviation accidents or aviation incidents.

It should be stressed that current statistics are based on reports made by persons other than drone operators and pilots, which means they can hardly be considered as anything more than official statistics on UA activity made by "traditional aviation" organizations. The vast majority of such reports are classified as incidents. The analyzed data also shows that most of the incidents are reported by the Polish Air Navigation Services Agency. However, reports from airport managers and air operators are also becoming all the more common. According to publicly available information, among all incidents involving UA reported between 2012 and 2016 (a total of around 60 cases), almost half of them concerned UA violating airspace restrictions[348].

1.3.4. Statistics for other countries

Publicly available data on events involving UA can be found in documents published by the UK CAA. The UK CAA 2016 Safety Report states that about 300 UA reports were noted in 2016, 87 of which were reported as so-called airprox, which is a UA observed in dangerous proximity to a manned aircraft[349].

According to press information published by DFS[350] (Germany), pilots reported the following number of UA incidents in Germany: 88 in 2017 and 158 in 2018.

---

348 Data from the Report on the State of Civil Aviation Safety for 2017, CAA.

349 UK Aviation Safety Review for 2016, CAP 1595.

350 https://www.dfs.de/dfs_homepage/en/Press/Press%20releases/2019/12.03.2019.-%20Growing%20risk%20of%20drones%20to%20air%20traffic/

However, the most detailed statistics on drone-related incidents reported by pilots / controllers are published by the FAA (USA). Nearly 200 events involving UA are currently reported via the Aviation Safety Reporting System (NASA ASRS)[351] every month. Data available for 2017 and 2018 (data published with report descriptions) contain statistics which indicate over 200 reports per month. In total, there were 2 124 incidents in 2017 and 2 312 of them in the USA in 2018. Available data for previous years confirm the upward growth trend in the number of drone incident reports.

It should be clarified, however, that there are three systems for reporting UA-related incidents currently in force in the USA. The aforementioned ASRS is an incident reporting system dedicated to manned aviation personnel (an incident reporting system based on Regulation 376/2014 is the European equivalent here). Then, there is the NTSB for reporting accidents and serious incidents, some of which are subject to investigations (equivalent of Regulation 996/2010). There is also an independent, complementary system for drone pilots for reporting specific incidents involving UA directly to the FAA (PART §107.9). These specific incidents involve incidents resulting in:

(a) serious injury or loss of consciousness,
(b) damage to property other than the UA, if the value of the damage exceeds $ 500.

There is no similar obligation in EU legislation. However, as a condition for obtaining UA operator certification, regulations envisage an internal security management system which is used to report and analyze UA safety-related events[352]. But it must be clarified that UA operator certification continues to be voluntary under EU regulations.

1.3.5. An analysis of available data on incidents involving UA

The analysis of available statistics on incidents involving UA leads to the conclusion that the vast majority of these events concern situations where pilots report encountering a UA or a device that resembled a UA. These are situations in which UA pilots were carrying out operations in airspace they should not have been in. Analyses of safety statistics kept by national or European authorities are publicly available. For example, a British UA operational safety document[353]

351 https://www.faa.gov/uas/resources/public_records/uas_sightings_report/
352 UAS LUC 030 Regulation 2019/247.
353 Drone Safety Risk: An Assessment, CAP 1627.

provides more detailed statistics on reported UA incidents for 2016 and 2017. These include the reported altitude at which the pilot/controller saw a UA. It is worth noting that the vast majority of UAS flight observation reports concerned operations at altitudes below 4,000 feet, with most of these being operations below 2,000 feet (approx. 700 meters). What's more, the FAA's UA safety report[354] also includes similar statistics. These show that almost a third of reported incidents occurred at more than 3,000 feet (approx. 1000 m).

Reporting such events allows for monitoring the overall state of safety. Such data lets states and organizations assess whether UA operations really do pose a threat to manned aviation safety. As indicated, reporting incidents and analyzing such data makes it possible to assess whether the regulatory requirements for UA operations are sufficient in maintaining present levels of safety[355]. In other words, reporting and analyzing are the most appropriate methods of assessing whether existing UA safety regulations meet the objectives of enabling UA operations while maintaining the safety of third parties and manned aviation.

Two types of events, which for obvious reasons are of the subject of public interest, require particular attention.

The first is events involving drones operating near airports, i.e. in controlled airspace where UA should not, in principle, carry out any operations. It is increasingly the case that such events cause significant difficulties in airport operations. Take the Gatwick incident for example, which was so widely covered in the media. The incident resulted in the suspension of flights, complications during Christmas, and the closure of the airport for over 30 hours[356]. There are several aspects of this situation that are worth noting. First of all, the authorities decided to use military drone detection systems to confirm that the airport could continue its operations without any threats to safety. Second of all, the police launched a wide-ranging investigation, the findings of which indicated that the UA operations in question were organized by a group of people. The investigation alone cost more than £800 million[357]. Third of all, the authorities finally took systemic measures and proposed, among others[358]:

354 https://www.oig.dot.gov/library-item/35367.

355 J. Guzetti, op. cit.

356 https://www.bbc.com/news/uk-england-sussex-46623754

357 https://www.bbc.com/news/uk-england-sussex-49846450

358 https://www.gov.uk/government/publications/government-response-to-future-of-drones-in-the-uk-consultation

- the introduction of a drone registration system,
- the introduction of mandatory on-line exams for drone pilots,
- changes to the borders of UA-prohibited zones around airports.

Most of these changes have been in force since November 2019.[359]

Polish media also reported on a short-term suspension and reorganization of air traffic at Warsaw Chopin Airport, which took place due to reported UA activity in the airport's controlled airspace[360].

The issue of carrying out UA operations near aerodromes requires further analysis, particularly concerning the rules on the use of airspace.

The second type of drone-related incident of particular interest to the public is confirmed collisions with manned aircraft. Until recently, available studies indicated no such events have ever taken place. However, the 2018 UK AAIB report indicated two collisions in the air that happened in 2015[361]. Interestingly, both cases involved so-called ultra-light aircraft (manned) and models (unmanned) of very little mass (from 0.5 to 2 kg). The models were completely destroyed, and the ultra-light aircraft required minor or major repairs. This is important because in most countries (including Poland), the rules regarding ultra-light aircraft flights are quite liberal. For example, they allow for carrying out flights in areas other than airports or registered airstrips.

There have been more and more incident reports on collisions between manned aircrafts and UA other than models in recent years.

Information on the available reports on these events is provided below.

1. Drone collides with Beechcraft King Air BE100 (Canada, 2017)

On October 12, 2017, a plane with a 2-man crew and 6 passengers on board collided with a UA. The collision took place within the controlled space of an airport where the UA was not allowed to fly. As a result of the collision, the drone was wrecked and the plane sustained minor damage to one of its wings[362].

---

359 https://www.caa.co.uk/Consumers/Unmanned-aircraft/Our-role/Drone-and-model-aircraft-registration/

360 https://dlapilota.pl/wiadomosci/dlapilota/zblizenie-b777-z-dronem-po-startcie-z-epwa
https://dlapilota.pl/wiadomosci/dlapilota/drony-wstrzymaly-ladowania-na-epwa

361 https://www.gov.uk/aaib-reports/aaib-investigation-to-robin-dr-400-180-f-gsbm-and-sas-wildthing-radio-controlled-model-glider
https://www.gov.uk/aaib-reports/aaib-investigation-to-pioneer-300-g-opfa-and-valenta-ray-x-s037996

362 http://www.bst-tsb.gc.ca/eng/rapports-reports/aviation/2017/a17q0162/a17q0162.pdf

2. DJI drone collides with UH60 helicopter (USA, 2017)

The collision between a DJI-type drone and a UH60 military helicopter occurred on September 21, 2017, over the New York Bay. As a result, the drone was destroyed and the helicopter's main rotor blade was slightly damaged. According to an NTSB report on the incident, the cause of the accident was the drone operator performing the flight beyond line of sight and being unaware of the applicable air traffic rules[363].

3. Drone collides with GC2 helicopter (Switzerland, 2018)

On May 25, 2018, a helicopter flying toward Locarno airport collided with a drone, resulting in damage to the helicopter's rotor blades. Fortunately, the helicopter reached the airport and landed safely. It was found that the drone pilot was operating within restricted airspace as the area around the airport was considered a no-fly zone (5 km). The drone was destroyed.

4. Phantom4 collides with R44 helicopter (Israel, 2018)

On August 14, 2018, a Phantom 4 drone collided with a civilian R44 helicopter performing a field spraying flight. The drone was destroyed and the spraying system installed on the helicopter was damaged. The Israeli investigative commission report showed that the drone operator was properly licensed to perform a photo mapping operation of a construction site located near the farmland. However, he didn't notice the helicopter in time and the two collided, despite the drone having its emergency landing system activated[364].

The occurrences discussed were not classified as air accidents or serious incidents. The UA involved were small drones and the destruction of such a drone does not qualify to be investigated as an air accident, since these drones are not subject to certification. The manned aircraft, on the other hand, sustained only minor damage, which also does not qualify for an investigation (only serious damage is tantamount to investigation). The above occurrences were classified only as incidents; however in light of their significance, it seems all the more appropriate to investigate such events.

363 See NTSB link https://app.ntsb.gov/pdfgenerator/ReportGeneratorFile.ashx?EventID=20170922X54600&AKey=1&RType=HTML&IType=IA%EF%BB%BF [access: January 2, 2020].

364 http://aiai.mot.gov.il/NOTES/NAI_1256.pdf

1.3.6. Conclusions

The above analysis of the regulations on reporting incidents involving UA and related statistics leads to the following conclusions:

Current regulations on reporting incidents involving UA seem to view the issue from the perspective of manned aviation, be it in the US (the ASRS system) or in the EU (Regulation 376/2014, the ECCAIRS system). The vast majority of reported events concern situations where the crew of a manned aircraft spots a drone or a drone-like object. Obviously, it is very difficult to determine the identity of the UA operator in such situations. In some cases, there is a similar difficulty in verifying whether the observed object was actually a UA (a so-called false-positive)[365]. Nevertheless, reporting these types of events is necessary as it provides the basis for identifying one of the main threats related to the widespread use of UA – violation of the rules on airspace use. Ultimately, all regulations have the goal of preventing collisions between manned and unmanned aircraft. Unfortunately, events like this have already happened and it seems necessary to investigate them, even if the aircraft involved did not sustain any serious damage. Investigations allow us to pinpoint the exact causes of such events.

Regardless of the fact that certain incidents simply need to be investigated (prevention), incident reporting in itself allows for an in-depth analysis of aggregated data. Data collected from incident reporting allows for scientific and institutional analyses of safety procedures and the clearer identification of risks. As mentioned earlier, the results of these analyses allow for assessing whether the applicable safety requirements for UA operations are sufficient. These requirements are intended to ensure the safety of third parties, i.e. people on the ground, as well as that of crews and passengers involved in manned aviation.

Thus, reporting incidents involving UA has its point. Nevertheless, there are three main challenges in reporting and analyzing incidents involving UA.

First, there are no uniform standards on what types of data should be collected when reporting drone incidents[366].

Second, reporting these types of events is obligatory only for manned aviation personnel, at least in the EU. Part 107.9, which obligates UA operators to report certain types of incidents to the FAA, has no equivalent in the EU.

---

365 J. Guzzetti, op. cit.

366 G. Wild et al., A Post-Accident Analysis of Civil Remotely-Piloted Aircraft System Accidents and Incidents. Journal of Aerospace Technology and Management, Vol. 9, No 2, 2017.

Third, there are no standards for analyzing UA incidents. Certain regulations in this regard have been adopted, but these are related only to accidents subject to mandatory investigation. It should be noted that accidents constitute only a small part of all events. So when it comes to occurrences other than accidents or incidents, it seems justified to develop basic principles related to their classification and analysis. Even if no actual accident occurred, conducting an analysis is the only method for discovering its causes. From a preventative point of view, it is much more advantageous to determine the cause of recurring problems with, for example, loss of communications, than to investigate a fatal accident caused by a UA that has lost communications. Critical to this is the issue of how UA users perceive the safety of UA operations. As mentioned before, all incidents have been reported "from the perspective of manned aviation" and not UA users. Reporting UA incidents, as long as the incident had no effect on manned aviation, has not been and is still not obligatory under EU regulations. Therefore, it is either up to national legislators (if they want to regulate the obligation to report incidents) or the public (using existing systems or within UA operator communities) to make a difference in this regard.

When analyzing the available data on drone incidents, there is a very clear increase in incident reporting across the EU as of 2015. Data from other countries, including the US, confirm this trend. However, it has not been noted in Poland. Why?

In Poland, national regulations on UA operations have been in force since mid-2013. However, the first reports of drone incidents were recorded in 2015. From 2015 to 2018, the number of these reports remained at a similar level of about a dozen events per year. An analysis of this data shows that these are mostly situations where UA are spotted near airports or by manned aviation personnel. Comparing this number of event reports year after year with trends observed in other countries shows that there is a very limited number of events that take place. This may indicate both a relatively high level of safety of UA operations in Poland, as well as the lack of sufficient awareness among UA operators of the need to report such events. However, it should be borne in mind that only manned aviation personnel and organizations are obliged to report UA-related incidents, so the dozen or so events per year are mostly just UA spotted in zones they were not supposed to be flying in. Manned aviation personnel are aware of their obligation to report such situations, which is proven by statistics. Therefore, there is no reason to assume that the actual number of events involving UA reported by manned aviation personnel is much higher than what is officially made public. One could argue that UA operations in Poland are just carried out in a relatively safe manner, at least when it comes to their impact on the safety of manned aviation. This state of affairs may be caused by existing national regulations regarding UA operations, a large number of trained operators (holders of qualifications certificates), or the availability of a system that supports operation performance, among other factors. However, this can only be confirmed after verifying the available data on events involving UA and analyzing data on the total number of UA operations taking place in Polish airspace.

Chapter 6 Drones as aircraft – finding solutions to civil liability cases

1. Liability for damage caused by the use of unmanned aircraft for air transport (contractual liability)

1.1 International conventions and liability for damage caused by the use of unmanned aircraft

1.1.1. Liability for damage caused to passengers transported using unmanned aircraft

"The Drone Taxi market size is forecasted to grow from an estimated USD 74 million in 2025 to reach USD 860 million by 2030, at a CAGR of 63.0% from 2025 to 2030. The recent technological developments in the drone taxi market hold a promising future whereby cities are expected to adopt next-generation transportation systems using unmanned systems. Cities around the world are facing transportation challenges due to the increasing road traffic which causes major problems for mass transportation. Moreover, growth in disposable income coupled with the reducing cost of automobiles for personal use have led to an increase in the number of automobiles, thereby increasing environmental concerns."[367]

In May 2013, a Jetstream aircraft became the first UA to perform a pioneering passenger flight, largely under control of a pilot on the ground. The flight took off from Warton near Preston, Lancashire, and landed in Inverness. On its 500-mile journey, the 16-passenger plane shared the airspace with passenger flights. There was nobody on board except for two pilots. This event can undoubtedly be considered a new chapter in the history of aviation.[368]

---

367 Dublin, July 30, 2021 (GLOBE NEWSWIRE) – The "Drone Taxi Market by Range (Intercity, Intracity), Propulsion (Fully Electric, Hybrid, Electric Hydrogen), Autonomy (Fully Autonomous, Remotely Piloted), Passenger Capacity (Up to 2, 3 to 5, More than 5), System, End Use & Region – Global Forecast to 2030".

368 M. Prigg, Welcome to drone air: First passenger plane piloted remotely flies across the UK in pioneering trial: https://www.dailymail.co.uk/sciencetech/article-2324358/Welcome-drone-air-First-passenger-plane-pilot-flies-UK-pioneering-trial.html [access: October 31, 2018]; S. Michaelides-Mateou, Ch. Erotokritou, Flying into the Future with UAVs: The Jetstream 31 Flight. Air and Space Law, Vol. 39, Issue 2, 2014, p. 112.

At the Consumer Electronics Show (CES) in Los Angeles in 2016, Chinese company Ehang presented a so-called Personal Flying Vehicle, PFV (Ehang 184) capable of carrying one passenger (weighing up to 100 kg) on board. The vehicle reaches a speed of 100 km/h, an altitude of 3,300 m and has range of about 20 km. It can carry out flights in manual or autonomous modes with a pilot–passenger and a maximum airtime of 23 minutes.[369]

In 2017, a German company called Lilium Jet tested its fully electric drone, which was capable of vertical takeoff but could fly like a jet. The company was proud to announce that this was "the world's first electric vertical takeoff and landing jet." The all-electric aircraft has a range of 300 km and a top speed of 300 km/h, while creating less noise than a motorbike.[370]

Airbus created a prototype of a flying autonomous taxi called Vahana. The taxi can be summoned with a smartphone and then transports passengers to their destination. In January of 2018, Vahana completed its first test flight at the Pendleton UAS Range in the state of Oregon. The vehicle reached an altitude of 5 meters and landed safely.

Also in 2018, in cooperation with a German company Volocopter, Intel presented Volocopter VC200, a passenger aerial taxi, which had carried out a few test flights in North America and Dubai. It can be operated by a pilot or fly on its own, and is fully electric. Currently, it can fly for 30 minutes with a max range of 17 miles. Volocopter has already been authorized to fly in Germany.[371]

In December of 2019, Airbus carried out the first test flight of its 4-person multicopter in Donauwörth, Germany. CityAirbus is an international project run by Airbus Helicopters aimed at creating an electric unmanned air taxi.

During the 2020 edition of the Farnborogh Air Show, Aston Martin presented its Volante Vision concept intended to transport three people. The aircraft takes off and lands vertically and uses a hybrid engine to power its propellers.

Uber is another company that is working on developing shared air transport within the framework of the Uber Elevate program. Its introduction is planned for 2023 and the project is intended to operate in suburban and urban areas. On

369 A.J. Hawkins, Ehang's passenger-carrying drones look insanely impressive in first test flights, The Verge 5 February 2018, https://www.theverge.com/2018/2/5/16974310/ehang-passenger-carrying-drone-first-test-flight [access: November 6, 2018].

370 B. Marr, 6 Amazing Passenger Drone Projects Everyone Should Know About, Forbes: https://www.forbes.com/sites/bernardmarr/2018/03/26/6-amazing-passen ger-drone-projects-everyone-should-know-about/#73a41c9a4ceb [access: February 18, 2020].

371 Ibidem.

January 6, 2020, Uber and Hyundai Motor Company announced a new partnership to develop Uber Air taxis and unveiled their new full-scale aircraft concept at CES. Hyundai is the first automotive company to join Uber Elevate, offering manufacturing capabilities at an automotive scale and record mass production of electric vehicles.[372]

For now, the future of passenger drones remains uncertain. For example, ICAO explicitly states that we will not see commercial passenger drone flights in the foreseeable future (2.7 Cir 328). However, the development of innovative technologies seems to clear the fog of uncertainty around this mode of transport.[373] Innovations in the areas of drone technology, air traffic management, the integration of manned and unmanned aviation, and collision avoidance systems may lead to the introduction of commercial passenger transport by UA. Before that happens, society as a whole must overcome a number of technological and operational challenges. The psychological barrier seems to be the most serious, and breaking this barrier is key to popularizing flights with passengers but with no crew on board. Nevertheless, should drone passenger flights become a reality, then in the event of possible liability for damages caused to passengers, the rules resulting from the international contractual liability regime could apply. In particular the Warsaw–Montreal system, which consists of the Warsaw Convention of 1929[374] and the Montreal Convention of 1999. The Warsaw system consists of the Warsaw Convention of 1929 and the acts amending or supplementing it – the Hague Protocol of 1955[375], the Guadalajara Convention of 1961, the Guatemalan Protocol of 1971, and the four Montreal Protocols of 1975. The Warsaw Convention, drawn up in French, was signed by representatives of 23 states and ratified by 153 countries. It entered into force on February 13, 1933. The Montreal

372 H. McNabb, Uber and Hyundai Have Established a Drone Taxi System That Just Might Work, Drone Life: https://dronelife.com/2020/01/10/uber-and-hyundai-have-established-a-drone-taxi-system-that-just-might-work/ [access: February 18, 2020].

373 See E. Darack, Are Dubai's Drone Taxis For Real?, Air & Space Magazine: https://www.airspacemag.com/articles/fly-through-air-greatest-ease-180962272/ [access: February 18, 2020].

374 The Convention for the Unification of Certain Rules Relating to International Carriage by Air signed in Warsaw, Poland on October 12, 1929; Convention for the Unification of Certain Rules for International Carriage by Air signed in Montreal, Canada on May 28, 1999.

375 Protocol to Amend the Convention for the Unification of Certain Rules Relating to International Carriage by Air signed in Warsaw, Poland on October 12, 1929, signed in Hague, The Netherlands on September 28, 1955.

Convention, drawn up in 6 languages, was signed on May 28, 1999, by representatives of 53 states and ratified by 86 countries[376]. It entered into force on November 4, 2003.

The conventions apply on the basis of a contractual route of transport and they apply to any international air transport of passengers, baggage, or cargo carried out for remuneration. They also apply to free transport carried out with an aircraft by an airline company[377]. When transporting passengers, there should be no doubt that an UA should be recognized as an aircraft and not a robot. In order for this to happen, the aircraft will have to meet all of the stringent technical and operational requirements that apply to manned aviation. According to the new European drone regulation (EU Regulation 2019/945), an UA used for passenger transport qualifies for the so-called *certified* category, which is associated with activities with the highest risk and its requirements mirror those expected of manned aircraft. This category requires certification of the drone itself, the operator and, in some cases, obtaining a license by the drone pilot. In addition, the competent authority, based on a risk assessment, may decide that the risk of an operation cannot be adequately mitigated without the certification of the UA and of the UA operator and, where applicable, without licensing of the remote pilot (art. 6 of Regulation 2019/947). Such obligations should be introduced in the event of commercial passenger transport with the use of UA. Moreover, in the case of providing services to passengers, these requirements should be supplemented with the requirements applicable to the provision of services to consumers (including the requirement to obtain a license, and many others).[378]

It would be worth considering whether the provisions of the Warsaw Convention would apply to air transport services (taxi or other) provided for remuneration by entities other than air carriers. The provisions of the Convention do not state that an air carrier is the only entity allowed to carry out air transport. They apply to all international passenger transport services performed by aircraft for remuneration. However, the provisions of public law indicate that if an entity intends to provide such services (transport of people), it needs to obtain

376 The current list of countries can be found at www.icao.int/icao/en/leb. Poland ratified the Convention on October 6, 2005. It entered into force on March 18, 2006 – government statement of October 16, 2006. (Journal of Laws of 2007, No. 37, item 236).

377 For a detailed discussion of the premises and principles of liability, see A. Konert, Odpowiedzialność cywilna przewoźnika lotniczego, Warsaw, 2010, passim.

378 Certain interpretations of the provisions of Regulation 1008/2008 could constitute the basis for a possible license requirement concerning drone carriers.

a license or some kind of concession[379]. Therefore, as a rule, if a taxi company is licensed, the provisions of the Convention could apply. Public law may limit the possibility of concluding contracts by persons who are not carriers. Moreover, the Warsaw–Montreal regime does not introduce the obligation to transport passengers from an airport to an airport *expressis verbis*. International carriage means any carriage in which, according to the contract made by the parties, the place of departure and the place of destination, whether or not there be a break in the carriage or a transshipment, are situated either within the territories of two High Contracting Parties (different states), or within the territory of a single High Contracting Party, if there is an agreed stopover within a territory subject to the sovereignty, suzerainty, mandate, or authority of another Power, even though that Power is not a party to the Convention. The Convention does not apply to domestic transport. However, it should be borne in mind that European legislators decided to extend carrier liability rules within the EU by introducing the obligation to apply the provisions of the Montreal Convention to all domestic flights in all EU countries (art. 1 of Regulation 889/2002[380])[381]. Therefore, international conventions will, in principle, be applicable to potential UA passenger flights in Poland, for example on a flight from Warsaw to Cracow.

When analyzing the provisions of both conventions, we come to the conclusion that their application to the transport of people by UA may raise a number of doubts, or even turn out to be impossible for technical, organizational, and practical reasons. First, their main purpose was to regulate the issue of liability for the carriage of passengers with the use of a licensed crew. The authors of the conventions likely never thought of the need to include UA in their provisions. Art. 8 of the Chicago Convention explicitly treats UA flights as something exceptional (their flights require a special permit and are allowed only if they do not jeopardize the safety of civil aviation). Many regulations apply to cabin crew or "persons acting on behalf of carriers." Second, in the event of an accident involving a drone, there exists a debatable possibility of the carrier discharging themselves of liability and proving they were not at fault. Third, some might say that it would be inconsistent with social principles to apply a compensation cap

379 See Commission Regulation (EU) No 965/2012 of 5 October 2012 laying down technical requirements and administrative procedures related to air operations pursuant to Regulation (EC) No 216/2008 of the European Parliament and of the Council (Journal of Laws L 296/1 of 25.10.2012)

380 Journal of Laws L 140 of 30.5.2002.

381 This is what the Polish legislator did in Art. 208 of the Aviation Law.

for death or bodily injury caused by an unmanned aircraft. Certainly, there will be groups who will claim that the compensation limits provided in the conventions are too low. New technological solutions usually require introducing new, more stringent liability rules concerning the issue of who is to reap the financial benefits of novel activity, which, due to its innovative nature, carries risks that may directly affect those using it. Nonetheless, technological development must be supported as it ultimately makes life easier for everyone. Questions arise from trying to apply mechanisms developed for decades-old, manned air transport to a sphere of aerial operations that is still in its infancy. For example, the Warsaw Convention introduced limits, justified by the need to protect carriers in the early years of the air transport system. Applying these solutions to drones, which technologically pose completely different challenges than air transport did back in the 1920s, would be unjustified. In layman's terms, this would be like using postal telegraph conventions for liability for deeds performed on the Internet. The mechanism of the Warsaw Convention is deeply rooted in the air carriage system, which back in the day used to perform 40 million operations annually (4 billion passengers). While a shift from risk-based rules to fault-based ones in such a system can be accepted, it is very difficult to imagine the same being done in the case of new drone technology. Fourth, it should be postulated that the evidentiary proceedings proving gross negligence of an air carrier (operator) must be mitigated in the case of victims of accidents involving UA. Finally, it is worth highlighting that many issues in manned aviation, such as successive carriage (that is, carriage carried out by different successive carriers, etc.), are not encountered in unmanned aviation operations.

The application of the provisions of the Warsaw–Montreal system to international transport raises questions about its applicability to passenger drone flights. While it is possible to imagine that one day we will have passenger drones (taxis) operating over short distances and at low altitudes, long-distance passenger flights using larger aircraft (only then is it profitable) are an even more distant vision. Admittedly, the global discussion on unmanned passenger flights that is currently taking place is on a purely theoretical level. However, it seems that in the future, if no specific regulations are drafted, IATA could issue specific (so-called model) requirements for UA carriage.

1.1.2. Liability for goods transported by unmanned aircraft

The carriage of goods with UA is already taking place. This method of transport interests not only large shipping companies, but also other entities such as restaurants or private entrepreneurs.

Many courier companies have declared plans to deliver parcels using drones. Amazon, DHL, and UPS are industry leaders in this category. Amazon plans to deliver packages weighing up to 2.3 kg in no more than half an hour and is currently developing an air distribution system (entire logistics facilities for drones) as part of a program called Prime Air[382]. In April 2017, Amazon became the first company in the United States to commercially deliver a package (sunscreen) with a drone.[383]

MD4-100, made by German company MicroDrones, is the first UA to perform cargo flights commercially in DHL's fleet. This UA transports drugs several times a week between the German island of Juist (North Sea) and Norddeich, a city in the North of Germany, and flies in a special airspace zone designated by the German Air Control Service (DFS).[384]

The provisions of the Montreal Convention, which applies to any commercial international transport of passengers, luggage, or cargo, may apply to the international transport of goods by drones as well as to domestic transport between EU Member States (Regulation 889/2002). The Convention also applies to carriage performed free of charge by an airline company with the use of an aircraft. The subjective scope of this application may be interpreted differently than in the case of passenger transport. There is no doubt that the Convention will apply to air carriers using drones to transport goods, but will it apply to private companies, couriers, hospitals, emergency departments, etc.? According to the assumptions of ICAO and EASA, a certified UA operator becomes the responsible entity in more advanced operations. Therefore, a hospital wanting to transport e.g. medication by drone, will always have two options – it can either use the services of a certified entity or undergo a certification process itself.

The Warsaw–Montreal system concerns contractual liability, i.e. a situation where we have two parties to the contract. But will we have to deal with a contract of carriage to support rescue operations (e.g. transport of a defibrillator set or blood for transfusion to the scene of an accident)? Most likely, such situations

382 https://www.amazon.com/Amazon-Prime-Air/b?ie=UTF8&node=8037720011 [access: November 6, 2018].

383 See http://dlapilota.pl/wiadomosci/aero-newsnet/usa-pierwsza-dostawa-paczki-za-pomoca-drona [access: November 6, 2018].

384 W. Lorenc, M. Chodnicki, P. Kordowski, M. Nowakowski, Drony transportowe – nowa era transportu towarów i ludzi, Efektywność transport, Autobusy: technika, eksploatacja, systemy transportowe no. 6/2016.

will involve a paid contract of carriage (e.g. using a helicopter belonging to the Polish Aviation Rescue Service).

There are many possible scenarios to consider. We must determine whether they fall within the scope of the provisions of the Warsaw–Montreal regime. These could be, for example, any of the following cases: the transport of blood from hospital to hospital for a fee, transport of film or photography equipment to a movie set for a film crew for a fee, a restaurant (e.g. a pizzeria) offering home delivery, DHL delivering parcels, the post office delivering letters, an agritourism company delivering organic fruit and vegetables to a fair, pharmacies transporting drugs, etc.

When analyzing the individual provisions concerning the scope of application of the abovementioned conventions, we come to a few conclusions. First of all, the condition of "payment" has been met in all cases (the transport takes place for remuneration). Second, the answer to the question of whether we are dealing with "aircraft" is not always obvious and unambiguous. It seems that when drones are used on a large scale by companies that have no connection with aviation (e.g. pharmacies, restaurants, farmers) and do not employ pilots but only use a "quasi-autonomous system" (drones equipped with AI-based systems), they are closer to being classified as robots than as aircraft. Nevertheless, if, for example, DHL delivers goods by UA between countries using the services of air carriers, the conventions do apply. In this case, it is the carrier, and not DHL, who is the liable entity. However, one more important condition must be met. "International carriage" is carriage between airports in two different countries (in the case of the EU also between two ports within one country), so the carriage of goods should, in principle, take place between two airports. The current cargo system is based on the airport-to-airport principle. Admittedly, there is already a project to build small airports for drones in Africa, which assumes the creation of a logistics network based on UA and small airports in well-connected parts of the continent, where drones would deliver supplies (weighing up to 10 kg) within a radius of 100 km from these airports. The cargo itself is to be airdropped to its designated destination[385]. Nevertheless, drones will not land at an airport when being used to transport goods (in most situations), e.g. when delivering pizzas, letters, or parcels to specific addressees.

The conventions themselves do not feature the term "airport" in the definition of "international carriage", and only state that "the place of departure and

385 W.Lorenc, M. Chodnicki, P. Kordowski, M. Nowakowski, Drony transportowe – nowa era transportu towarów i ludzi.

the place of destination are situated either within the territories of two High Contracting Parties". The Convention later mentions the term "airport" when defining "air transport time", which is the period of time in which the goods are under a carrier's supervision, excluding carriage by land, sea, or inland waters.

Furthermore, it should be borne in mind that the Warsaw–Montreal regime also applies when the carriage is performed free of charge by aircraft belonging to an air carrier.

As for postal services, the Convention admits *expressis verbis* that it does not apply to these types of services in art. 2 p. 2.

In view of the above, it should be stated that in a situation where air carriers start using UA to transport goods (especially between airports), the Warsaw–Montreal regime would be applicable.

When transporting goods, a carrier issues a so-called air waybill (AWB). In IATA terminology, the term "cargo shipment" means one or more pieces of goods received by the carrier from one shipper at one place and time with a confirmation of receipt, to be transported under one waybill for one recipient and one address[386]. The rights and obligations of the parties to the contract for the carriage of goods have also been regulated quite broadly.[387]

Several problems or ambiguities may arise when applying the provisions of the Convention to the international transport of goods by drone. First, any comments related to passenger transport remain relevant here. Apart from the already mentioned problem related to defining drones as "aircraft", and the necessity to transport goods from airport to airport, it is usually the recipient who receives the goods. This is not always possible when it comes to drones. Moreover, there are certain obligations and requirements that a sender has to meet, such as requirements for the carriage of dangerous goods (IATA Dangerous Goods Regulations). For example, some goods cannot be transported at all by air, while others can be transported only on specific aircraft. Finally, one should consider whether the strict principle of liability for the destruction, damage, or loss of goods would be acceptable for various parties involved, such as courier companies. On the one hand, we can compare this situation to 1929 when the Warsaw Convention was drafted and the transport of passengers and goods was rare, or rather a novelty. Back then, the carrier, who was considered to be the weaker part of the contract, was assigned the presumption of guilt. On the other

386 M. Żylicz, Prawo lotnicze: międzynarodowe, europejskie i krajowe, Warsaw, 2011, p. 411.

387 See. A. Konert, Odpowiedzialność cywilna przewoźnika lotniczego, p. 160.

hand, it is in the (mainly financial) interest of these enterprises to modernize methods for delivering goods, ensuring that these do not have a negative impact on consumers.

In view of the above, it seems that the Warsaw–Montreal regime will apply to the carriage of goods by UA only to a limited extent (an air carrier performing cargo operations with UA between airports). As for other cases, it seems that other regulations should be in force. Due to the lack of international or European regulations in this regard, we should look to national law for solutions.

Involving IATA could be another solution. The organization could supplement existing regulations or introduce new ones, but these would only apply to air carriers. Provisions not arising directly from the conventions could be supplemented or changed by the carriers themselves in their General Conditions of Carriage, introducing specific regulations for the carriage of goods by UA. This, however, may turn out to be insufficient. IATA is an air carrier association, not a courier association, and does not seem to have the competences to determine the rules for delivering pizzas or letters.

In the case of domestic transport of goods by drone (local deliveries), we should introduce special national regulations (possibly by temporarily applying transport laws).

In any case, the operator will have to closely monitor the information, declarations, and content of the cargo to be shipped.

2. Liability for damage caused by unmanned aircraft operators

Applying the tort liability regime (for damages caused by an UA operator) is much more likely than applying the contractual liability regime (for the transport of passengers or goods). This is because we are dealing with all kinds of situations not related to transport for remuneration, e.g. when a drone user causes bodily injury or damage to property while performing a recreational flight. Another situation might be during commercial flights, when, for example, damage is caused while filming at an event or during a test flight, etc.[388]

When analyzing the issue of liability for damage caused by UA other than in transport, we should recall the classification of drones indicated in Chapter

388 W. Sarnowski, Dron poczty spadł 50 metrów od przedszkolaków. Loty wstrzymane: https://cyfrowa.rp.pl/technologie/36293-dron-poczty-spadl-50-metrow-od-przedszkolakow-loty-wstrzymane [access: June 21, 2020].

I (which are based on flight control criteria). The first type of aircraft is an operator-controlled aircraft. The second type includes drones capable of flying without human intervention. In the former situation, the operator is present at a remotely controlled unmanned aircraft system (remotely piloted aircraft or remotely piloted aircraft system, RPAS). This category also includes so-called automatic flights, i.e. operations in which a UA automatically takes off and lands at a designated location and flies along a pre-programmed route. The operator only supervises the operation remotely, retaining the possibility of immediately taking remote control over the UA or taking other action in the event of a dangerous situation. There are also FPV operations (First Person View), i.e. operations in which the remote pilot has a first-person view outside the UA. When carrying out an operation of this type, the operator controls the model without maintaining direct eye contact with it, determining its position in the air through video data transmitted to them in real time by devices mounted onboard the UA. So-called autonomous flights take place without human intervention. The subchapter below analyzes all types of operations controlled, to a greater or lesser extent, by a remote pilot or operator (i.e. excluding autonomous flights).

2.1. Liability for damage caused by operator-controlled UA

2.1.1. Liability and international law

The regime of liability for damage caused by aircraft traffic has been regulated at an international level (the Rome–Montreal system). On May 29, 1933, the first convention for the Unification of Certain Rules Relating to Damage Caused by Foreign Aircraft to Third Parties on the Surface (the Rome Convention of 1933)[389] was adopted. It is binding for only five countries. Another attempt at unifying this regime gave us the so-called Second Rome Convention of 1952[390]. This convention was drawn up in 3 original versions – in English, French, and

389 The wording of the Convention and conference materials are available in ICAO Doc 106 – CD: http://www.icao.int/publications/Pages/default.aspx [access: December 16, 2013].

390 Convention on Damage Caused by Foreign Aircraft to Third Parties on the Surface signed in 1952 in Rome, ICAO Doc. 7634, JALC 447/1952. In 1978, a protocol was adopted to amend the Convention – Protocol to Amend the Convention on Damage Caused by Foreign Aircraft to Third Parties on the Surface, ICAO Doc 9257/2195 UNTS 372.

Spanish. It entered into force on February 4, 1957,[391] and was ratified by 49 countries[392]. However, it does not function in practice, as its provisions have never been applicable to air accidents involving third parties[393]. Poland has not ratified it either. In order to improve the so-called "Rome System", two new conventions were created. The first was the *Convention on Compensation for Damage Caused by Aircraft to Third Parties, in case of Unlawful Interference*[394]. The second was a more general convention regulating liability for damage caused by aircraft to third parties on the ground (*Convention on Compensation for Damage Caused by Aircraft to Third Parties)*[395]. Both conventions were finally adopted at a diplomatic conference in Montreal in 2009[396]. Neither of them has entered into force yet as they have not been ratified by a sufficient number of countries (the first has been ratified by four and the second by seven countries).

In light of this, we can only analyze the issue of liability of UA operators on the basis of the provisions of the Rome Convention of 1952, provided that we are dealing with an aircraft and an operator. Autonomous flights are not taken into account.

When analyzing the provisions of the Rome Convention of 1952, one can point to several limitations that it poses. These make it difficult to apply the Convention's provisions to UA. First, only 49 countries have ratified the Convention. What's more, those countries which most actively contribute to the development of the UA industry, such as the United States, France, or Great Britain, are not on the list of signatories. Second, the Convention applies to damage caused on the territory of a given state by an aircraft registered in another state, which is a

391 A. Tobolewski, Monetary limitations of liability in air law: legal, economic and socio-political aspects, p. 40.

392 The list of countries that have signed the 1952 Rome Convention is available on the ICAO website: http://www.icao.int/icao/en/leb/rome1952.pdf

393 See A. Konert in: M. Żylicz (ed.), Prawo lotnicze. Komentarz, p. 839.

394 Text of the draft of May 1, 2008 (LC / 33-WP / 3-24) with the rapporteur's statement (LC / 33-WP / 3-3).

395 Text of the draft of May 1, 2008 (LC / 33-WP / 3-25) with the rapporteur's statement (LC / 33-WP / 3-4).

396 Compensation for damage caused by aircraft to third parties arising from acts of unlawful interference or from general risks. ICAO headquarters, Montréal, Canada 20 April – 2 May 2009 http://www.icao.int/DCCD2009/. Convention on Compensation for Damage Caused by Aircraft to Third Parties, ICAO Doc. 9919 and Convention on Compensation for Damage Compensation for, Resulting from Acts of Unlawful Interference Involving Aircraft, ICAO Doc. 9920.

party to the Convention (art. 23 sec. 1), irrespective of the origin of the injured person(s) and the aircraft operator. Therefore, aircraft registered in the state of incident are excluded. Third, the Convention applies to damage caused on the surface of the earth. Thus, damages caused "in the air", i.e. damages caused to another aircraft in flight (as well as their passengers and baggage on board), are clearly excluded as well. Therefore, this also excludes situations involving mid-air collisions between an aircraft and a drone, and any possible liability of the drone operator for damage caused to the manned aircraft's passengers. In recent years, we have witnessed an increasing number of breaches of drone no-fly zones, including UA operations taking place in the vicinity of airports. For example, the British Airline Pilots Association (BALPA) reported that there were seven drone incidents in the UK in December 2015, four of which were classified as Category A incidents (severe collision hazards)[397]. The US, on the other hand, counts as any as over 100 incidents per month[398]. These concern UA approaching manned aircraft or, again, breaching the borders of no-fly zones. For example, on July 22, 2014, the pilot of an A320 landing at Warsaw's Chopin Airport reported seeing a drone directly ahead as they were nearing the runway at an altitude of 700 meters AGL. There were 180 people on board the plane at that time. Another example that perfectly illustrates both the legal and security-related implications of such breaches is the incident that took place at London Gatwick Airport where drones were spotted in the vicinity of one of its runways. Traffic at the airport was suspended for two days, between 19 and 21 of December, 2018, causing major disruptions which affected app. 140,000 passengers and 1,000 flights.

Fourth, the Convention does not apply to damage caused by state aircraft. Fifth, compensation caps based on the weight of the aircraft would be a rather controversial issue. According to the provisions of the Convention, the upper compensation limit depends on the total mass of the aircraft and is divided into five categories:

- 500,000 francs for aircraft weighing 1,000 kg or less;
- 500,000 francs plus 400 francs per kg over 1,000 kg for aircraft weighing more than 1,000 but not exceeding 6,000 kg;
- 2,500,000 francs plus 250 francs per kg over 6,000 kg for aircraft weighing more than 6,000 but not exceeding 20,000 kg;

397 http://di.com.pl/samolot-pasazerski-zderzyl-sie-z-dronem-prawdopodobnie-54803 [access: May 31, 2017].

398 https://www.faa.gov/uas/resources/uas_sightings_report/ [access: May 31, 2017].

- 6,000,000 francs plus 150 francs per kg over 20,000 kg for aircraft weighing more than 20,000 but not exceeding 50,000 kg;
- 10,500,000 francs plus 100 francs per kg over 50,000 kg for aircraft weighing more than 50,000 kg.[399]

So, for example, if a Jetstream 31 drone weighing 6,500 kg caused damage on the ground, the operator's liability would be limited to 2,500,000 francs plus 250 francs for each kg above 6,000 kg (i.e. about 200,000 USD). Such an amount hardly seems like enough should such an aircraft fall from the sky and injure several people.

On the one hand, information on the weight of the UA may actually be significant and affect the estimated value of the damages it causes. For example, a drone weighing 25 kg can cause serious damage to no more than one person. On the other hand, the weight of a UA does not have to affect the value of the damages it may cause. After all, a drone weighing 5 kg can, under certain conditions, cause more damage than a heavier plane if, for example, it collides with the engine of a passenger plane or flies into with something flammable, e.g. at a gas station. There was an accident in Great Britain in 2015 in which a drone's propeller cut the eye of an 18-month-old boy. Oscar Webb was playing in a neighbor's garden while his dad watched family friend Simon Evans, 29, fly his GBP 300 drone. The drone clipped a tree as Evans was trying to land it and spiraled out of control, hitting the toddler in the face. As a result, the little boy lost one of his eyes.[400] A drone weighing 50 kg can cause damage in the form of serious injury to several people. Will the limit of 500,000 francs be sufficient in such a situation? Surely not.

Moreover, the scope of the Convention would be limited in such situations since the drone should be classified as an aircraft and the entity performing the flights as an operator. Although the definition of an operator is much broader and more flexible than the definition of an air carrier, there may still be some subjective restrictions.[401] Finally, the Rome Convention does not provide full

399 Art. 11.

400 https://www.huffingtonpost.co.uk/2015/12/01/toddler-drone-eye-blind_n_8686366.html?guccounter=1&guce_referrer=aHR0cHM6Ly93d3cuZ29vZ2xlLmNvbS8&-guce_referrer_sig=AQAAACoLIc6Jl3KK7_eTtEWi5ydiOKr4Qr5zFs8cNDzRbawCH-q5wU6OSjs7NJTu25mE1m9rQ9IXad87Uum3N-dWTs6HyHfs59_is94f97HjlVyNPJ39Pcu4LFxmiui1gODZIE2n-Wi67G0Oqm-85pSN7KMK-P-4Ctf3BeEivC2DuVCr [access: March 18, 2020].

401 The term "aircraft operator" was interpreted according to the Polish law and remains valid under the provisions of the Rome Convention.

and effective legal protection in many issues related to manned aircraft, so why should it be effective for unmanned aviation?[402]

2.1.2. *Liability of unmanned aircraft operators under national law*

2.1.2.1. *Examples of solutions in selected countries*

This part of the publication considers liability for damages caused by the use of UA as liability for personal injury and damage to property caused in either a direct (e.g. as a result of colliding with a person or property) or indirect manner (e.g. as a result of a collision with another aircraft which damages other property). Drones can also hinder rescue operations, thus indirectly causing greater damage to property. For example, 2015 saw an incident in which firefighters were forced to ground an aerial firefighting aircraft due to the presence of drones in the same airspace. That day, 36,000 acres of land burned in Southern California.[403] JARUS and EASA also point to the risk of UA operations damaging critical infrastructure, e.g. when a drone falls on power lines and cuts off power to an urban area.

Most countries do not provide for special regulations on civil liability of drone operators. An interesting and rather unique solution was introduced in Italy, which happens to be the only country that directly implements the rules resulting from the Rome Convention of 1952 into its liability system for drone operators. When amending the Aviation Code (*Codice della navigazione*) in 2005, the Italian legislator proposed a new definition of the term "aircraft". Art. 743 was amended to state that remotely operated aircraft systems are also recognized as aircraft in accordance with certain provisions issued by the civil aviation authority. The amendment also covered military aircraft in accordance with other regulations issued by the Ministry of Defense. As a consequence of this decision, all the rules of the Code on manned aircraft are, as far as possible, applicable to UA as well.[404]

At the same time, the rules on civil liability of the operator for damage caused on the ground were also amended. The amended art. 965 provides that the

---

402 See also S. Michaelides-Mateou, Ch. Erotokritou, Flying into the Future with UAVs: The Jetstream 31 Flight, p. 124.

403 V. Sehrawat, Liability Issue of Domestic Drones. Santa Clara High Technology Law Journal, Vol. 35, No. 1, November 2018, p. 117.

404 A. Massutti, Drones for Civil Use: European Perspective on Third-Party Liability and Insurance. Journal for International Trade and Transport Law, 2016, nr 16, p. 243 et seq.

operator's liability for damage caused to persons or property on the ground is subject to the international law in force in the country, which also applies to liability for damage caused on Italian territory by aircraft registered in Italy. The international law in force in Italy is the Rome Convention of 1952, which was ratified in 1963. These changes resulted in a situation in which any aircraft – manned or unmanned – registered in Italy is subject to the same rules, and the Rome Convention is also a part of national law.[405]

In most countries, however, general rules on civil liability under aviation or civil law apply. In Australia, it is the Damage by Aircraft Act of 1999. France has its own transport law (art. s L. 6131-1 et L. 6131-2 du code des transports). In Belgium – the Civil Code (La responsabilité du fait personnel – art. 1382, La responsabilité du fait d'autrui des maîtres et commettants – art. 1384, alinéa 3, La responsabilité du fait de la chose viciée – art. 1384)[406]. The situation is similar in the Netherlands (art. 162 Book 6 of the Civil Code). China applied an interesting solution in terms of drone operator responsibility based on rules rooted in tort law regarding liability for ultra-hazardous activities (art. 71 Tort Liability Law of the People's Republic of China), which declare that the operator shall be objectively liable, regardless of fault, and shall be released of liability only if they demonstrate that the damage was caused through the victim's fault.[407]

In the US, existing federal laws do not regulate liability for damage caused by UA operations. State laws governing the use of drones do not cover liability issues. Therefore, the UA operator may be held civilly liable for personal injury and damage to property under general regulations. Here, the *ordinary principles of negligence law* apply. The operator can be held liable if they lose control

---

405 S. Busti, Le sanzioni in materia di trasporto marittimo, aereo, terrestre e codice della strada, in: Responsabilità per i danni a terzi dal volo di aeromobile, A. Cagnazzo, S. Toschei and C. Pozzi, Giappichelli (ed.), Turin, 2012, p. 388 et seq. and A. Masutti, Drones for Civil Use: European Perspective on Third-Party Liability and Insurance, p. 243 et seq.

406 For more, see L. Poncelet, L'arsenal législatif relatif à la responsabilité civile en Belgique, est-il suffisant pour pallier aux risques liés à l'utilisation des drones?, These, Université catholique de Louvain, 2016 and A.Cassart, Droit des drones: Belgique, France, Luxembourg, Bruxelles 2017 and L. Archambault, A. Mazous, L'Envol des Drones Civils: Appréhension par le droit français d'une pratique émergente., 40 Annals of Air and Space Law 2015.

407 For more, see B. Scott (ed.), The Law of Unmanned Aircraft Systems. An Introduction to the Current and Future Regulation under National, Regional and International, Kluwer Law International, The Netherlands, 2016.

of the drone, allowing it to hit a third party causing death, personal injury, or damage to property. Courts may rely on the *principle of negligence* by ordering the claiming party to prove four elements of negligence:

- existence of a duty from the defendant in favor of the plaintiff
- breach of duty, which considers proving that the operator did not act "reasonably" and that they did not maintain a reasonable degree of care/ordinary care,
- there were damages resulting from the incident,
- the breach of duty was the proximate cause of the damage – the actions of the operator must be a significant factor in the cause of injury (injury as a direct result of the breach).

In most cases, investigating the above can help establish what actually led to the damage being caused. However, this also involves costly and lengthy legal proceedings. The plaintiff must prove that the drone operator did not maintain "reasonable care" when performing their operation. The borders of "reasonable care" should be clearly defined. It seems that any breach of the operational rules on the use of UA should be treated as a failure to maintain reasonable care. Furthermore, the plaintiff must establish a causal link between the lack of reasonable care on the operator's part and the cause of the damage.

These classic elements of breach of duty apply when the improper operation of a drone causes an accident. According to the *principle of negligence*, everyone is obliged to avoid foreseeable risks of harm. If a person violates this rule and their actions directly result in damage, then they shall be deemed liable. An example of this *breach of duty* could be failure to follow basic principles of safe drone exploitation or the lack of regular technical check-ups (e.g. resulting in a drone colliding with a car as a result of a damaged rotor). An operator who uses a drone with a low power reserve level shall be held liable if a loss of power causes the device to collide with a person or property and result in damage.

Instead of proving the abovementioned four elements, the court could apply *res ipsa loquitur* – the principle of objective liability, which assumes that the owner of the drone is liable for any damage caused by its use, irrespective of their role in causing the damage. Such a solution would provide victims with an effective means of redress, placing the risk on drone owners and subjecting them to strict principles of liability. Creating a new, hybrid type of responsibility could be another solution.

According to the Article 206 of Polish Aviation Law Act of 2002 liability for damage caused by the movement of aircraft is subject to civil law for liability for damage caused by the use of mechanical means of communication raised by the forces of nature. Thus, this Article refers to the Civil Code, and particularly to

Articles 435 and 436. Article 435 (1) C.C. establishes the rule of strict liability for injuries caused by enterprises or establishments which are set in motion by natural forces like steam, gas, electricity, and fuel. The enumeration is not exclusive and atomic energy should be included. The same liability is imposed by Article 435 (2) C.C. on establishments manufacturing or using high explosives, for instance, mines. The person who is operating the enterprise on his/her own account is liable on proof of injury caused by accident unless he/she proves that the damage was the result of force majeure or incurred through the exclusive fault of the person injured or of a third party. Article 436 refers to traffic accidents caused by motor vehicles. According to the Article, the liability depends on possession of the vehicle and not on ownership. The result is that in the case of theft, the owner of a car ceases to be liable. There are two important exceptions to this rule. Principles of liability based on fault are applicable when persons are transported gratuitously and in the case of a collision (see Art. 436 (2) C.C.). A gratuitous guest must prove the fault of the possessor (or his/her servant). In the case of a collision, general principles decide how far the fault of each driver contributed to the damage. [408] The liability of an operator is therefore strict and he/she cannot escape of it unless he/she proves that the damage was the result of a force majeure or incurred through the exclusive fault of the person injured or of a third party.[409] Therefore, it is important for a drone operator to purchase insurance (third party liability insurance).[410]

3. Future international regulations. Governing law

It is only a matter of time before passengers are transported by UA. We still have to wait for the transport of passengers but this is only a matter of time. It seems best that such means of transport are subjected to harmonized rules resulting from the Warsaw–Montreal system, as these are not open to interpretation. International regulations will not apply to damage caused to third parties mainly due to the small number of countries that have ratified the Rome Conventions, as well as the inability to apply certain provisions in them to UA. Therefore, there

---

408 See more: A. Szpunar, The Law of Tort in the Polish Civil Code, The International and Comparative Law Quarterly, Vol. 16, No. 1, January 1967, pp. 86–102.

409 See more: A. Konert, Odpowiedzialność za szkody spowodowane przez ruch statku powietrznego na ziemi, Warszawa 2014 (Liability for damages caused by aircraft to third parties on the ground).

410 P. Kasprzy, A. Konert, UAS safety operation – Legal issues on reporting UAS incidents. Journal of Intelligent & Robotic Systems, 2021.

are three possible solutions. First, national law will apply to mid-air collisions and damage to the ground as *lex loci domicili*. According to art. 33 of the Act of 4 February 2011, Private International Law[411], the law applicable to liability for a non-legal incident is laid down in Regulation (EC) No 864/2007/EC of the European Parliament and of the Council of 11 July 2007 on the law applicable to non-contractual obligations (Rome II)[412]. Under this regulation, the law applicable to a non-contractual obligation arising out of a tort/delict shall be the law of the country in which the damage occurs, irrespective of the country in which the event giving rise to the damage occurred and irrespective of the country or countries in which the indirect consequences of that event occur (art. 4 sec. 1).

The second solution is to create a new international convention that would take into account the specificities of UA and their operations, including autonomous flights, leading to greater harmonization and the application of uniform rules for remote operators.[413]

A third option is for the EU to implement the provisions of the Rome Convention of 1952 in all Member States, as it did in the case of air carrier liability by implementing the provisions of the Montreal Convention of 1999 with Regulation 889/2002. However, it is important to consider the shortcomings of the Rome regime when doing so.

Regardless, it seems necessary to motivate national legislators to draft their own solutions until action is taken at an international or regional level to create new legislation to fill this legal void.

4. Liability insurance for damage caused by unmanned aircraft operations

4.1. Introduction

Liability insurance protects UA operators and is also a guarantee of compensation for victims.[414] It can cover four groups of cases: damage to a passenger,

411 Journal of Laws of 2011, No. 80, item 432.

412 OJEU L 199 of 31.07.2007, p. 40.

413 This solution is supported by, among others, A. Masutti, Drones for Civil Use: European Perspective on Third-Party Liability and Insurance,, p. 243 et seq. and S. Michaelides-Mateou, Ch. Erotokritou, Flying into the Future with UAVs: The Jetstream 31 Flight, p. 112.

414 The risks covered by the insurance related to the use of unmanned aircraft, in addition to civil liability, include damage to property, breach of privacy, breach of personal data, cyber risk, etc.

damage to luggage, damage to goods, and damage to a non-passenger (third party). The Montreal Convention of 1999 first introduced compulsory liability insurance for air carriers toward passengers[415]. Under the Rome Convention of 1952, unlike the one from 1933, persons utilizing aircraft are not required to have liability insurance for damage to third parties.[416] The Montreal Convention of 2009 harmonizing liability for damage caused by aircraft traffic to third parties on the ground (which has not yet entered into force) introduced compulsory liability insurance.[417]

4.2. Minimum liability insurance requirements in the EU

In order to ensure the transparent, non-discriminatory, and harmonized application of minimum insurance requirements, the European Parliament adopted Regulation (EC) No 785/2004 of the European Parliament and of the Council of 21 April 2004 on insurance requirements for air carriers and aircraft operators[418], which also applies to certain UA. Art. 2 sec. 2 of the Regulation provides that it does not apply to model aircraft with an MTOM of less than 20 kg and aircraft (including gliders) with a MTOM of less than 500 kg which are used for non-commercial purposes. Therefore, if we interpret it literally, the scope of the regulation covers flying models weighing more than 20 kg and all commercial UA. "Commercial operation" means any operation carried out for remuneration (art. 3 letter i). It seems that carriage for remuneration by drone is currently solely under theoretical consideration, as this would require obtaining an AOC certificate whilst the requirements for drone transport have not been developed yet.

Another problem also arises from the use of the term "flying model", which is not defined in the Regulation, which was adopted at a time when drones were not as popular as they are now. It is therefore safest to assume that, since the Regulation does not define what a model is, the law of a Member State can clarify this. Poland and the United Kingdom recognize models as aircraft used for recreational or sporting purposes. This is also the general principle adopted in the SERA Regulation[419].

---

415 For a discussion on international legal acts regulating the issue of air carrier liability toward passengers, see Chapter 2.

416 For a discussion on international legal acts regulating the liability of an aircraft operator for damage caused to third parties, see Chapter 1.

417 For more, see A. Konert w: M. Żylicz (ed.), Komentarz. Prawo lotnicze, op.cit., p.

418 Journal of Laws L 138, April 30, 2004.

419 Commission Implementing Regulation (EU) No 923/2012 of 26 September 2012 laying down the common rules of the air and operational provisions regarding services

The Preamble of the 2018 Basic Regulation defines "model aircraft" as UA for the purposes of this Regulation and used primarily for leisure activities. Delegated and implementing acts concerning UA, adopted on the basis of the Regulation, should take into account that such model aircraft have so far had a good safety record, especially those operated by members of model aircraft associations or clubs which have developed specific codes of conduct for such activities. In addition, when adopting those delegated and implementing acts, the European Commission should take into account the need for a seamless transition from different national systems to the new EU-wide regulatory framework, so that model aircraft can continue to operate as they do today, as well as take into account existing best practices in individual Member States (p. 34).

In addition, Regulation 947/2019 provides that model aircraft are considered as UAS and, given the good safety level demonstrated by model aircraft operations in clubs and associations, there should be a seamless transition from the different national systems to the new EU regulatory framework, so that model aircraft clubs and associations can continue to operate as they do today, as well as taking into account existing best practices in individual Member States.

Regulation No 785/2004 applies to all air carriers and aircraft operators operating within, to, from, and above the territory of an EU Member State.[420] Under its provisions, "aircraft operator" means a person or entity, not being an air carrier (an air carrier company with a valid license), who has continual effective disposal of the use or operation of the aircraft. This definition undoubtedly covers operators of UA, including operators of remotely controlled UA, who may alter a UA flight's parameters at any moment. However, autonomous operations that do not allow for operator interference are excluded from the regulation. With regard to third parties, "flight" means the use of an aircraft from the moment when power is applied to its engines for the purpose of taxiing or actual takeoff until the moment when it is on the surface and its engines have come to a complete stop. Additionally, it shall mean the moving of an aircraft by towing and push-back vehicles or by powers which are typical for the drive and the lift of aircraft, particularly air streams (art. 3 letter d).

---

and procedures in air navigation and amending Implementing Regulation (EU) No 1035/2011 and Regulations (EC) No 1265/2007, (EC) No 1794/2006, (EC) No 730/2006, (EC) No 1033/2006 and (EU) No 255/2010.

420 For more, see A. Konert, Ubezpieczenia lotnicze, Warsaw, 2014 and Prawo lotnicze. Komentarz in: M. Żylicz (ed.), p. 870.

For UA taking off using methods other than taxiing, the moment that engines are started and the aircraft takes off from the ground should be considered the beginning of a flight. Here, we can reference Regulation 996/2010[421]. In the case of UA, it recognizes the moment when the aircraft is ready to move until it stops at the end of a flight and its primary propulsion system is turned off as the beginning of a flight.

With regards to civil liability for damage caused to passengers, the minimum insurance cover is SDR 250,000 per passenger[422]. As for liability for luggage, the minimum insurance cover in commercial transport amounts to 1,288 SDR per passenger. For cargo liability, the minimum insurance cover is 22 SDR per kg for commercial transport.[423] These limits should be increased in relation to the 2019 revaluation of the limits provided for in the Montreal Convention of 1999.

As for third parties, insurance should cover death, personal injury, and damage to property as a result of air accidents, depending on the weight category of the aircraft (art. 7).

The provisions of the regulation do not regulate the exclusion of the insurer's liability. Therefore, cases of such exclusion are usually included in the general terms and conditions of an insurance policy, which are in accordance with national law[424]. In Poland, the insurer is also liable for damages caused intentionally or as a result of gross negligence of the policyholder or persons for whom they are responsible (art. 9 of the Compulsory Insurance Act).[425]

---

421 A. Konert (ed.), Aspekty prawne badania zdarzeń lotniczych w świetle Rozporządzenia 996/2010, Warsaw, 2013.

422 However, for non-commercial operations of aircraft with an MTOM of 2,700 kg or less, EU countries may set a lower level of minimum coverage, provided that the coverage is at least SDR 100,000 per passenger.

423 Due to the fact that ICAO determined that from the date the Montreal Convention entered into force (November 4, 2003) the inflation rate exceeded the value of 10%, which is the threshold beyond which the liability limit should be changed, the Commission issued Regulation (EU) No 285/2010 of 6 April 2010 amending Regulation (EC) No 785/2004 of the European Parliament and of the Council on insurance requirements for air carriers and aircraft operators (OJEU L 87/19 of April 7, 2010), which increased the liability limits accordingly.

424 According to the Polish Civil Code (Art. 805–834) and the Act of May 22, 2003 on Compulsory Insurance, Insurance Guarantee Fund and the Polish Motor Insurers' Bureau (Journal of Laws No. 124 item 1152 as amended).

425 A. Konert w: M. Żylicz (ed.), Prawo lotnicze. Komentarz, p. 870.

Regulation 2019/947 of May 24, 2019, on the rules and procedures for the operation of UA does not introduce any new insurance regulations[426]. It only provides for the requirement to present the UAS insurance policy number when registering a UA, if EU or national law requires such insurance.

Category	**MTOM (kg)**	**Minimum Insurance (SDR in million)**
1	< 500	0.75
2	< 1000	1.5
3	< 2700	3
4	< 6000	7
5	< 12,000	18
6	< 25,000	80
7	< 50,000	150
8	< 200,000	300
9	< 500,000	500
10	500,000	700

4.3. Liability insurance requirements in Poland

Regulation of the Minister of Transport, Construction and Marine Economy of March 26, 2013, on the exclusion of the application of certain provisions of the Aviation Law Act to certain types of aircraft and specifying the conditions and requirements for the use of these crafts[427] introduced mandatory liability insurance for aircraft users as to whom Regulation 785/2004 does not apply. Annex 7 of the 2013 regulation specifies the requirements for third-party liability insurance for people who use gliders, paragliders, parachutes, flying models, and UA weighing up to 20 kg.

426 Only the Parliament and the Council are competent to regulate third party liability insurance.

427 Journal of Laws of 2013 item 440.

When concluding a third-party liability insurance contract, it is not necessary to specify the particular aircraft model (only the type of aircraft is specified). Third-party liability insurance may also be concluded by a training entity or other entity conducting flights, parachute jumps or airdrops, as collective and nameless insurance without the need to individually conclude such an agreement by each participant of a training, flight, jump or drop.

Within the meaning of art. 206 of the Act, third-party liability insurance of aircraft operators covers the civil liability of these persons for damages caused during the period of insurance coverage, caused by the movement of aircraft or any person, animal, or object falling out of an aircraft and by the use of a parachute for rescue purposes. Third-party liability insurance covers damages such as bodily injury, health impairment or death of a third party, or damage to third party property on the ground, water, or in the air.

In terms of insurance, carriage of mail is covered by Regulation (EC) No 1008/2008 of the European Parliament and of the Council of 24 September 2008 on common rules for the operation of air services in the Community[428]. Pursuant to section 5 of the Regulation of the Minister of Finance of 27 December 2012 on compulsory third-party liability insurance for air carriers, businesses providing ground services, and air navigation service providers, the minimum amount of liability insurance for an incident, the effects of which are covered by the insurance contract, is the PLN equivalent of 22 SDR for each kg of mail in the event of destruction, loss, damage, or delay in the transport of mail. However, civil liability insurance does not cover damage resulting from the fault of the sender or recipient, resulting from a hidden defect or natural properties of the mail, or consisting in contractual penalties caused by the policyholder's actions or omissions after the expiry, withdrawal, or suspension of the concession unless the damage is a consequence of events that had occurred before the day of the incident. However, the regulation applies to "air carriers", whom the Aviation Law Act defines as entities authorized to provide air transport services under a license (in the case of a Polish air carrier), or on the basis of a relevant act of a competent authority of a foreign country (in the case of a foreign air carrier). The regulation of the Minister of Finance of December 27, 2012, does not apply to UA as currently there is no such type of UA air carriage that would require a license. The amount of the minimum guaranteed sums for air carriers was established on the basis of the limits of air carrier's liability for the carriage of passengers, baggage, goods, and delays set out in the Montreal Convention. These limits should be

428 Journal of Laws L 293 of October 31, 2008.

increased in connection with the 2019 revaluation of the limits provided for in the Montreal Convention.

When analyzing legal acts at European and national levels, one could conclude that UA have been categorized for the purposes of third-party liability insurance. We can distinguish four of the following categories:

- UA weighing between 5 and 20 kg;
- UA with a mass exceeding 20 kg;
- UA without a weight category;
- UA used for the carriage of mail.

There are no obligations to insure aircraft over 500 kg MTOW (min. 750,000 SDRs).

Analyzing the causes of accidents involving UA, especially those posing the greatest risk in drone operation, can help insurers better define the details of their insurance policies.

4.4. Liability insurance requirements in the U.S.

In the U.S., insurance is not currently required for either recreational or commercial operations. However, there are UA insurance offers on the market and they consist of two separate types:

(a) protection against liability for damage to persons and property ("hull") for UA owners/operators, and
(b) protection against product liability for UA manufacturers and subcontractors.

The "hull" option protects the policyholder against personal injury and property damage claims that may arise as a result of commercial UA activity. Usually, liability limits start at $500,000 and can be negotiated up to as high as the insured person requires. "Hull insurance" is designed to protect the policyholder against financial costs associated with physical damage caused by a UA. Typically, the coverage is assessed on a so-called "Agreed Value" basis.

A separate type of insurance is "payload" insurance[429]. For example, a UA has many cameras or sensors. This type of insurance protects the policyholder against any damages to such equipment.

---

429 'Payload' means instrument, mechanism, equipment, part, apparatus, appurtenance, or accessory, including communications equipment, that is installed in or attached to the aircraft and is not used or intended to be used in operating or controlling an

Many companies have entered the business of insuring UA in the US. Among them, we can find such entities as Unmanned Risk Management, Aerial Park, AIG, Sutton James Incorporated, Avalon Risk Management, Global Aerospace, Aviation Insurance, Driessen Assuadeuren (Drone-Insurance.com), UAV Protect, SkySmith, Harpenau Insurance Agency, and Coverdrone.

4.5. Liability insurance requirements in selected countries

In Germany, as drones are considered aircraft, the provisions on aircraft operator liability and compulsory insurance also apply to UA operators. According to art. 37 of the German Aviation Act (Luftverkehrsgesetz / LuftVG[430]), UA with a takeoff mass of less than 500 kg also require civil liability insurance, which covers at least 750,000 SDRs. Moreover, pursuant to art. 113 of the Insurance Act, insurance must be provided by an insurance company authorized to provide insurance cover in Germany. Proof of insurance must be provided and maintained throughout the course of any operation.

In Australia, in accordance with the Civil Aviation Safety Regulations, there is no obligation to hold civil liability insurance and there is no registration requirement. Larger UA are an exception, defined as "UA with a takeoff mass greater than 150 kg."[431] Therefore, in the event of damage caused by a UA with a takeoff mass of 100 kg, the aggrieved party may have problems with claiming compensation due to the lack of identification of the operator. [432]

In Canada, a person carrying out business activity with a UA must have a minimum insurance policy of $100,000.

4.6. Comparative analysis. Comments *de lege ferenda*

The above analysis of regulations concerning the insurance of UA operations shows a variety of solutions. Uniform regulations exist only at an EU level, but only in the field of UA with a take-off mass exceeding 20 kg.

There is also a mutual obligation to insure UA, but this applies only to those with a MTOW above 500 kg (in the amount of min. 750,000 SDRs). Regulations

aircraft in flight, and is not part of an airframe, engine, or propeller (Art. 2 of Regulation 947/2019).

430 BGBl. no. 253/1957 and BGBl. I, no. 83/2008.

431 Civil Aviation Safety Regulations 1998 (Cth), reg 101.240.

432 Consultations on the draft amendments to Part 101 Civil Aviation Safety Regulations 1998 are currently underway: https://www.casa.gov.au/standard-page/project-us-1418-post-implementation-review-certain-aspects-part-101-casr

do not cover drones below this mass. What's more, issues may arise in attempting to identify the operator of a UA that caused an accident. So far in Poland, the police and the prosecutors have not been able to find the person(s) responsible for nearly causing the aforementioned collision between a drone and a civil aircraft, putting lives of several hundred passengers at risks. SCAAI classified this occurrence as a serious incident, but a report on the matter has not yet been published. On July 1, 2019, Commission Delegated Regulation (EU) 2019/945 of 12 March 2019 on UAS and on third-country operators of unmanned aircraft systems introducing harmonized technical requirements applicable to UAS and additional elements for remote identification operated in accordance with the principles set out in Commission Implementing Regulation (EU) 2019/947 of 24 May 2019 on the rules and procedures for the operation of unmanned aircraft entered into force.

There is no obligation to insure in the US at all. However, since the FAA has made it mandatory for all UA operators to register, there is no problem identifying a person who may cause damage. Of course, the issue of whether such a person has adequate resources to cover the damage is a separate yet very important issue. Nevertheless, it may turn out that it will be more probable for damaged parties to win compensation in the US than in countries where insurance is compulsory and UA registration is not. In most cases, unregistered drone operators are unlikely to buy private insurance. The sole possibility of being identified forces the necessity to purchase insurance. UA insurance policies in the US cover three main areas of risk: security, cyber security, and privacy.

The main challenges for insurers is the lack of historical data on the actuarial approach to underwriting.[433] In such a case, they could turn to data on aviation risks and past experiences with military drones. Finally, we must not forget about the fact that the drone industry is a highly regulated one.

433 David K. Beyer, Donna A. Dulo, Gale A. Townsley, Stephen S. Wu, Risk, Product Liability Trends, Triggers, and Insurance in Commercial Aerial Robots, p. 20.

Chapter 7 Drones as a new technology – finding solutions to civil liability

1. Introduction

The question of liability for UA that do not remain under human control without any decision-making capabilities is part of a broader problem that has sparked lively discussions in recent years, namely the role of civil liability in the development of new technologies. We are living in times where a tidal wave of new technologies, such as smart home technologies, is flooding the market day after day. Household items including ovens, security cameras, or coffee makers can now be operated remotely using smartphones and tablets. Moreover, technology is also expanding into other uncharted territory with phenomena such as artificial intelligence (AI), the Internet of Things (IoT), 3D printing, robots, or automated (autonomous) motor vehicles. A report by the McKinsey Global Institute (MGI) indicates 12 areas of technology that have a huge impact on people's lives, work, and economic development. Its authors try to assess the potential economic impact that each of these sectors will have on various fields in the year 2025[434]. These fields include advanced robotics (automation) and autonomous or semi-autonomous vehicles.

The Internet of Things (IoT)[435] should be considered the fourth industrial revolution, simply because of the fact that it enables two independent IoT devices to communicate directly with one other. And without a doubt, drones are ready to become part of this revolution.

There are scenarios in which UA are connected to the Internet, thus connecting with ordinary devices (such as computers or tablets, which can be used

---

434 Disruptive Technologies: Advances That Will Transform Life, Business, and the Global Economy, May 2013:

https://www.mckinsey.com/~/media/McKinsey/Business%20Functions/McKinsey%20Digital/Our%20Insights/Disruptive%20technologies/MGI_Disruptive_technologies_Full_report_May2013.ashx [access: November 5, 2019].

435 See the report "Internet of Things – Polska Przyszłości" of the Internet of Things (IoT) Working Group at the Ministry of Digital Affairs: https://www.gov.pl/web/cyfryzacja/grupa-robocza-ds-internetu-rzeczy-internet-of-things-iot [access: June 3, 2020].

instead of specialized devices for navigation or recording and storage of audio or video data) in order to save costs. So, what liability rules should apply in the event of damages caused by a programming or production error in the software?

We should also consider a scenario in which damage is not caused by a software or operator error, but due to a failure of a mobile telephone network. Rules on product liability would not apply to the network operator (who is neither a manufacturer, importer, nor seller of the product in question).[436] New technologies and their features often cause unknown problems in shaping regulations concerning liability for damage, like in the case of determining a common standard of care or when attempting to define what a product defect is.[437]

Presently, the civil use of unmanned aircraft that are not under an operator's direct control is forbidden by law. However, the drone market has been developing many concepts regarding UA autonomy which would undoubtedly facilitate carrying out beyond visual line of sight operations, as well as those that take place over large distances. It must be noted that before safe autonomous UA flights are introduced, technological infrastructure including operation management systems, operation registration and monitoring systems, anti-drone systems, and many others must first be developed.[438] After this has been done, there will remain the need to define regulations that will be used for determining liability for damages.

Today, in the absence of standardization of technical solutions that would guarantee operational safety in all conditions, the public – and therefore legislators – are reluctant to welcome the widespread use of fully autonomous drones that are not supervised in real time and can't be controlled by operators. Currently, there is always somebody supervising a UA operation to a greater or lesser extent, which facilitates the pursuit of possible claims for damages caused during these operations. Oftentimes, UA operators used to have to pass state exams and obtain state certificates (e.g. certificates for commercial VLOS operations and BVLOS operations). In Poland, it had been possible to carry out BVLOS operations since 2019 based on the regulation of the Minister of Infrastructure of December 20, 2018, amending the regulation on the exclusion of certain provisions

436 A. Newstead, Drones and robots: liability for designers, manufacturers and insurer.

437 P. Machnikowski, Perspektywa uegulowania odpowiedzialności cywilnej związanej z nowymi technologiami, in: A. Dańsko-Roesler, M. Leśniak, M. Skory, B. Sołtys, Ius Est Ars Boni et Aequi, Księga pamiątkowa dedykowana Profesorowi Józefowi Frąckowiakowi, Wrocław, 2018, p. 688.

438 Biała Księga Bazzałogowych Statków Powietrznych, p. 14.

of the Aviation Law Act for certain types of aircraft and determining conditions and requirements for the use of these aircraft. This applies to operational, special, automatic, and training flights. This was the first step in paving the way for autonomous flights in the future.

While BVLOS operations were still banned in many countries, this regulation provided operators holding valid certificates of competency and BVLOS rating to conduct such flights after meeting certain requirements. These certificates were scheduled to remain valid until July 1, 2021, on basis of art. 21 of the Commission Implementing Regulation (EU) 2019/947 of 24 May 2019 on the rules and procedures for the operation of UA. However, due to the situation related to the COVID-19 pandemic, most EU Member States, including Poland, asked the European Commission to change the date of application of the regulation. The European Commission complied with the request and the application date has been postponed by 6 months. This means that the provisions of Regulation 2019/947 entered into force on December 31, 2020. According to the announcement of the Civil Aviation Authority, in Poland, until the new regulations entered into force, national regulations had applied to UAV operators[439].

The main goal of this chapter is to find a solution for civil liability for damages caused by autonomous drones. The obvious consideration will be a manufacturer liability but is it enough? This chapter indicates the necessity to adapt existing regulations on liability for defective products to the world around us, which is changing constantly due to the ongoing fourth industrial revolution. Moreover, the chapter highlights the need to link UA product liability regulations with public law safety standards (CE marking). There is also the issue of qualifying autonomous drones as robots from a legal perspective, and therefore subjecting them to regulations that widely differ from those found in aviation law.

2. Liability for damages caused by autonomous UA operations

When analyzing the basic premises of liability, the biggest problem may lie in the fact that causal relationship (causation) will be linked to a machine, and not to human activity. This will mean that machines will be considered as legal entities. Taking matters one step further leads to dilemmas caused by trying to

439 https://ulc.gov.pl/pl/aktualnosci/5002-przesuniecie-daty-wejscia-w-zycie-przepisow-dotyczacych-dronow [access: June 10, 2020 r.].

determine legal relationships between different machines (i.e. machine-to-machine or M2M).

The number of responsible entities in an autonomous UA operation can be very large. This may include the owner of the UA, its manufacturer, an app developer, a provider of telecommunications services necessary for its proper functioning, or a data provider for the UA's operating system. As it turns out, determining a single entity's responsibility in such a complicated system may be impossible. For instance, let's imagine a situation in which two autonomous UA collide in mid-air because wrong assumptions on traffic rules entered into their software, causing damage to a person on the ground. Or another example – incorrect data on restricted zones causes an UA to enter a restricted airport zone, where it collides with a manned airplane. More complicated examples would concern situations in which autonomous UA are part of a smart city or the IoT.

However, situations in which damages are caused by an autonomous decision made by a UA's operating system, which are not related to a system malfunction or incorrect data entered into its software, are the biggest challenge. Applying current regulations could be difficult due to complications in establishing causal relationships. Adopting new solutions together with introducing a statutory causal relationship, just like in the case of air carrier liability under the Montreal Convention of 1999, could be a solution here.

Some argue that new regulations on determining liability for damage caused by robots should follow the concept adopted when determining liability for damage caused by animals (under Civil Codes). Could such laws serve as a benchmark for liability regulations concerning autonomous drones? Under the analyzed liability regime, an animal must cause damage driven by its own urges. Therefore, any damage that occurs results from its instinctive behavior, and not from the animal obeying human commands. Here, we find a certain analogy with autonomous drones, as the operator does not actually have the ability to "execute" commands for the machine. Nevertheless, this theory has many disadvantages.

There is one more issue that requires regulation in the case of autonomous UA. When it comes to non-autonomous UA, there is always somebody supervising the operation and that person, in most cases, is required to have a certificate of competency. In such a case, the UA operator (holder of the certificate) is responsible for its operations. Autonomous operations, on the other hand, might not need an operator/pilot at all. Many companies that are neither related to aviation nor employ people who are licensed UA operators will be performing these types of operations. For example, restaurants will deliver pizzas, courier companies will deliver parcels, companies will deliver medical equipment to the scene of an accident, and state services may perform air quality/smog control tests, etc. Therefore, in such situations, it will be necessary to perceive these operations as conducted by a machine, and not a person. This, once again, raises the question – should we recognize machines as legal entities? And if so, what rights should machines be granted?[440]

The issues mentioned above lead to the conclusion that current civil liability regulations need to be adjusted to consider the problems raised in the event of damages caused by autonomous UA. Channeling responsibility onto manufacturers is an alternative here. But full responsibility? Given the lack of actual control over subsequent UA operations, manufacturers cannot be deemed the sole liable entity. Thus, introducing new regulations, for example by amending the national Aviation laws, might be a solution. There is no doubt that the legislator will have to introduce a principle of liability of an entity that is unable to exercise full control over a UA. The principle of guilt does not apply here, because the subject could easily exculpate itself. Moreover, the guilt principle gives rise to other issues, such as difficulties in establishing a group of responsible entities. The case of *Richardson v. Bombardier*[441] serves as an example that shows the complexity and need for expertise in the evidentiary process, in which it had to be proven that the accident in question was caused by a malfunction of the autopilot system installed in an aircraft.[442]

In light of the foregoing considerations, it therefore appears that liability for damage caused by an autonomous UA should be the objective. There is no doubt that the law should provide for exoneration in cases where damage was caused solely by the person claiming compensation, or by the person from whom he or she has acquired his or her rights. When introducing such a strict principle of liability, it seems necessary to simultaneously introduce an appropriate

---

440 See considerations on the issue of machine as legal entity and the issue of legal relationship of two machines (the so-called machine to machine – M2M): G. Borges, Liability for machine-made decisions: Gaps and potential solutions, OECD Conference AI, 27 October 2017, Paris; Ch. Wendehorst Robotics, Artificial Intelligence, and MachinetoMachine(M2M) Contracts, European Parliament, Brussels, 21 April 2016; Verma, Pawan & Verma, Rajesh & Prakash, Arun & Agrawal, Ashish & Naik, Kshirasagar & Tripathi, Rajeev & Khalifa, Tarek & Alsabaan, Maazen & Abdelkader, Tamer & Abogharaf, Abdulhakim, Machine-to-Machine (M2M) Communications: A Survey. Journal of Network and Computer Applications, Vol. 66, 2016.

441 United States District Court, M.D. Florida, Tampa DivisionNov 16, 2005Case No. 8:03-cv-544-T-31MSS, (also docketed in 8:03-cv-539-T-31MSS) (M.D. Fla. Nov. 16, 2005).

442 K. Wojdyło, Kto odpowiada za robota?, p. 16.

(mandatory?) liability insurance system. Moreover, it seems justified that the issue of liability for autonomous UA should be regulated on at least a regional level (EU).

The introduction of autonomous flights will undoubtedly contribute to improving the efficiency of UA. Ironically, UA autonomy could become a reality far quicker than the autonomy of motor vehicles, mainly for psychological reasons. Therefore, there is no doubt that it is necessary to regulate possible civil liability for damages caused by autonomous UA operations.

3. Product liability

Product liability is one of the biggest challenges for UAS manufacturers. Civil liability for defects in aviation products, i.e. broadly understood as unmanned aircraft systems, is liability for damages to persons and property caused by malfunctioning unmanned aircraft or elements of an unmanned aircraft system necessary for its control. These elements include: a load platform equipped with data acquisition sensors, a *flight control system* (FCS), an avionics system for remote or autonomous flight control, propulsion, batteries, a data transmission system, data processing software, ground control station (GCS), etc.

Product liability covers defects in software, the manufacturing process, materials, or a lack of information or warnings about possible damages that may arise as a result of regular use. The circle of potentially liable entities includes UA component and software designers, manufacturers, subcontractors, and suppliers.

In addition, UA often collect data, including personal data, which then they send to the manufacturer or operator. This extends the scope of protected goods to privacy and protection of personal data. Although this issue is the subject of the next chapter, it is worth considering whether the scope of protected goods should be extended under the current product liability regime.

At the design stage, an UA must be carefully crafted with regard to its maximum weight, shape and weather conditions in which it will be operating. Moreover, manufacturers must ensure that the device is capable of maneuvering and landing safely without causing damage to people or property. Demonstrating an error in any of these areas may lead to liability claims against the UA designer or the computer technology the device uses.[443] Also, manufacturers need to ensure

443 A. Newstead, Drones and robots: liability for designers, manufacturers and insurer, http://www.inhouselawyer.co.uk/legal-briefing/drones-and-robots-liability-for-designers-manufacturers-and-insurers/?pdf=1713 [access: July 23, 2019].

that their UA conform to design specifications and that they all have passed sufficiently stringent quality control tests. They take these steps in order to make sure that their products meet the required design and safety standards.

3.1. Manufacturer liability. A need for new regulations?

"Product safety and compensation for damage caused by defective products are social imperatives that must be met in the internal market." The answer to these requirements was, inter alia, enactment of a Council Directive 85/374/EEC of 25 July 1985 on the approximation of the laws, regulations, and administrative provisions of the Member States concerning liability for defective products which created a regime of strict liability for defective products applicable in all member states of the European Union.

The directive adopted 30 years ago, as well as the internal regulations of individual EU Member States, may prove insufficient in ensuring the protection of the public in the era of new technologies, robots, autonomous vehicles, smart cities, the Internet of Things, etc.

In 2018, the Commission prepared a report for the European Parliament, the Council, and the European Economic and Social Committee on the Council Directive on the approximation of the laws, regulations, and administrative provisions of the Member States concerning liability for defective products (85/374/EWG)[444]. The report contained an assessment of the Directive, which also regarded the latest technological developments and assessed whether the Directive was effective in achieving its original objectives; was effective at all; was consistent with relevant EU legislation; remained useful by taking into account the latest technological developments; and whether the EU legislation on product liability continued to provide added value for businesses and citizens.[445]

The Commission paid particular attention to the development of new technologies, also examining whether the Directive did not unnecessarily discourage manufacturers from marketing innovative products. The assessment showed that the Directive had a few loopholes, particularly in areas concerning emerging digital, autonomous, and intelligent technologies. The terms that were clearly defined 30 years ago when the Directive was adopted, such as "product", "manufacturer", "defect," or "damage", have become less clear today. What was needed was an in-depth analysis of the impact of technological changes (e.g. autonomous

444 Brussels, May 7, 2018 COM(2018) 246 final.
445 Ibidem, p. 2.

products) on product liability. The Commission set up a liability expert group which operated in two configurations – the first group's objective (representatives of Member States, industry, consumer organizations, civil society and academia) was to interpret and possibly update the Directive in the light of changes in European and national case laws, the impact of new and emerging technologies, and any other changes in the area of liability for products. The second group's objective (independent academics and practitioners) was to assess whether an overall liability regime was appropriate enough to facilitate the deployment of new technologies by promoting investment sustainability and consumer confidence.[446]

3.1.2. Manufacturer liability under the new European drone law (the so-called Delegated Regulation)

The drone law indicates a significant role played by the manufacturer. Commission Delegated Regulation (EU) 2019/945 of 12 March 2019 on unmanned aircraft systems and on third-country operators of unmanned aircraft systems entered into force on July 1, 2019. It introduced harmonized technical requirements for unmanned aircraft systems and additional equipment for remote identification used in accordance with Commission Implementing Regulation (EU) 2019/947 of 24 May 2019 on the rules and procedures for the operation of unmanned aircraft.[447] These rules are supposed to be the same in every European Union and EASA Member State.

The Delegated Regulation concerns the design, production, and introduction of the so-called open category of unmanned aircraft to the internal European Union market.[448]

According to the Regulation, open category UA can only become available on the EU market if they meet the requirements set out in the Regulation and do not pose any threats to the health and safety of people, animals, or property. Market availability means any form of supplying said product to the market for purposes of distribution, consumption, or use. Therefore, the Regulation applies not only to producers, but also to distributors. The Regulation specifies the requirements for open category UAS and introduces conformity assessment procedures, including those with a harmonized standard.

---

446 Ibidem, p. 11.

447 The provisions of both regulations are discussed in Chapter 2.

448 For an overview of all of the categories, see Chapter 2.

The Regulation applies to four categories of entities (so-called economic entities):

- "manufacturer", which is any natural or legal person who manufactures or orders the design and production of a product, and markets that product under his name or trademark;
- "authorized representative", which is any natural or legal person established within the Union who has received a written mandate from a manufacturer to perform specified tasks on his behalf;
- "importer", which is any natural or legal person established within the Union who places a product from a third country on the Union market;
- "distributor", which is any natural or legal person in the supply chain, other than the manufacturer or the importer, who makes a product available on the market.

The Annex to the Regulation sets out detailed requirements (weight, maximum airspeed, maximum achievable altitude above the take-off point, operating manual, noise level, etc.) for individual UA classes within the open[449] category (with the exception of UAS designed for private use) and for additional elements for remote identification.

The Regulation imposes most of these obligations on manufacturers[450]. When introducing products to the EU market, they must ensure that they have been designed and manufactured in accordance with the requirements set out in the Annex to the Regulation.

Manufacturers are required to compile technical documentation provided for in Art. 17[451], update it regularly, and carry out appropriate conformity assessment procedures referred to in Art. 13 (they can be carried out by subcontractors as well). All of this must be done in accordance with the requirements of the Regulation and relevant harmonized standards. So, the assessment is solely the manufacturer's obligation. It must be based on one of three procedures indicated in Art. 13, point 2:

---

449 The Regulation also introduces requirements for "certified" and "specific" category UAS (3).

450 For the obligations of authorized representatives, see Art. 7, importers – Art. 8; and the distributors – Art. 9 of the Delegated Regulation.

451 The content of the technical documentation is specified in Part 10 of the Annex to the Delegated Regulation.

- internal production control as set out in Part 7 of the Annex, when assessing the compliance of a product with the requirements set out in Parts 1, 5, or 6 of the Annex, subject to the condition that the manufacturer has applied harmonized standards, the references of which have been published in the Official Journal of the European Union, for all the requirements for which such standards exist;
- EU-type examination followed by conformity to type based on internal production control as set out in Part 8 of the Annex;
- conformity based on full quality assurance as set out in Part 9 of the Annex, excepted when assessing the compliance of a product which is a toy within the meaning of Directive 2009/48/EC.[452]

If the conformity assessment procedure demonstrates that the product complies with the requirements set out in the Annex to the Regulation, the manufacturer draws up an EU declaration of conformity (in accordance with the form available in Part 11 of the Annex, translated into the language or languages required by the Member State where the product is marketed) and affixes the CE marking on the packaging. Regulation (EC) No 765/2008 of the European Parliament and of the Council of 9 July 2008 setting out the requirements for accreditation and market surveillance relating to the marketing of products and repealing Regulation (EEC) No 339/93[453] states that by affixing or having affixed the CE marking, the manufacturer indicates that they take responsibility for the conformity of the product with all applicable requirements set out in the relevant EU community harmonization legislation providing for its affixing (Article 30, point 3).

According to Art. 36, market surveillance authorities of a Member State shall assess the product to check if it meets the requirements of the Delegated Regulation. Where the market surveillance authorities of one Member State have sufficient reason to believe that a product presents a risk to the health or safety of persons or to other aspects of public interest protection, they shall, without delay, require the relevant economic operator to take all appropriate corrective actions to bring the product into compliance with those requirements, to withdraw the product from the market, or to recall it within a reasonable period, commensurate with the nature of the risk, as they may prescribe.

---

452 For more, see M. Ostrihansky, M. Szmigiero, Prawo dronów. Bezzałogowe statki powietrzne w prawie Unii Europejskiej oraz krajowym, p. 206 et seq.

453 Journal of Laws of August 12, 2008 L 218, p. 30.

In Poland, open category UA must comply with the rules indicated in, but not limited to, the Act of Parliament of 13 April 2016 on conformity assessment systems and market surveillance[454] and the Act of 30 August 2002 on conformity assessment system[455].

Some of the procedures, on the basis of which a manufacturer will be able to assess the conformity of their product before making it available on the market, take certification procedures into account, i.e. an assessment of conformity carried out by a third party (a notified certification body, independent of the manufacturer or of the consumer).

Starting January 1, 2021, manufacturers will be able to distribute products that comply with requirements and relevant harmonized standards on European markets. This also means that, from that date only, conformity assessment bodies, which have been notified under the Delegated Regulation and in accordance with the relevant national legislation (including the aforementioned Acts), will be allowed to carry out conformity assessment procedures mentioned in the Regulation. In Poland, the Ministry of Infrastructure and the CAA are consulting the issue of implementing a conformity assessment system. The other consultation party in this case consists of entities that have sufficient resources and competences that are interested in getting accredited for carrying out conformity assessment tests and certification of UA.[456] Moreover, the Polish Centre for Accreditation is currently working on an accreditation system. The national market surveillance authority is obliged to verify whether UA available on its market are safe. The notifying authority is responsible for drafting and implementing procedures necessary to assess notified bodies and inform the European Commission about entities that comply with the requirements set out for them. Obtaining the status of a notified body takes place after positive verification carried out by a notifying entity, accreditation from the national accrediting authority (Polish Centre for Accreditation), and notifying the European Commission about such a body.[457]

454 i.e. Journal of Laws of 2019, item 544.

455 i.e. Journal of Laws of 2018, item 155.

456 http://cedd.pl/2019/09/17/spotkieta-dotyczace-c certacji-bsp-z-jednostkami-oceniajacymi-zgodnosc/ [access: February 29, 2020]. See The PC-BSP unmanned aircraft (drone) certification program: https://www.cnbop.pl/uslugi/c certacja-drony/program-pc-bsp.pdf [access: February 29, 2020].

457 For more, see: https://www.ulc.gov.pl/pl/drony/wdrazanie-przepisow-ue/4717-certy fikacja-bsp-zgodna-z-wymogami-ue [access: February 29, 2020].

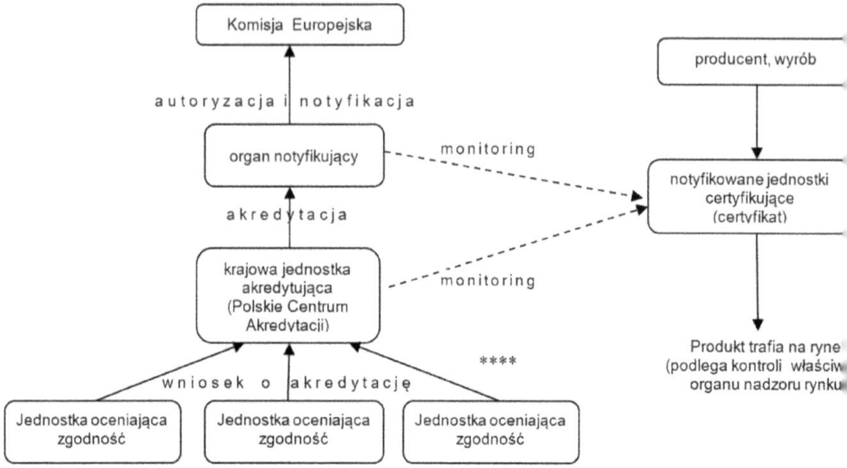

Diagram showing The accreditation process and the role of a notified body in the certificatic of products

Source: CAA

In 2014, ISO created the Unmanned Aircraft Systems committee – ISO/TC 20/ SC 16. It consists of 17 Member States (including China, France, Germany, India, Japan, Russia, the United Arab Emirates, the United States of America, Great Britain) and 6 other observer-countries (Poland is represented by the Polish Committee for Standardization). The committee focuses on the standardization of unmanned aircraft systems, i.e. their classification, design, production, operation, maintenance, and operation safety management.[458]

In December 2019, after 12 months of consultations, a document entitled "ISO 21384-3 Unmanned aircraft systems – Part 3: Operational procedures" saw the light of the day. It was the first international UA standard. It specified the requirements for safe commercial UAS operations.[459]

At a European level, we have the Drone Standardisation Request Ad-Hoc Group (SRAHG) which consists of representatives of the European Committee

458 R Fellner, R Kochańczyk, T Stechnij, A Wilisowski, P Sitko, Aspekty prawne oraz certyfikacyjne bezzałogowych statków powietrznych w świetle wybranych regulacji międzynarodowych, Katowice 2019, p. 37.

459 https://www.iso.org/news/ref2461.html

for Standardization (Comité Européen de Normalisation CEN), the European Committee for Electrotechnical Standardization (Comité Européen de Normalisation Electrotechnique CENELEC), and the European Association for the Coordination of Consumer Representation in Standardisation (ANEC).[460]

Both European and ISO standards are not binding. Nevertheless, entities following these standards show that their products are of a certain level of quality, safety, and reliability.[461]

Admittedly, the provisions of the Delegated Regulation are of public nature and do not narrow down the potential liability of manufacturers or other commercial entities enough. Nonetheless, we should postulate binding the rules of product (UAS) liability with public safety standard regulations. First, the current provisions on civil liability for products are insufficient and do not reflect real-life challenges (i.e. the ongoing development of new technologies, including drones). Second, EU legislators decided to put the heaviest legal burden (obligations) on manufacturers, since they have detailed knowledge of the design and production process (point 18 of the preamble of the Delegated Regulation). Third, when affixing the CE marking, manufacturers declare that the product conforms to all of applicable requirements specified in the EU standardizing laws describing the conditions of obtaining such marking. Finally, these provisions are the basis for safety standards, which must be met in order for a product to be made available on the market. Manufacturers are no longer anonymous entities, and if their products turn out to be nonconforming with the requirements in force, then they should have never been made available to consumers on the European market.

If the market surveillance authority obliges a manufacturer to withdraw their product from the market, they do not do so and then the said product causes damages to a third party, then this may be "exploited" under private law, for example in the form of increased manufacturer liability, shifting the burden of proof or not having to prove all the premises of liability.

Taking the above considerations into account, the rules on manufacturer liability should be partially based on public law when it comes to the open category. The other two categories do not have any standards for manufacturers. The entire responsibility for the safe performance of operations under the specific and certified categories rests with the operator, who is obliged to carry out a risk analysis in order to prove to the aviation authority (CAA) that the operations

460 R Fellner, R Kochańczyk, T Stechnij, A Wilisowski, P Sitko, Aspekty prawne oraz certyfikacyjne bezzałogowych statków powietrznych, p. 39.

461 Ibidem.

they plan to undertake are safe. It should not be forgotten that ultimately it is the aviation authority that allows a given unmanned aircraft (system) to fly, ensuring that it does not pose a threat to human health or life.

4. The civil liability and legal status of robots in the EU

In the case of UA, the issue of product liability is undoubtedly part of a bigger problem – namely civil liability related to the development of new technologies, and particularly the issue of civil liability for robots[462].

In 1942, Isaac Asimov introduced the three laws of robotics in his novel "Runaround":

- the First Law: a robot may not injure a human being or, through inaction, allow a human being to come to harm;
- the Second Law: a robot must obey orders given to it by human beings except where such orders would conflict with the First Law;
- the Third Law: a robot must protect its own existence as long as such protection does not conflict with the First or Second Laws.[463]

Later, he added the "Zeroth Law", according to which a robot may not injure humanity, or, by inaction, allow humanity to come to harm. These laws have become both an inspiration and a basis for the ongoing debate on the legal status of robots and civil liability for damages caused by them.

In the years 2012–2014, a research paper entitled "Regulating emerging robotic technologies in Europe: Robotics facing law and ethics" was carried out under a project financed under the Seventh Framework Program of the European

462 For more, see: C.E.A. Karnow, The application of traditional tort theory to embodied machine intelligence, [in:] R. Calo, A.M. Froomkin, I. Kerr (ed.), Robot Law, Cheltenham, Northampton 2016; Santosuosso, Amedeo & Boscarato, C. & Caroleo, F. & Labruto, Roberto & Leroux, Christophe, Robots, Market and Civil Liability: A European Perspective, 2012; Sebastian Lohsse, Reiner Schulze, Dirk Staudenmayer (ed.) Liability for Artificial Intelligence and the Internet of Things Münster Colloquia on EU Law and the Digital Economy IV, 2019; Cindy Van Rossum, Liability of robots: legal responsibility in cases of errors or malfunctioning, thesis Ghent University 2017; E. Schaerer et al., Robots as Animals: A Framework for Liability and Responsibility in Human-Robot Interactions, 18th IEEE International Symposium on Robot and Human Interactive Communication 2009, https://papers.ssrn.com/sol3/papers.cfm?abstract_id=2271466.

463 L. McCauley, AI Armageddon and the Three Laws of Robotics. Ethics Inf Technol, Vol. 9, 2007, pp. 153–164

Union.[464] The aim of the project was to define the laws and regulations necessary for the introduction of robotics technologies. The project identified the legal and ethical implications of new robotics technologies and determined whether the existing legal framework was adequate to cope with such a level of technological advancement.[465] A report published by the ROBOLAW team analyzed the impact of robotics technologies on laws in Europe, including issues related to autonomous vehicles. The team pointed to the need to build artificial intelligence into the vehicles themselves, not road system, and highlighted the currently existing legal barriers.[466]

The European Commission is to develop regulations on the civil liability and legal status of robots within the next few years. These regulations should be in line with the recommendations of the European Parliament.

In February 2017, a two-day seminar on the development of robotics and artificial intelligence took place in the European Parliament. Its participants analyzed the "European Civil Law in Robotics" report prepared by the JURI committee[467], which formed the basis for the European Parliament resolution of 16 February 2017 with recommendations to the Commission on Civil Law Rules on Robotics.[468]

The European Parliament (EP) points out that between 2010 and 2014, the average increase in sales of robots was 17% per year, with sales increasing by 29% in 2014, the highest year-on-year increase in sales ever. Moreover, the number of robotics patent applications tripled in the last decade[469]. In the long term,

---

464 "Regulating emerging robotic technologies in Europe: Robotics facing law and ethics" (ROBOLAW). Project URL: http://www.robolaw.eu [access: October 25, 2019].

465 https://cordis.europa.eu/project/rcn/102044/brief/pl [access: October 25, 2019].

466 For more on the theory of UA being a robot rather than an aircraft, see Mikromakro Institute reports: 2013 – Człowiek – maszyna – bezpieczeństwo; 2014 – Roboty w przestrzeni publicznej; 2015 – Rynek dronów w Polsce. Księga popytu i podaży; 2017 – Rynek dronów w Polsce. Świt w dolinie śmierci; 2018 – Rynek dronów w Polsce. Jutrzenka: https://www.5zywiolow.pl [access: March 19, 2019].

467 https://www.europarl.europa.eu/RegData/etudes/STUD/2016/571379/IPOL_STU(2016)571379_EN.pdf [access: March 3, 2020].

468 2015/2103 (INL). The resolution contains provisions on: general principles for the development of robotics and artificial intelligence for civilian, research, and innovation purposes; ethical principles, establishment of a European agency, intellectual property rights and data flow, standardization, safety, and security, autonomous means of transport, care robots, medical robots, repair and improvement of the human body, education and employment, environmental impact, responsibility.

469 Ibidem, letter D.

according to the Parliament, the current trend toward designing intelligent and autonomous machines that can be trained and make their own decisions holds not only the promise of economic benefits, but also many concerns about their direct and indirect impact on society.[470]

The resolution states that the current legal framework will not be sufficient to account for damages caused by next-generation robots. These robots will have the capability to adapt and learn, which can bring some degree of unpredictability to their behavior. Such robots will learn independently from their own varied experiences and interact with their environment in a unique and unpredictable way.[471]

The EP proposes that liability for damage caused by robots should be proportionate to the level of instruction given to the robot and its degree of autonomy.[472]

MPs point to the need to create universally accepted and flexible definitions of the terms "robot" and "artificial intelligence" which will not hinder innovation, stressing that we are dealing with a broad category that requires additional clarification. For example, the development of autonomous vehicles (including autonomous drones) should be approached systemically as it requires the creation of infrastructure and control systems. This, in turn, involves the need to agree on many standardization requirements. Moreover, works on UA regulations conducted at an international, European, and national level prove how many control issues need to be resolved before the discussion on the autonomy of machines can even begin.[473]

We can find clear references to drones in the Parliament's Resolution (remotely piloted unmanned aircraft – UA[474]). The EP indicates remarkable progress in the development of drone technology, especially in the field of search and rescue. It also underlines the importance of European legal framework in terms of protecting the safety and privacy of EU citizens and calls on the Commission to act on the recommendations made in the resolution of the European Parliament of 29 October 2015 on safe use of remotely piloted aircraft systems (RPAS), commonly known as unmanned aerial vehicles (UAVs), in the field of civil aviation. The Commission should also assess the widespread use of drone

470 Ibidem, letter G.

471 Ibidem, letter AI.

472 p. 56.

473 P. Rutkowski, Świat dla robotów, Co do zasady. Studia i analizy prawne. 2017: http://www.codozasady.pl/swiat-dla-robotow/ [access: March 3, 2020].

474 Ibidem, p. 30.

technology from a safety perspective and examine the requirement for a mandatory UA identification and tracking system that would allow determining the position of these aircraft in real time. Furthermore, the Parliament recalls that Regulation (EC) No 216/2008 of the European Parliament and of the Council provides for measures that ensure the homogeneity and safety of UA.

When analyzing the basic premises of liability, a causal relationship may be the biggest problem as it will have to be linked to a machine's operations and not human activity. This opens the door for recognizing machines as entities with legal capacity. The problem here is that machines themselves could be held liable if the robot is independent and its operations were contrary to its manufacturer's intentions. The European Parliament proposed a solution to this problem – the introduction of the term "electronic person", which would allow machines to be held accountable. In the Resolution, the Parliament uses this term when referencing the most advanced autonomous robots. This solution is strongly supported by manufacturers, who would thus avoid liability. On the other hand, it raises objections, especially among experts, on artificial intelligence. Legal personality is automatically associated with the assignment of rights and obligations that are closely correlated with human morality. So, what rights could a robot get?

The EP notes that the development of robotic technologies will require a greater understanding of the need for a common foundation necessary for combined human and robot activity. This activity should be based on two relationships of interdependence, i.e. predictability and controllability, which are important in determining what information should people and robots share between one another and how to establish common ground for humans and robots to enable their smooth cooperation.[475]

The Parliament points to the fact that the Commission will have to make an in-depth assessment to determine whether to apply strict liability or a risk management-based approach. The latter focuses on the entity itself, which can minimize risks under certain circumstances by taking action.[476]

Moreover, a system of compulsory insurance for manufacturers or robot owners is also being considered. It would be supplemented with a fund compensating for damages not covered by insurance.[477] However, the creation of such

475 p. 50.
476 p. 53 and 55.
477 p. 57 i 58.

a fund raises several questions. How would it be funded? If it were to be funded through contributions, who would pay them? Would it cover all kinds of robots?

The EP suggests introducing a strict principle of objective liability, regardless of fault. At the same time, it points to the possibility of moderating the liability of manufacturers, programmers, owners, and users of robots by taking advantage of liability limitations, if they were to pay contributions to the compensation fund.[478]

There is also a proposition to introduce individual registration numbers, which would be kept in a special EU register. This would allow anybody to get information on the nature of the fund, the limitations of liability in the event of damage to property, or names and functions of the persons who contributed to the creation of a certain machine.[479]

On April 25, 2018, the Commission issued a Communication which presented steps to help society take advantage of the benefits of artificial intelligence (AI) and increase the EU's competitiveness in this area.[480] Artificial Intelligence has been defined as systems that exhibit intelligent behavior by analyzing their environment and taking action to achieve specific goals with a certain level of autonomy. AI-based systems can be software-based and exist in a virtual world (like a voice assistant), or they can be embedded in computer hardware (e.g. advanced robots, autonomous cars, drones, or Internet of Things applications).

The emergence of AI, which includes a complex ecosystem and autonomous decision-making, requires reflection on the adequacy of certain civil liability laws. Social acceptance and public trust in new technologies are crucial here – they can be achieved only by ensuring a high level of safety and an effective redress mechanism.[481]

A preliminary analysis of product liability legislation, machine-related directives, and the current liability framework in the light of AI and emerging technologies has already been carried out. The Expert Group is presently carrying out a further analysis of these challenges.

---

478 p. 59 (c).

479 p. 59 (e).

480 COMMUNICATION FROM THE COMMISSION TO THE EUROPEAN PARLIAMENT, THE EUROPEAN COUNCIL, THE COUNCIL, THE EUROPEAN ECONOMIC AND SOCIAL COMMITTEE AND THE COMMITTEE OF THE REGIONS Artificial Intelligence for Europe COM/2018/237 final, Brussels, April 25, 2018.

481 Ibidem, p. 18.

5. Manufacturer's liability for damages caused by autonomous UA in light of comparative considerations regarding regulations of autonomous vehicles and vehicles using autopilot equipment

The 1980 American comedy "*Airplane!*" features a scene that seems to predict the future. An aircraft's crew has been poisoned, so Ted Striker, a former military pilot who is reluctant to fly since the war, comes in to save the day. Upon falling ill, the pilot of a plane yells at a flight attendant to turn on the autopilot. She frantically searches the control panel and finds the right switch, flipping it. In that very moment, a plastic, inflatable, fully-uniformed pilot pops out of an empty seat and takes control of the airplane with inflatable plastic hands. Everyone is relieved, but moments later air begins escaping from the "autopilot" and the plane starts falling toward the ground. Panic sets in until the flight attendant is able to pump the pilot back up again. After that terrifying flaw is resolved, everyone in the cockpit seems overly confident in the autopilot's ability to keep the plane airborne safely. Indeed, the fact that these movie characters blindly trust an inflatable automatic pilot is one of the funniest aspects of the movie. The audience would probably never trust a plastic "pilot" to fly a plane without supervision, so their willingness to do so is both hilarious and terrifying.[482]

However, recent experience has taught us that autopilot scenes from movies may turn out to be more real than we could have ever imagined, at least when it comes to human reactions to automation. Over the past few years, many car manufacturers have started introducing new forms of automation to their vehicles.[483]

As pointed out by the European Commission, autonomous vehicles will change our lives and shape the future of road transport. They can significantly reduce transport costs, support the creation of many new services, improve mobility (e.g. for the elderly or disabled), support car-sharing services and "mobility as a service", contribute to the development of electrification and electromobility, free up space currently used for parking lots, and revolutionize urban planning.[484] Moreover, autonomous vehicles could significantly

482 T.H. Pearl, Hands on the Wheel: A Call for Greater Regulation of Semi-Autonomous Cars. Indiana Law Journal, Vol. 93, Issue 3, 2018, p. 714.

483 Ibidem.

484 COMMUNICATION FROM THE COMMISSION TO THE EUROPEAN PARLIAMENT, THE COUNCIL, THE EUROPEAN ECONOMIC AND SOCIAL

improve road safety as human error is estimated to play a role in 94% of road accidents.[485]

For several years, people have been lively discussing the issue of civil liability for damage caused by autonomous vehicles. In Polish, they are referred to as self-propelled. English, however, uses various different names such as *autonomous car, driverless car, self-driving car,* or *robotic car.* [486] Americans have distinguished four levels of vehicle autonomy.[487]

Autonomous vehicles are currently mainly being tested in the US, China, Japan, and Singapore. In Japan, autonomous driving has been identified as a key innovation to stimulate the country's economic growth. Some EU member states (e.g. Germany, France, the United Kingdom, Sweden, and the Netherlands) have already taken a number of initiatives in this field, which include testing opportunities. The European Commission, on its way to develop a common European strategy for connected and automated driving, has taken action to promote the development of infrastructure and connectivity services that support automated vehicles.[488]

In the US, state authorities took the lead in creating autonomous vehicle regulations. In May 2018, twenty states passed regulations for driverless cars. While the provisions of individual state statutes differ in many aspects, there are also some similarities.[489] For example, at least three states define a person who engages a car without a driver (i.e. starts the engine) as the "operator" of that vehicle. Likewise, four states and the District of Columbia enacted laws that would

---

COMMITTEE, THE COMMITTEE OF THE REGIONS On the road to automated mobility: An EU strategy for mobility of the future, Brussels, May 17, 2018 COM(2018) 283 final, p. 1.

485 Ibidem.

486 D.J. Fagnant, K. Kockelman, Preparing a Nation for Autonomous Vehicles: Opportunities, Barriers and Policy Recommendations. Transportation Research Part A: Policy and Practice, Vol. 77, 2015.

487 See S.P. Wood, J. Chang et al., The Potential Regulatory Challenges of Increasingly Autonomous Motor Vehicles. Santa Clara Law Review, Vol. 52, No. 4, 2012, p. 1423 et seq.

488 COMMUNICATION FROM THE COMMISSION On the road to automated mobility: An EU strategy for mobility of the future.

489 These regulations have been described in detail, inter alia, in Tracy Hresko Pearl, Fast & Furious: The Misregulation of Driverless Cars, 73 N.Y.U. ANN. SURV. AM. L. 19, 30–34 (2017).

require drivers (people) to take control of their autonomous vehicles under certain circumstances.[490]

Source literature presents a view that existing state laws ignore the differences between semi-autonomous and fully autonomous vehicles. In many cases, they put unjustified liability on drivers (people) and encourage people to act like traditional drivers instead of letting cars drive themselves, which could actually be less safe. Legal setbacks arising from these regulations may discourage the development of the autonomous vehicle market.[491]

The US Senate is also working on new regulations that should significantly accelerate the popularization of fully autonomous cars. These new laws concern authorizing vehicle drivability and using autonomous cars. Still, liability for accidents and determining which party is to bear the possible legal consequences (driver or manufacturer) remain the most controversial issues. These new regulations require manufacturers to check and ensure that their vehicles are able to detect all types of other road users. In addition, manufacturers would be required to implement a system under which they would inform the relevant authorities of any potential safety issues with their products. Vehicle registration, insurance, licensing, and safety checks would be the responsibility of state authorities.[492]

Autonomous vehicles can have defects that conventional vehicles do not. These can be mechanical, electronic, or software-related. For example, there may be mechanical or physical defects in an autonomous control system or in the sensors used by said system, defects in the electrical components of sensors or a control system, or software defects. However, from the point of view of civil liability, the most dangerous and controversial potential defects are autonomous driving software defects e.g. not recognizing certain patterns which can lead to an autonomous vehicle not being able to recognize pedestrians or other obstacles, or maneuvering errors (turning, maintaining safe distances, changing

490 T.H. Pearl, Hands on the Wheel: A Call for Greater Regulation of Semi-Autonomous Cars, op.cit., p. 724–725.

491 Ibidem, p. 725.

492 See https://www.govtrack.us/congress/bills/115/hr3388 [access: March 6, 2020]. For more on regulations in the USA, see: M.A. Geisfeld, A Roadmap for Autonomous Vehicles: State Tort Liability, Automobile Insurance, and Federal Safety Regulation. California Law Review, Vol. 105, 2017; Andrew Swanson, "Somebody Grab the Wheel!... Vehicle Legislation and the Road to a National Regime, Marquette Law Review, Vol 97, Issue 4, 2014; T.H. Pearl, Hands on the Wheel: A Call for Greater Regulation of Semi-Autonomous Cars. Indiana Law Journal, Vol. 93, Issue 3, 2018.

speeds, avoiding collisions) and errors arising from improper communication between an owner / passenger and the vehicle's computer.[493]

The British issued the *Vehicle Technology and Aviation Bill*[494], according to which insurance policies should cover any eventual financial consequences arising from traffic accidents – regardless of whether the vehicle was driven by a driver or autonomously. The aggrieved party has the direct right to claim compensation from a car insurer and, in turn, the insurer has the right to recourse to the responsible entity to the extent of liability under applicable law, including laws on product liability. The government explained that automated vehicles will allow the driver to fully pass the task of driving onto the vehicle itself when automatic systems are active, without the need to intervene or even monitor the situation, which in turn creates a problem for vehicle insurance. British law requires all drivers to have insurance, so when a driver uses a vehicle's automatic driving mode, loopholes in insurance provisions emerge which can make it difficult for victims to pursue claims.[495]

The adopted bill allows two exceptions to this rule. First, the insurer will be able to refuse to pay compensation if the car owner has introduced unauthorized changes to the car's software. Second, if the car owner has neglected to update the software as required by its terms of use.

It is worth noting that the bill does not contain any provisions regarding UA, despite numerous groups calling for such regulations. In light of the increasing number of accidents involving drones and passenger aircraft, as well as other incidents related to the inappropriate use of drones, the government was called upon to create a set of safety rules for the use of UA. Additionally, those investing in the drone industry see the possibilities that the improved regime brings as key to the development of this lucrative market in the UK. Several members of the House of Lords have expressed their surprise and concerns about the lack of regulations on UA. On March 16, 2017, 3 MPs – MacDonald, Foxcroft, and Burton – introduced an amendment that would have forced the government to present UA regulations within 6 months of receiving the so-called Royal Assent.

---

493 S. Wu, Product Liability Issues in the U.S. and Associated Risk Management. In: M. Maurer, J. Gerdes, B. Lenz, and H. Winner (eds.), Autonomes Fahren. Springer Vieweg, Berlin, Heidelberg, pp. 563–564.

494 HL Bill 82 of 2017–19

495 Department for Transport, Impact Assessment: Pathway to Driverless Cars – Insurance for Automated Vehicles, 7 October 2016: https://www.parliament.uk/documents/impact-assessments/IA17-008A.pdf [access: April 5, 2019].

The suggested subject material included geofencing, a registration process, and the regulatory role of the CAA. However, the amendment was withdrawn due to a lack of support in its second reading. Since the legislator clearly refused to regulate the issue of drones in the bill, it seems that its provisions on civil liability will not apply to autonomous UA operations.

At a European Union level, the European Commission has taken a number of actions to promote the implementation of communications infrastructure and services that support automated vehicles. These actions include, among others, creating a strategy for the fifth-generation mobile network (5G network), intelligent transport systems, a space strategy, an artificial intelligence initiative supporting autonomous vehicles, and a strategy for autonomous mobility with recommendations for automated and connected vehicles.[496]

Liability for accidents caused by motor vehicles is regulated at a European level through legal instruments such as the Motor Insurance Directive and the Product Liability Directive. In addition, each Member State provides for a number of local tools such as traffic regulations, civil law regulations (liability regulations), and product liability regulations that implement the Directive in this respect. As there are currently no specific solutions that would regulate the issue of liability for damages caused by autonomous vehicles, the principles resulting from the abovementioned legal acts should apply.

However, the European Commission points out that the essential issue here is the real chain of events that lead to damage or an accident, and therefore proposes that automated vehicles be equipped with data recorders to identify the person driving (i.e. an actual driver or an autonomous vehicle system) in the event of an accident.[497]

The Commission underlines that damages qualified under the Motor Insurance Directive are compensated quickly. The Directive has recently been assessed and it was concluded that there was no need to introduce changes in regard to automated vehicles as they will have to be insured in accordance with the same Directive. At the same time, the Commission points out that the insurer may then take legal action against the vehicle manufacturer under the Product Liability Directive if the automatic driving system had malfunctioned or was defective.[498] However, the Commission's optimistic approach may turn out to be

---

496 COMMUNICATION FROM THE COMMISSION On the road to automated mobility: An EU strategy for mobility of the future p. 7

497 Ibidem, p. 13.

498 Ibidem.

incorrect in practice. Today, motor insurance premiums are estimated based on factors related to the driver (age, experience, number of accidents, etc.). In the case of autonomous vehicles, insurers will have to take other criteria into account, especially tech-related (e.g. technical condition of the vehicle) and the condition of road infrastructure.

Due to the relatively new regime of liability for damages caused by the use of UA and the lack of official court rulings, it is necessary to analyze the rulings on accidents related to the use of autopilot.

In the case of *Nelson v American Airlines, Inc.*,[499] the plaintiff – Mary Nelson – was a passenger on a flight to Los Angeles. Shortly after the plane reached cruising altitude, the pilots engaged the autopilot to maintain level flight. However, the autopilot made the plane dive down suddenly, causing the plaintiff to suffer bodily injury. The Court of Appeal ruled that the carrier could have shown that it had exercised its best efforts by proving that it had not caused the accident or that the cause of the accident was unavoidable and unknown. The Court of Appeal indicated that the autopilot malfunction could have caused the accident, but nevertheless no evidence to eliminate the carrier's negligence was found.[500]

In the case of *Ferguson v Bombardier Services Corp.*[501] the injured persons filed a lawsuit against the manufacturers of a plane and the manufacturers of its autopilot after a plane belonging to the National Guard was involved in an accident. The most important issue at hand was to establish who was to be blamed. The plaintiffs pointed to various shortcomings in the autopilot system. The defendants argued that the plane had been loaded improperly, and that when the pilot left the cockpit to move to the rear of the plane, the plane became unstable and a gust of wind caused the plane to lose control. The Court of Appeal ruled that it was appropriate for the lower court to exclude an expert's testimony on autopilot defects, which the injured parties invoked, as said expert admitted during a pre-trial hearing that information from the flight data recorder was as consistent with the theory that the aircraft was improperly loaded as it was with the theory that the autopilot was flawed, and therefore his testimony would not have helped the jury understand the evidence they were handed. Another plaintiffs' argument was based on a different expert's testimony on federal aviation regulations,

499 Court of Appeal of California, First District, Division Four Jul 9, 1968263 Cal.App.2d 742 (Cal. Ct. App. 1968).

500 Interestingly, Nelson did not file a lawsuit against the manufacturer of the autopilot or the aircraft.

501 244 Fed. App'x 944 (11th Cir. 2007).

in which it was claimed that regulations required manufacturers to mount a warning device in the autopilot system. However, the expert was not able to show that the regulations did indeed contain such a requirement. Thus, the aggrieved parties were not able to prove the "defect" of the product in question.

In the *Moe v. Avions Marcel Dassault-Breguet Aviation*[502] case, the plaintiffs pointed to a defect in the autopilot as the cause of the accident, claiming that if the pilots had not disabled the autopilot, there would have been no warning when the pilots tried to manually control the aircraft. In fact, the aggrieved parties claimed that the autopilot would have caused the plane to act against the pilots' manual control inputs. However, they were unable to provide sufficient evidence to support these claims.

In the case of *Glorvigen v Cirrus Design Corp.*, [503] the main claim was that the company had voluntarily undertaken the obligation to train their pilot in the use of the autopilot system, and yet had not provided them with adequate training, advanced training in particular. According to the plaintiffs, the accident took place because the pilot did not know how to use the autopilot system under weather conditions that required manual control. The court ruled that the aggrieved parties had not proved that the cause of the damage was a defect in the autopilot system. Moreover, the aggrieved parties could not use the so-called "implied warranty" because the company had renounced these warranties when it had bought the plane. So, the only argument left was the theory of negligence. The Minnesota Court of Appeal ruled, in accordance with the negligence theory, that Cirrus had not been required to provide further pilot training. However, it had been required to provide appropriate instructions for the autopilot system, and the lack of sufficient instructions caused the accident.

In the cases discussed above, the aggrieved parties were to prove that a product defect was the cause of the damage, without the need to prove manufacturers' fault. Looking at these rulings, one could say that proving guilt may be easier than proving that damage was caused by a product defect.

When analyzing other cases related to the use of autopilot, we see that courts pay special attention to the human factor, i.e. a pilot's behavior when using the system. For example, in the *Brouse v United States*[504] case, the court ruled that it

---

502 United States Court of Appeals, Tenth Circuit, Jan 30, 1984, 727 F.2d 917 (10th Cir. 1984).

503 United States District Court, D. Minnesota Feb 11, 2008, Civil No. 06-2661 (PAM/JSM) (D. Minn. Feb. 11, 2008).

504 United States District Court, N.D. Ohio, E.D Mar 25, 194983 F. Supp. 373 (N.D. Ohio 1949).

had been the pilot's duty to pay attention to potential collisions while the flight had been under autopilot control.[505]

In disputes over unmanned vehicles and vehicles with autopilot, the issue of product liability will almost always come into play, in addition to operators' liability. Our analysis of autopilot rulings leads us to the conclusion that courts seem to focus on classic product liability issues, such as the actual cause of the accident, and whether the device in question had any defects.[506]

The use of autopilot blurs the line between manned and unmanned aviation.[507]

6. The standard of care for robotics manufacturers vs. the standard of care for human operators of machines

Disputes over unmanned and autopilot vehicles mention two regimes of liability: operator's liability and manufacturer's liability. Therefore, one should consider the standard of care for both of these.

The Arnold v Reuther[508] ruling showed the differences in treating a robot/system (manufacturer) and a person (operator). The Louisiana Court of Appeal found that a human, no matter how effective, is not a robot and doesn't possess supernatural powers to detect danger before it happens. One should always keep in mind certain human weaknesses and reaction times. A human being needs a fraction of a second to react, and even then cannot react with mechanical speed and accuracy, unlike robots/systems equipped with radars and anti-collision devices.

This ruling could translate into the near future, when autonomous unmanned aircraft are be widely used. Courts should therefore apply a high-care requirement to manufacturers in order to avoid collisions, as robots/systems can operate faster and more accurately than humans. Moreover, if one day human driving turns out to be more dangerous than typical autonomous driving, people might even start giving up on their urge to drive. If such a day comes, will not using a robot/system be perceived as culpable action?[509]

---

505 Automation in various means of transport, for more, see H. Perritt, Jr., Who Pays When Drones Crash?. UCLA Journal of Law and Technology, Vol. 21, Issue 1, 2017, p. 7 et seq.

506 S. Wu, Unmanned Vehicles and US Product Liability Law. Journal of Law, Information and Science, Vol. 21, Issue 2, 2012, p. 234 et seq.

507 See also A. Konert, A. Kunert-Diallo, Odpowiedzialność operatora kosmicznego względem turystów kosmicznych, Państwo i Prawo nr 6/2019.

508 Court of Appeal of Louisiana, Orleans, February 18, 1957, 92 So.2d 593 (1957).

509 S. Wu, Unmanned Vehicles and US Product Liability Law.

A UA operator, as a human, will always be obliged to avoid accidents, even if operation is handed over to a robot/system. This liability may arise when using semi-autonomic machines, such as autopilot, and above all when using unmanned aircraft systems.

When studying subject literature, one may encounter an opinion expressed commonly during the technological development of manned aircraft in the 1960s that gives priority to technological progress – according to this view, there is a need for experiments in the age of extraordinary technological development and therefore sporadic failures may occur. This should even be expected, as any pioneering industry is reaching far beyond the current state of knowledge. Without experiments, progress in our society would be significantly slowed. The author criticizes those who argue that technological innovation should be punishable by imposing liability for trying to develop improvements.[510]

It seems that this opinion can be applied to modern times and the current development of unmanned aircraft systems. Therefore, should we accept a certain degree of imperfection in robots/devices? And if so, to what degree? Or should we follow the rules introduced in *Arnold v Reuther*, according to which only man can make mistakes and a machine should be perfect?

There is no doubt that the standard of care for manufacturers should be significantly higher than that for UA operators. The assessment of due diligence in economic activity is, of course, stricter than the one generally required. Necessary expertise, which includes not only purely formal qualifications but also experience resulting from professional practice and customary standards of requirements, somehow constitute the essence of economic activity.[511] Economic entities should be subject to equally high standards of care as legal professionals.[512]

Finally, a financial aspect must be considered. Manufacturers should take the potential risk (of failure) on themselves at the expense of financial self-development.

However, if a UA operator is an entrepreneur, the standard of care should be the same for them as the one for manufacturers. It therefore appears that when an aircraft is not autonomous, and an operator is in control of a flight, the standard of care should be the same for the manufacturer as it is for the operator.

---

510 W.E. Maloney, Current Trends in Aviation Product Liability Law. Journal of Air Law and Commerce, Vol. 36, Issue 3, 1970, p. 545.

511 Supreme Court ruling of September 22, 2005, IV CK 100/05, also see Supreme Court ruling of May 7, 2004 I CK 625/03, LEX no. 479 350.

512 Supreme Court ruling of July 25, 2013, II CSK 613/12.

Chapter 8 Privacy and data protection

1. Introduction

An article entitled "Right to Privacy" by Samuel D. Warren and Louis de Brandeis, published in the Harvard Law Review in 1980 was the first to introduce the right to privacy. Today, the two authors are considered the creators of the concept of the right to privacy.[513] They defined it as the right to exclusivity, distinctness, mystery, solitude, and the *right to be alone.*[514] The right to privacy, borne in American law in the 1980s, is a very specific institution which includes personal copyrights and significantly differs from the protection of privacy as a personal right, protected by the Polish legal system by the absolute subjective right.

Ensuring the protection of citizens' privacy is a huge challenge in the era of UA, considering their technological capabilities – a potential breach of individual privacy through the use of UA is a serious issue. Drones can be equipped with video or audio recorders, letting drone operators easily come into possession of large amounts of private data that allows for the identification of persons who have not consented to this.

Recording video in real time, taking photos while flying over private property and storage of these materials at later stages pose a great threat to privacy. Drones can collect personal information, including video, audio, and location-based data, so their use can be compared to that of a surveillance system.

Drones can process images, sound, geolocation data, or other electromagnetic signals related to an identified or identifiable natural person and process this data using onboard devices, which may have an impact on privacy and data protection and therefore trigger data protection laws.[515]

Depending on the type of onboard technology, data can be collected without being in direct line of sight (e.g. through roofs, debris, or clouds), over long periods of time, and over large areas without interruption.[516]

---

513 J. Sieńczyło-Chlabicz, Naruszenie prywatności osób publicznych przez prasę, Zakamycze 2006, p. 25.

514 S.D. Warren, L. Brandeis, The Right to Privacy. Harvard Law Review, Vol. IV, December 1890, p. 193–220.

515 Opinion 01/2015 on Privacy and Data Protection Issues relating to the Utilisation of Drones, ARTICLE 29 DATA PROTECTION WORKING PARTY, 01673/15/EN WP 231, p. 7.

516 Ibidem, p. 8.

Today, we could be under surveillance from UA so small that they are virtually unperceivable to humans, e.g. insect-sized drones. The fact that such devices cannot be easily spotted poses a great threat to our privacy, and their small size does not affect the quality of the materials they record. Moreover, they are widely available and can be used by anyone.

The European Commission has highlighted these issues on numerous occasions. First, the Article 29 Working Party published an opinion in 2015 on privacy and personal data protection issues in the context of the use of drones. This document indicates that drones themselves do not pose a threat to privacy, but rather their unlawful use. Second, the Commission decided to fund an "awareness-raising campaign" under the 2014–2020 COSME program (Program for the Competitiveness of Enterprises and Small and Medium-sized Enterprises) to help better understand the legal framework and restrictions related to the use of UA in Europe. The project was called DroneRules PRO. Its purpose was to contribute to developing a culture of privacy and personal data protection among UA operators, manufacturers, and pilots by providing them with access to reliable information and high-quality educational resources online.[517]

In civil aviation, the protection of privacy and personal data has so far been associated mainly with the processing of personal passenger data through ICT systems (Passenger Name Record, PNR).[518] However, there are no separate regulations regarding the protection of privacy for drone operations. Therefore, the general principles on the protection of privacy and personal data guaranteed at an international, European, and national level apply. The purpose of this chapter is to analyze these regulations in terms of the use of UA using a legal–dogmatic approach. A distinction should be made between protection of privacy under civil law and administrative law (public law), as the two rely on different legal grounds, premises, scopes of protection and measures. Civil law relies on the provisions of public law to establish unlawfulness (especially when trying to revoke a presumption).

The other purpose of this chapter is to determine the limits of the protection of property rights – it will answer questions that fall within the scope of property rights, such as: does someone have the right to shoot down a drone that is flying

517 https://dronerules.eu/pl/ [access: January 8, 2020].

518 Zob. D. Zadura, Importance of personal data protection law for commercial air transport, Transactions of the Institute of Aviation, No. 1 (246), Warsaw, 2017, p. 35 et seq. and A. Kunert-Diallo, "Kontrola tożsamości w przewozie lotniczym" in: Prawo lotnicze i kosmiczne oraz technologie, pub. University of Rzeszów, pp. 78–95.

over their property? A comparative analysis will look at infringements of the right to privacy as a tort.

2. The right to privacy and protection of personal data – international regulations

2.1. General issues

The right to privacy is a broad concept covering family life, domestic peace, personal rights, human integrity, protection of personal data, secrecy of correspondence, and an individual person's private sphere.[519] At a Nordic Conference of Jurists held in Stockholm in 1967, experts pointed to the negative aspects of the right to privacy, which forbids to:

- interfere with private, family, and home life;
- interfere with physical and mental integrity;
- violate somebody else's reputation;
- misrepresent an individual;
- reveal embarrassing, shameful facts about an individual's private life;
- use an individual's name, image, or other data related to the identity of an individual;
- track, spy on;
- interfere with secrecy of correspondence;
- disclose information considered a trade secret;
- abuse private means of communication.[520]

The right to privacy is guaranteed by international, European, and national laws. At all of these three levels, the instruments of law aimed at protecting this right are significantly developed. These include (at an international and European level):

- Universal Declaration of Human Rights – 1948;
- European Convention on Human Rights – 1950;
- Hesse Personal Data Protection Act – 1970;
- Resolutions 22 and 29 – 1973 and 1974;

519 M. Pryciak, Prawo do prywatności: M. Sadowski i P. Szymianiec (ed.). Prawa człowieka – idea, instytucje, krytyka. Wrocław, 2010, p. 214.

520 Quoted after J. Sieńczyło-Chlabicz, Naruszenie prywatności osób publicznych przez prasę, op.cit., pp. 212–213.

- OECD guidelines – 1980;
- Council of Europe Convention No. 108–1981;
- Directive 95/46/EC – 1995;
- Charter of Fundamental Rights of the European Union (2000/C364/01) – 2000;
- General Data Protection Regulation – 2016[521]

The most important legal acts regulating the right to privacy at an international and European level include: the Universal Declaration of Human Rights, the International Covenant on Civil and Political Rights, the Convention for the Protection of Human Rights and Fundamental Freedoms, and the EU Charter of Fundamental Rights.

Article 12 of the Universal Declaration of Human Rights states that no one shall be subjected to arbitrary interference with his privacy, family, home, or correspondence, or to attacks upon his or her honor and reputation. Everyone has the right to the protection of the law against such interference or attacks.

Article 17 of the International Covenant on Civil and Political Rights indicates that, first of all, no one shall be subjected to arbitrary or unlawful interference with his or her privacy, family, home, or correspondence, or to unlawful attacks on his or her honor and reputation. Second, the article emphasizes that everyone has the right to the protection of the law against such interference or attacks.

Article 8 of the Convention for the Protection of Human Rights and Fundamental Freedoms states that everyone has the right to respect for his or her private and family life, his or her home and his or her correspondence.

Article 7 of the EU Charter of Fundamental Rights underlines that everyone has the right to respect for his or her private and family life, home, and communications.

Moreover, Article 8 of the same charter indicates that everyone has the right to the protection of personal data concerning him or her and that such data must be processed fairly for specified purposes and on the basis of the consent of the person concerned or some other legitimate basis laid down by law. Everyone has the right to access data, which has been collected concerning him or her, and the right to have it rectified. Compliance with these rules shall be subject to control by an independent authority.

---

521 L. Kępa, Ochrona danych osobowych. Praktyczny przewodnik dla przedsiębiorców, Warsaw, 2018, p. 4.

The right to privacy is therefore a fundamental human right that is closely related to the protection of personal data. In fact, the protection of privacy is "closely related to the extent to which information protection mechanisms are effective".[522] Personal data protection is therefore a kind of specialized structure, the purpose of which is to protect the same values that protect the right to privacy.[523]

In June of 2015, the Article 29 Working Party published an opinion on the issues related to the protection of privacy and personal data in the context of the use of drones. This opinion was supposed to contribute to better protection of personal data when using drones, and its recommendations applied to people who use UA for purposes other than private, unless a private person shares personal data they obtained through the use of a UA, e.g. uploads it online.

A drone operator who collects personal data must fulfill their information obligation toward those entities whose data is processed as soon as possible, no later than the moment of first disclosure. However, fulfilling this obligation by the operator may prove difficult. In the case of flights over facilities, for example when performing operations at major sporting events, the information obligation may be fulfilled by providing event participants with relevant information, e.g. leaflets or by means of electronic communications. The situation becomes even more complicated when we are dealing with spontaneous flights. The Party suggests publishing information on flights on operators' websites. This seems impossible in most cases. A generally available UA flight registration system could be the solution here. The system would allow easy identification of data administrators by, for example, using so-called smart license plates.[524]

Personal data protection has been regulated in detail in Regulation (EU) 2016/679 of the European Parliament and of the Council of 27 April 2016 on the protection of natural persons with regard to the processing of personal data and on the free movement of such data, and repealing Directive 95/46/EC.

522 J. Sieńczyło-Chlabicz, Naruszenie prywatności osób publicznych przez prasę, op.cit., p. 70.

523 P. Sarnecki, Art. 47, [in:] Konstytucja Rzeczypospolitej Polskiej. Komentarz, III, ed. L. GARLICKI, Warsaw, 2003, p. 4.

524 https://ec.europa.eu/justice/article-29/documentation/opinion-recommendation/index_en.htm [access: June 9, 2020].

2.2. Redress for breaching the provisions of the Convention for the Protection of Human Rights and Fundamental Freedoms

Violation of the right to privacy may result in a complaint being filed with the European Court of Human Rights in Strasburg, pursuant to Art. 8 of the European Convention for the Protection of Human Rights and Fundamental Freedoms[525]. There is no legal definition of the term "private life" in Art. 8 sec. 1 of the Convention, but there is a tendency to broadly interpret this concept to include, inter alia, the right to the protection of physical and mental integrity, the right to the protection of personal data, the right to respect for one's home, or the right to identity.

Violation of Art. 8 of the Convention may also take place in the event of more widespread use of drones by the State, e.g. for crowd surveillance, crime monitoring, or for military purposes. Here, an obvious problem arises – limiting the sphere of privacy of individuals. This is often justified by the activities of specialized state institutions, the aim of which is to fight against and prevent threats to public safety. For example, let's consider a situation in which the police use a drone to surveil a suspect at his home. In the meantime, they record the man's neighbor during an intimate situation and then share this recording (intentionally or not) online.[526] People have brought many complaints to the European Court of Human Rights (ECtHR) against different states for activity related to the surveillance of individuals.[527]

---

525 Poland acceded to the European Convention for the Protection of Human Rights and Fundamental Freedoms. (Journal of Laws of 1993, No. 61, items 284–286).

526 The first time photos taken by a police drone were used as evidence was in a Canadian court after local police used a drone in 2007 to photograph a homicide scene. "Canadian Police Push Limits of Civilian UAV Laws", Homeland Security News Wire, 17 Feb 2011: http://homelandsecuritynewswire.com/canadian-police-push-limits-civilian-uavs-laws [access: January 20, 2019].

527 See: Friedl v. Austria (January 31, 1995, case no. 15225/ 89) Herbecq v. Belgia (January 14, 1998, case no. 32200/96 and 32201/00) P.G. and J. H. v. United Kingdom (September 25, 2001, case no. 44787/98); Allan v. United Kingdom (November 5, 2002, case no. 48539/99); Peck v. United Kingdom (January 28, 2003, case no. 44647/98); Perry v. United Kingdom (July 17, 2003, case no.63737 / 00); Martin v. United Kingdom (February 19, 2004, case no. 63608/00); Association for European Integration and Human Rights and Ekimdzhiev v. Bulgaria (June 28, 2007 case no. 62540/00); Szypusz v. United Kingdom (September 21, 2010, case no. 8400/07); Köpke v. Germany (October 5, 2010, case no. 420/07.

The ECtHR has not created a definition of the "right to privacy" that could be commonly used. In many of its rulings, the Court points to the close relationship between the right to privacy and the public sphere. In one of its judgments, the Court noted that private life "encompasses the right for an individual to form and develop relationships with other human beings, including relationships of a professional or business nature"[528]. In another, the Court states that "Article 8 also protects a right to personal development, and the right to establish and develop relationships with other human beings and the outside world"[529]. Moreover, the Court indicates that the notion of "private life" does not exclude activities of a professional or business nature, since it is, after all, in the course of their working lives that the majority of people have a significant opportunity of developing relationships with the outside world.[530]

The deliberate use of drones as lethal weapons is a much more dangerous issue that's also related to their exploitation. We are already living in times where pilotless aircraft have become a part of modern warfare. Some of the characteristics of unmanned combat aircraft – such as flying at high altitudes, the ability to collect information, and their impact on civilians – influence decisions on the legality of these weapons. Moreover, the sheer distance between the aircraft's operator and their military targets affects the principles of international humanitarian law[531]. The use of drones (notably by the US)[532] has sparked a fierce debate about the

---

528 See: C. v. Belgium, August 7, 1996, § 25, Reports 1996-III.

529 See: Pretty v. United Kingdom, no. 2346/02, § 61, ECHR 2002-III).

530 See: Niemietz v. Germany, December16, 1992, § 29, Series A no. 251-B.

531 M.E. O'Connell, Remarks: The Resort to Drones under International Law. Denver Journal of International Law and Policy, Vol. 39, 2011; R. Mousazadeh, A. Basiri, M. Babaee, A. Tabasi, Analyzing the Legal Dimensions of Unmanned Combat Aerial Vehicle in the International Law. Journal of Politics and Law, Vol. 9, Issue 10, 2016; R. Vogel, Drone Warfare & the Law of Armed Conflict. Denver Journal of International Law & Policy, Vol. 39, Issue 1, 2011; R. Alberstadt, Drones under International Law. Open Journal of Political Science, Issue 4, 2014; G.J.A, Knoops, Legal, Political and Ethical Dimensions of Drone Warfare under International Law: A Preliminary Survey. International Criminal Law Review, Issue 12, 2012; M. P. Kreuzer, RPAs and Non-International Conflict – A Strategic/Legal Assessment. Cardozo Law Review, Vol. 36, Issue 2, 2014. (passim).

532 For a detailed discussion of the possibility of pursuing claims against the United States or its officials for personal and property damage suffered as a result of drone attacks, see ninter alia, Rosen, Richard D., Drones and the U.S. Courts. William Mitchell Law Review, Vol. 37, Issue 5, 2011;. Q. Eijkman i M. Bakker, Access to an Effective Remedy and Reparations for Civilian Victims of Armed Drone Strikes, in: B. Custers (ed.),

legality of performing targeted killings by UA under international law[533]. Assuming that drone attacks on suspected terrorists and in armed conflicts violate international law, do actual or potential victims have the opportunity to obtain redress? Drones are also used outside of armed conflicts. In order to assess the legality and legitimacy of deliberate killings with the use of armed drones, we must distinguish between what constitutes an armed conflict situation[534] and a non-armed conflict situation (*law enforcement*). The principles of redress outside the context of an armed conflict are largely dictated by international public law – human rights in particular. The ECtHR announced the criteria for the use of force in so-called *law enforcement* operations.[535]

In order to kill a person, he or she must pose a concrete threat to human life and at the same time be suspected of having committed a serious crime. Thus, the protection of human life is the only argument justifying a deliberate killing of a person.[536]

The most decisive criterion for the use of drones by *law enforcement officials* is reflected in Principle 9 of the UN's Basic Principles on the Use of Force and

---

The Future of Drone Use, Information Technology and Law Series, Springer 2016; M. Matthews, M. McNab, Clarifying the Law Relating to Unmanned Drones and the Use of Force: The Relation-ships between Human Rights, Self-Defence, Armed Conflict and International Humanitarian Law. Denver Journal of International Law and Policy, Vol. 39, 2011. (passim).

533 T. Hattan, Lethal Autonomous Robots: Are They Legal under International Human Rights and Humanitarian Law?. Nebraska Law Review, Vol. 93, 2014.

534 For more on the use of drones in armed conflicts, see Q. Eijkman and M. Bakker, Access to an Effective Remedy and Reparations for Civilian Victims of Armed Drone Strikes, in: B. Custers (ed.), The Future of Drone Use, Information Technology and Law Series, Springer 2016; Blum G, Heymann, Law and policy of targeted killings. Harvard Journal of National Security issue 1, 2012; M. P. Kreuzer, Drones and the Future of Air Warfare: The Evolution of Remotely Piloted Aircraft, Routlege, 2016; Ch. Enemark, Armed Drones and the Ethics of War. Military Virtue in a post-heroic age, Routlege 2013; H. Perritt Jr., Eliot O. Sprague, Domesticating Drones: The. Technology, Economics, and Law of Unmanned Aircraft, Routlege 2018. (passim).

535 G.J. Knoops, Drones at Trial. State and Individual (Criminal) Liabilities for Drone Attacks. International Criminal Law Review, Vol. 14, 2014, p. 66.

536 Nilz Melzer, 'Targeted killings in operational law perspective', in: Terry D. Gill and Dieter Fleck (eds.), The Handbook of the International Law of Military Operations (Oxford: Oxford University Press, 2010), p. 287; L. Garlicki, Commentary to Art. 2 of the ECtHR in: L. Garlicki (ed.), Konwencja o Ochronie Praw Człowieka i Podstawowych Wolności, Vol. 1, CH Beck, Warsaw, 2010, p. 73 et seq.

Firearms by Law Enforcement Officials. It states that law enforcement officials shall not use firearms against persons except in self-defense or defense of others against the imminent threat of death or serious injury, to prevent the perpetration of a particularly serious crime involving grave threat to life, to arrest a person presenting such a danger and resisting their authority, or to prevent his or her escape, and only when less extreme means are insufficient to achieve these objectives. In any event, intentional lethal use of firearms may only be made when strictly unavoidable in order to protect life.[537]

The ECtHR partially interpreted the notion of "strictly unavoidable" in its judgment of December 20, 2011, in the *Finogenov and others v. Russia*[538] case. The case was as follows. On October 23, 2002, a group of terrorists belonging to a Chechen separatist movement (more than 40 people) armed with machine guns and explosives took hostages inside the Dubrovka Theater in Moscow. For three days, over nine hundred people were held hostage in the theater. Eighteen suicide bombers were placed in the hall among the hostages. Another group of terrorists occupied the administrative premises of the theater. In the early morning of October 26, 2002, at around 5:30 a.m., Russian special forces pumped unknown narcotic gas into the main room through the building's ventilation system. Both the terrorists and hostages could smell the gas. A few minutes later, when the terrorists in control of the explosives and the suicide bombers in the audience lost consciousness, a special unit stormed the building. Most of the suicide bombers were shot when they were unconscious, others tried to resist but died during the shooting.[539]

The victims and their relatives filed a complaint against Russia with the ECtHR under Art. 2 (the right to life) of the European Convention on Human Rights. The plaintiffs argued that the raid was not an absolute necessity as there were other ways to end the siege, such as negotiations. In addition, the terrorists had no intention of killing the hostages, as they did not detonate their bombs after noticing the gas that was being spread into the theater. Finally, it was admitted that the authorities had failed to plan an adequate rescue operation, which

537 Basic Principles on the Use of Force and Firearms by Law Enforcement Officials, Adopted by the Eighth United Nations Congress on the Prevention of Crime and the Treatment of Offenders, Havana, Cuba, 27 August to 7 September 1990: https://www.ohchr.org/en/professionalinterest/pages/useofforceandfirearms.aspx [access: February 3, 2020].

538 Finogenov and others v Russia (case no. 18299/03 and 27311/03) December 20, 2011: https://hudoc.echr.coe.int/eng#{"itemid":["001-108231"]} [access: February 3, 2020].

539 Ibidem.

resulted in the deaths of 129 civilians and serious bodily and psychological injuries of those who survived the raid.

The ECtHR has three standards justifying the deliberate use of a lethal weapon. First, the operation must meet Art. 2 of the Convention. Second, there is a so-called "level of control" (the extent to which the operation has been monitored or assessed by national legal authorities). Third, an actual analysis of the deliberate use of a lethal weapon should be carried out.[540]

Regarding the first element, the Court found a causal link between the use of gas and the death of the hostages. Therefore Art. 2 applies. As to the second point, the Court emphasized that the national authorities had a certain "margin of appreciation", even if some later decisions taken by the authorities might be called into question. The Court stated that certain aspects of the situation went well beyond the Court's scope of expertise. The authorities had to act under extreme time pressure and their control over the situation was minimal. Therefore, derogation from the absolute requirement of necessity may be justified in some situations. Regarding the third criterion, the Court concluded that the raid did not violate Art. 2 of the Convention because there existed a real, serious, and immediate risk of mass human losses and that the authorities had every reason to believe that a forced intervention was the "lesser evil" given the circumstances. Therefore, the authorities' decision to end negotiations and storm the building did not run counter to Art. 2 of the Convention and the use of gas prior to the raid was not a disproportionate measure.[541]

Thus, when examining whether the lethal use of firearms by state authorities in a particular situation is justified, it is necessary to take into account the availability of information at the time, whether there are other reasonable ways to end a crisis (the requirement of proportionality) and whether possible precautionary measures to prevent additional (foreseeable) damages have been implemented. For *law enforcement drone operations*, the same parameters should apply.[542]

Although there are standards in line with international law that indicate that victims of armed drone attacks (e.g. as part of anti-terrorist operations) have the right to an effective judicial remedy (including the right to redress), the challenges concerning their implementation have been huge so far. In many cases,

540 G.J. Knoops, Drones at Trial. State and Individual (Criminal) Liabilities for Drone Attacks, p. 69.

541 Finogenov and others v Russia (app no. 18299/03 and 27311/03).

542 G.J. Knoops, Drones at Trial. State and Individual (Criminal) Liabilities for Drone Attacks, p. 70.

there is no formal public recognition that an armed drone attack has actually taken place, making it difficult for victims to confirm their victim status and seek any form of justice or compensation.[543]

As rightly noted in several sources, even in the case of targeted killings in the context of a conflict that is a legal state of war, Council of Europe Member States should be aware that their actions may be subject to the control of the European Court of Human Rights[544]. At the moment, there are no ECtHR judgments specifically targeting drone killings. However, we should expect such cases soon, given the scope of the extraterritorial application of the European Convention on Human Rights.[545]

2.3. Protection of privacy and personal data in the EU

2.3.1. GDPR

Data protection is regulated in detail in Regulation (EU) 2016/679 of the European Parliament and of the Council of 27 April 2016 on the protection of natural persons with regard to the processing of personal data and on the free movement of such data, and repealing Directive 95/46/EC.

According to Art. 4 of the GDPR, "personal data" shall mean any information relating to an identified or identifiable natural person (a "data subject"); an identifiable person is one who can be identified, directly or indirectly, in particular by reference to an identification number or to one or more factors specific to his physical, physiological, mental, economic, cultural, or social identity.

Personal data of natural persons must be protected regardless of what technological advances may occur in the future. The Preamble to the GDPR states that "rapid technological developments and globalization have brought new challenges for the protection of personal data. The scale of the collection and sharing of personal data has increased significantly. Technology allows both private companies and public authorities to make use of personal data on an unprecedented scale in order to pursue their activities. Natural persons increasingly make personal information available publicly and globally. Technology has transformed both the economy and social life, and should further facilitate the

543 Q. Eijkman and M. Bakker, Access to an Effective Remedy and Reparations for Civilian Victims of Armed Drone Strikes, p. 297.

544 A. Bodnar, I. Pacho, Targeted Killings (Drone Strikes) and the European Convention on Human Rights, Polish Yearbook of International Law, 2012, p. 208.

545 Ibidem.

free flow of personal data within the Union and the transfer to third countries and international organizations, while ensuring a high level of the protection of personal data" (point 6).

The provisions of the GDPR may apply to UA operators. It all depends on the way one uses a drone and handles the data they record. Collected, stored, and processed data, which includes someone's "personal data" such as their name, e-mail address, or telephone number must comply with the rules of the GDPR[546]. There is no doubt that most drones on the market are capable of collecting large amounts of such data.

GDPR provisions do not apply if the operator uses a drone for their own needs and the images recorded by them do not include data that could be used to identify other people, and this data is not shared further (e.g. online). If, on the other hand, the drone operator wants to share any materials they have recorded on the Internet, then they are obliged to ensure that the photos or videos of any recorded persons are not presented in a way that allows for their identification, or if it does, then their consent has been obtained first. For example, if an operator records a city panorama, and the recording can be used to identify persons or vehicle registration plates, then such activity may violate the provisions of the GDPR. However, if individuals are far away and their faces are blurred, then it is unlikely that such data would be considered personal information.

The provisions of the GDPR apply when a drone records details of a person's physical characteristics, behavior, private life, or professional activity. Such "less obvious" data can only lead to the identification of a specific individual when combined with other data.

In a situation where a drone's software automatically masks and anonymizes personal data, personal data is not processed. However, in the case where data is not anonymized, then it is assumed that it is being processed.

Drones used for taking photos or videos at weddings, during property mapping, filming, or any other commercial activity are subject to the GDPR as the data they collect contains images of people and information that allows for the identification of individuals. Photos used for informational (news) or art purposes are an exception here. Nevertheless, in these cases, consent from the persons shown

546 According to Art. 4 of the GDPR, "personal data" shall mean any information relating to an identified or identifiable natural person ("data subject"); an identifiable person is one who can be identified, directly or indirectly, in particular by reference to an identification number or to one or more factors specific to his physical, physiological, mental, economic, cultural, or social identity.

must be obtained before such content is shared. In addition, the provisions of the GDPR apply when carrying out inspections and monitoring, which are also situations in which people can be marked or identified. This usually does not include monitoring transmission lines or oil rigs, as well as using drones for agricultural purposes as the data they collect rarely includes identifying information. Using drones for mapping and surveying depends on the purpose for which the data is being collected. One should always filter the identifiable characteristics of individuals from geospatial information to protect personal data.

UA used for delivering goods will not be subject to the GDPR as they already have a delivery address as well as the consent of the person who requested the delivery. However, if such UA collect additional information in any way, a permit will be required.[547]

If a given type of UA operation is likely to result in a violation of the rights or freedoms of natural persons (due to its nature, scope, context, and objectives), then pursuant to Art. 35 sec. 1 of the GDPR, the UA operator (as the administrator), prior to the processing, is obliged to carry out a so-called assessment of the impact of the envisaged processing operations on the protection of personal data (*Data Protection Impact Assessment, DPIA*).

The Regulation clearly indicates that a DPIA is required in the case of a systematic and extensive evaluation of personal aspects relating to natural persons which is based on automated processing, including profiling, and on which decisions are based that produce legal effects concerning the natural person or similarly significantly affect the natural person; processing on a large scale of special categories of data; or a systematic monitoring of a publicly accessible area on a large scale. In other cases, such an assessment must be carried out by each entity independently, taking into account, for example, the size, organizational structure, technical capabilities, scope and type of data, or the purpose of their processing.

The DPIA is a process that helps organizations identify and minimize privacy risks and should focus on finding and implementing measures that minimize the risks associated with the violation of privacy rights as much as possible.[548]

547 For more, see A. Konert, M. Sakowska-Baryła, The Impact of the GDPR on the Unmanned Aircraft Sector. Air and Space Law, Vol. 46, Issue 4/5, 2021, p. 517 and A. Konert, M. Sakowska Baryła, Prawne uregulowania w zakresie używania bezzałogowych statków powietrznych przez media, International Journal of Legal Studies 2020, Tom 8, Nr 2.

548 For more, see A. Konert, Przetwarzanie danych osobowych przez operatorów bezzałogowych statków powietrznych, Ius Novum 2/2021.

A high risk of violation of the rights or freedoms of natural persons particularly occurs when recording people entering or leaving religious buildings, medical facilities, police stations, political party headquarters, brothels, etc. Also when flying over the same area regularly or for extended periods of rime.[549]

The GDPR also indicates a number of rights and obligations for operators of UA that are controllers or data processors.

The specific nature of the activities of police and judicial authorities in criminal matters requires differentiated rules on the protection of personal data in order to facilitate its free movement and to ensure appropriate cooperation between Member States in these areas. Therefore, if data is processed by public services for the purposes of crime prevention, investigation, detection, prosecution of prohibited acts, execution of penalties, protection against and prevention of threats to public safety, such data should be subject to a special EU legal act. Namely, Directive (EU) 2016/680 of the European Parliament and of the Council of 27 April 2016 on the protection of natural persons with regard to the processing of personal data by competent authorities for the purposes of the prevention, investigation, detection, or prosecution of criminal offences or the execution of criminal penalties, and on the free movement of such data, and repealing Council Framework Decision 2008/977/JHA (the so-called "Police Directive").[550] This directive aims to protect the right of natural persons to the protection of their personal data while guaranteeing a high level of public security.

2.3.2. Privacy Code of Conduct

In 2018, due to the complexity of the legal framework surrounding UA, a *Privacy Code of Conduct* was published as part of the DroneRules PRO project. The Code[551] is a practical guide to privacy and data protection requirements for drone operators and pilots.[552]

The European Data Protection Board and the Commission encourage the drawing up of codes of conduct to contribute to the proper application of the GDPR, taking account of the specific features of the various processing sectors

---

549 DroneRules PRO, A Privacy Impact Assessment Handbook and Template, p. 7 https://dronerules.eu/assets/files/DRPRO_Data_Protection_Impact_Assessment_EN.pdf [access: January 24, 2020].

550 JOEU L 119 of May 4, 2016, p. 89.

551 https://dronerules.eu/pl/ [access: March 20, 2020].

552 The Code is available at: https://dronerules.eu/assets/files/PCC_DR_final-for-printing_9-November-2018.pdf [access: January 8, 2020].

and the specific needs of micro, small, and medium-sized enterprises. A privacy code of conduct may form the basis of a legally recognized code of conduct pursuant to Art. 40 of the GDPR.

The Code is divided into 5 thematic parts:

- Establishing a legal framework for drone activities;
- Be informed and plan in privacy in mind;
- Act fairly, transparently, and proportionately;
- Treat data diligently;
- Ensure compliance with the GDPR in practice.

Each of these parts has been described in detail and includes a series of practical tips for UA users.

2.3.3. Solutions for the protection of privacy in the new Drone Regulation

Commission Delegated Regulation (EU) 2019/945 and the Commission Implementing Regulation (EU) 2019/947 present a comprehensive system of unified legal regulations on UA in three categories. They are categorized by risk assessment of UA operations for individual types of UA, their weight, and application.

The purpose of introducing these new regulations was, inter alia, privacy protection and protection of personal data while allowing free access to airspace for drones.

While there are no rules on surveillance, the EU has proposed so-called geofencing[553] systems as part of a list of mandatory requirements for drone operations. These systems use GPS and other satellite systems to automatically prevent UA from flying near forbidden areas, such as airports, prisons, or nuclear power plants.

Also, another significant legal change is the introduction of the obligation to register all UA weighing over 250 g (from July 1, 2010) in the open category.

The Preamble to Commission Implementing Regulation (EU) 2019/947 of 24 May 2019 on the rules and procedures for the operation of unmanned indicates that operators of UA should be registered where the operation of an aircraft presents risks to privacy, protection of personal data, security, or the environment (point 14). In addition, UA operators should be subject to registration if they

553 For more, see EASA report. https://www.easa.europa.eu/document-library/general-publications/study-and-recommendations-regarding-unmanned-aircraft-system [access: May 20, 2017].

operate an UA which is equipped with a device capable of collecting personal data. However, this should not be the case when the UA is considered to be a toy within the meaning of Directive 2009/48/EC of the European Parliament and of the Council on the safety of toys (point 16). National registration systems should comply with applicable EU and national laws on privacy and processing of personal data, and information stored in those registrations systems should be easily accessible (point 19).

In the specific category, in order to obtain a permit from the competent authority (CAA) for the performance of an operation, the UA operator must, among others, provide a statement confirming that the intended operation complies with any applicable EU and national rules relating to it, in particular, with regards to privacy, data protection, liability, insurance, security, and environmental protection (Art. 12 sec. 2 letter c). Considering the above, the drone operator should also take into account the provisions of the GDPR. Particularly Art. 35, which requires carrying out a Data Protection Impact Assessment (DPIA) if a given type of operation may result in a high risk of violating the rights or freedoms of natural persons.

Pursuant to Article 15 of the Regulation, when defining UA geographical zones for safety, security, privacy, or environmental reasons, Member States may: (a) prohibit certain or all UA operations, request particular conditions for certain or all UA operations, or request prior operational authorization for certain or all UA operations; (b) subject UA operations to specified environmental standards; (c) allow access only to certain UA classes; (d) allow access only to UA equipped with certain technical features, in particular remote identification systems or geo-awareness systems.

Article 18 requires the competent authority (CAA) to establish and maintain registration systems for UA whose design is subject to certification, as well as for UA operators whose operations may present a risk to safety, security, privacy, and protection of personal data or the environment.

3. Protection of privacy in the US

3.1. The Fourth Amendment to the United States Constitution

On December 15, 1791, the 4th Amendment to the US Constitution entered into force under the Charter of the Rights of the United States of America. It states that "the right of the people to be secure in their persons, houses, papers, and effects, against unreasonable searches and seizures, shall not be violated, and no Warrants shall issue, but upon probable cause, supported by Oath or affirmation, and particularly describing the place to be searched, and the persons or things to be seized."

This amendment puts restrictions on the monitoring of law enforcement activities during a "search". While the Supreme Court has not yet dealt with drones in the context of the 4th Amendment, it has established some important principles that are rooted in legal precedents for the application of the 4th Amendment to surveillance technology.[554]

However, it remains unclear when drone monitoring activities will constitute a "search" under the 4th Amendment and will require a warrant. It seems that this will depend on the following factors: privacy expectations of the public in the context of the area to be searched by monitoring operations (public, private), the technology used, and the duration of the surveillance operation.[555]

3.2. Breaching the right to privacy during UA operations

3.2.1. Violation of the right to privacy as a prohibited act

There is no one tort relating to a breach of the right to privacy. Civil law claims related to breaches of privacy are generally investigated on the basis of the Restatement (Second) of Torts. In the United States, there are four torts related to breaching the right to privacy:

- Publicity that unreasonably places the other in a false light before the public;
- Appropriation of the other's name or likeness;
- Unreasonable intrusion upon the seclusion or solitude of another;
- Unreasonable public disclosure of the other's private life.[556]

When it comes to the improper use of drones, we will most often deal with unlawful interference in the "seclusion" of an individual and his or her private

554 US Supreme Court, Katz v. United States, 389 U.S. 347 (1967); US Supreme Court, Florida v. Riley, 488 U.S. 445, 450 (1989); U.S. Supreme Court, Dow Chem. Co. v. United States, 476 U.S. at 239.

555 Study, p. 131. For more, see: Timothy T. Takahashi, Drones and Privacy, The Columbia Science and Technology Law Review, Vol. 14, 2012. p. 92 et seq. and T. Matiteyahu, Drone Regulations and Fourth Amendment Rights: The Interaction of State Drone Statutes and the Reasonable Expectation of Privacy. Columbia Journal of Law Social Problems, Vol. 48, 2014.

556 RESTATEMENT (SECOND) OF TORTS § 652A (1977). See: also W.L. Prosser, Privacy, California Law Review, 1960, nr 48, p. 384. See: Boon K, Lovelace D.C., The Domestic Use of Unmanned Aerial Vehicles, Oxford University Press, 2014, p. 252.

affairs. According to *§652B of the Restatement (Second) of Torts*, one who intentionally intrudes, physically or otherwise, upon the solitude or seclusion of another or his or her private affairs or concerns, is subject to liability to the other for invasion of his or her privacy, if the intrusion would be highly offensive to a reasonable person. The most important question posed in a liability investigation is whether the intended act of drone use is sufficient to result in an intrusion upon seclusion claim[557]. It is the plaintiff who will have to prove that the drone operator's actions have "highly offended a reasonable person".[558]

Privacy claims related to the use of drones may also concern the public disclosure of private facts. This may be the case when the drone is used to take photos or videos of private entities, which later are made public online or published in traditional media such as newspapers or magazines. The basis for assessing such claims is to examine whether the plaintiff was in a place where one could reasonably expect to maintain their privacy.

3.2.2. *Delict in the form of* trespass. *The limits of the protection of property rights*

Unlawful interference with another's property can make the use of UA burdensome for third parties. This issue concerns both natural persons (e.g. using a drone over a private garden) and legal persons, e.g. managers of national parks (using a drone may interfere with the surrounding natural habitat and pose a potential threat to visitors).

One of the oldest institutions of common law is *trespass* – that is infringement of real estate possession. This tort is regulated in all US states.[559] Compensation for damage caused by the *trespass* tort is possible when the aggrieved party holds the title to the real estate and physical trespass to the real estate has taken place without the consent of the owner.

Following a literal interpretation, if a person intentionally crosses a property line, they become a "trespasser". However, it is unclear whether flying a drone over someone else's property without physically entering it can be considered trespassing.

---

557 Benjamin D. Mathews, Potential Tort Liability for Use of Drone Aircraft, 46 ST. MARY'S L.J. 573, pp. 586–587.

558 See: Shorter v. Retail Credit Co., 251 F. Supp. 329, 332 (D.S.C. 1966).

559 R.L. Rausch, Reframing ROE: Property Over Privacy. Berkeley Journal of Gender, Law & Justice, Vol. 27, 2012.

Restatement Second of Torts clearly distinguishes between a property and the airspace above said property. Section 1588 of the Restatement of Torts sets out the elements of physical trespass to property. One is subject to liability to another for trespass if they intentionally: (1) enter land in the possession of another, or cause an object or a third person to do so, or (2) remain on the land, or (3) fail to remove from the land an object which they are under duty to remove.[560]

A person who intentionally infringes the possession of another person's property may be liable even if they have not caused any property damage.[561] In a situation where the three conditions of liability are met, the aggrieved party has the right to so-called *nominal damages*, *punitive damages*, and *injunctive relief* without the need to prove actual damage to property.[562]

Trespass upon property may also include an intrusion into the ground below or airspace above a property. In Great Britain, as early as in 1815, it was settled in the case of *Pickering v. Rudd* that a balloon flight over someone else's property was not trespass.[563] In the *Bernstein of Leigh v Skyviews & General Ltd* case,[564] the court stated that the landowner's right to the airspace was not absolute and was limited to the amount necessary to exercise their right of ownership.[565]

The flight of an aircraft into the airspace above the land of another person is considered trespass if *the aircraft enters into the immediate reaches of the airspace next to the land* and interferes *substantially with the other's use and enjoyment of the land*.[566]

Courts have long been trying to determine who owns the airspace above property and the extent of such ownership, knowing that the Heaven to Hell[567] doctrine is no longer applicable. In 1946, we saw a precedented ruling in the case of *United States v. Causby*[568], in which a farmer who was living near an airport at

560 RESTATEMENT (SECOND) OF TORTS § 158 (AM. LAW INST. 1979).

561 Dougherty v. Stepp, 18 N.C. 371, 372 (1835).

562 H. Perritt Jr., i E. Sprague, Law Abiding Drones. Columbia Scientific & Technology Review, Vol. 16, 2015, p. 439.

563 Pickering v Rudd (1815) 4 Camp 219.

564 [1978] QB 479.

565 See: W. Rannells, Aerial Navigation in the Law of Trespass, St. Louis L. Rev. 1919, Issue 4, p. 205.

566 RESTATEMENT (SECOND) OF TORTS § 159 (2) (AM. LAW INST. 1979).

567 C. L. Bouvé, Private Ownership of Airspace, Air Law Review 1930), Issue 1, p. 246 et seq.

568 328 U.S. 256 (1946).

which US military aircraft operated at low altitudes (80 feet) above his property suffered property damage from such flights.[569]

The Supreme Court ruled that the airspace that Congress had designated as public space is airspace above the minimum safe altitude (MSA) and outlined two key principles for airspace below the MSA. The Court stated that property owners have "exclusive control of the immediate reaches of the enveloping atmosphere" and that "the landowner owns at least as much of the space above the ground as they can occupy or use in connection with the land."[570] It also added that the property owner, if these conditions are met, is entitled to claim for damages in the event of any interference with their property. As a result, a plaintiff may have a valid claim for trespass to airspace if an airplane is flying at low altitude. Therefore, the Supreme Court ruled in favor of the farmer. However, it did not finally decide exactly where the limit of ownership of the airspace over the property was. In other words, it did not define the concept of "immediate reach" of the surrounding airspace. It merely stated that the Heaven to Hell doctrine no longer applied and that the airspace had become a "public highway" *("[t] he air is a public highway")*. The Supreme Court ruled that most flights over private property should not be considered trespass upon property because the airspace is "part of the public domain", except for the airspace in the immediate reach of the landlord's property.[571]

When analyzing this ruling, one can say that the Court's findings are prophetic observations regarding the confluence of technological innovation and law. The Court stated that if railroad tracks had been erected over the claimant's property at the exact height at which the planes were flying, there would have been no doubt that a partial seizure of the property had taken place, even if none of the elements of the structure would have been anchored to the claimant's land. This statement made over 70 years ago can be applied to the present day. A "drone highway" at a low altitude above private property would constitute an unjustified takeover of some part of the private property.

Congress amended the Federal Aviation Act of 1958[572] by creating a new definition of "navigable airspace", which means airspace at and above the minimum flight altitudes prescribed by the Federal Aviation Act of 1958, including airspace

---

569 Causbys' chickens were so frightened by the noise of passing planes that they died after hitting the walls of buildings they were in.

570 Ibidem.

571 United States v. Causby, 328 U.S. 256 (1946), 266.

572 Pub.L. No. 85-726, 72 Stat. 731.

needed for safe takeoff and landing.[573] An airplane flying over private property does not trespass upon property as long as it remains above the "minimum safe altitude" which Congress says is 500 feet or more.[574]

In 1962, the Supreme Court had a tough challenge to face in the case of *Griggs v. Allegheny County*.[575] It had to answer the question of whether there had been trespass upon private property during takeoffs and landings of planes over the owner's property over which an approach path was located. The takeoffs and landings were carried out below 500 feet. However, the airspace they were taking place in was not off limits within the meaning of the Federal Aviation Act of 1958. The Court found that, in such a situation, an infringement of the property right had in fact taken place in the form of "taking over some part of private property".[576]

In the following years, there was a trend among both state legislators and courts to protect aircraft operators from liability for infringement of property rights, unless the aircraft "significantly interfered" with the owner's enjoyment of their property. Some courts have even gone a step further, declaring that mere interference with regular enjoyment or possession was not enough. The owner had to demonstrate a significant interference with actual land use, even in cases where the aircraft was flying below the FAA regulated altitude.[577]

The way people perceive private airspace changed as the use of drones became more common. A question arose again – who owns the airspace above a property? And up to what height?[578]

The principle of "minimum safe altitude" is being modified in the case of UA. The rules limiting the maximum flight altitude for drones to 500 feet, proposed by the FAA, may not find backing. In most cases, UA fly below this altitude, e.g. at 50 feet. On the other hand, the greater the distance between a flying object and someone's land, the more difficult it is for the injured party to prove that the aircraft was in "direct reach of property ownership". Distances greater than

573 49 U.S.C. § 1301 (26) (1976).

574 Federal Aviation Act of 1958, Pub. L. No. 85-726, § 101(24), 72 Stat. 731.

575 369 U.S. 84 (1962).

576 369 U.S. 84 (1962), 88–89.

577 Smart v. City of Los Angeles, 112 Cal. App. 3d 232, 237 (1980); Drennen v. County of Ventura, 38 Cal. App. 3d 84, 87–88 (1974); Pueblo of Sandia ex rel. Chaves v. Smith, 497 F.2d 1043, 1046 (10th Cir. 1974).

578 J. Nicas, Drones Boom Raises New Question: Who Owns Your Airspace?, WALL STREET J. (May 13, 2015, 12:43): https://www.wsj.com/articles/drones-boom-raises-new-question-who-owns-your-airspace-1431535417 [access: October 11, 2019].

50 feet are unlikely to be interpreted as being "within the immediate reach of property".[579]

For aircraft operating between 50 and 500 ft, determining whether the aircraft is within the immediate reach of property will be based on the disruption the aircraft is actually causing to the enjoyment of the property. Unlike chickens' suicidal reactions to loud noise from military airplanes or strong winds from large planes flying low over the ground, drones do not cause the same physical annoyance and disturbance. They are relatively quiet, small, and almost undetectable.[580]

Assessing the severity of damages caused by UA requires a different level of consideration and takes different factors into account. The biggest threat related to the use of UA is not noise, but rather capturing audio or video data without consent or even without awareness.

First of all, we should consider whether altitude limits should apply here at all? UA can hover or fly at altitudes reaching hundreds of feet and still have the ability to record and capture data of people and objects on the ground. In other words, they act as a platform enabling visual observation (e.g. Wi-Fi sniffers, license plate readers, night vision cameras, facial recognition technology and other biometric devices, high-power telephoto lenses).[581]

Until recently, airspace below 500 feet was largely in the hands of state regulation. As a result, states can legally assign an airspace column to each property owner[582]. From June 2015, the state of Nevada allowed a landowner to bring a lawsuit against a UA operator who was to fly less than 250 feet above their property without a permit, if warned once[583]. Similarly, Oregon law also allows for civil lawsuits but the altitude requirement is less than 400 feet. In California, drones cannot fly at altitudes below 350 feet (approx. 107 m). This altitude has

579 RESTATEMENT (SECOND) OF TORTS § 159 cmt. l (AM. LAW INST. 1979).

580 H. Farber, Keep Out! The Efficacy of Trespass Nuisance and Privacy Torts as Applied to Drones. Georgia State University Law Review, Vol. 33, 2017, p. 387. See: F.E. Castillo-Ruiz, Property and Privacy Issues Arising from the Integration of Civil and Commercial Drones Into the Domestic Airspace of the United States. Annals of Air and Space Law, Vol. 40, 2015 and R.H. Gruber, Commercial Drones and Privacy: Can We Trust States with Drone Federalism. Richmond Journal of Law Technology, Vol. 21, Issue 4, 2014.

581 H. Farber, Keep Out! The Efficacy of Trespass Nuisance and Privacy Torts as Applied to Drones, p. 388.

582 Ibidem, p. 389.

583 Assemb. B. 239, 78th Leg., Reg. Sess. (Nev. 2015).

been found to be sufficient to protect against illegal tracking of private life of natural persons with the use of some of the devices mentioned earlier.

Currently, the FAA has set new rules, taking airspace below 500 feet under its jurisdiction, and taking into account the fact that UA can fly almost anywhere and the increasing pressure that is being exerted on it to integrate drones into national airspace. According to a new interpretation by the FAA, so-called "navigable airspace" includes all airspace outside of any enclosure. This space can be found anywhere from the ground up. Therefore, it can also be found in a private garden, etc. With this stance, the FAA essentially eliminated the concept of "immediate reach of the surrounding airspace" created by the US Supreme Court. Anyone using a UA in accordance with FAA rules has the right to fly in all such navigable airspaces. It is a federal offense to cause any disruptions to the flight of an aircraft and the FAA has classified UA as aircraft. Thus, private property owners and business owners must not prevent the use of drones in airspace, even if the airspace concerned is private property.

Should courts then treat navigable airspace as public in the same way they do with public highways? Does this also mean that if someone, while operating in navigable airspace, is simultaneously observing and recording somebody on the ground, they have the same right to do so as if they were at a public vantage point?

The claim that all airspace is "navigable" can hamper, if not eliminate, the right to enjoyment of property. In this way, anyone who builds a fence or a garage violates federally controlled airspace.

Federal law provides that the US Government has sole sovereignty over US airspace. The FAA develops plans and policies for the use of navigable airspace. Accepting the FAA's authority over all airspace raises serious concerns regarding property rights and so-called *air rights*, and could signal the end of private airspace. The owner retains the right to decide who can enter their garden, but not the airspace one meter above the ground. Taking these regulations into account, will a neighbor be able to say that they are using public airspace when placing a swing so that only its base stays on their property but all other elements use the airspace above a neighbor's garden? Is it possible to exercise rulership only over the ground without interfering with the airspace above that ground? The answer to these questions seems obvious. The FAA's interpretation leads to paradoxical situations.

Fortunately, the FAA recognizes that while it is the only authority that has the right to ensure security in US airspace, state and local authorities should take steps to strengthen privacy protection. The FAA further emphasizes that it does not replace or amend state and local privacy laws as the agency does not regulate privacy issues. And indeed, there is no exclusion clause in the latest *small UA* regulations.[584]

Regulations vary from state to state, but generally a landowner has the right to damage someone else's property to protect himself should they be in danger, or reasonably believes that they are in danger. Proportionality is key here. Some states have adopted the so-called "*Castle Doctrine*", which allows property owners to protect themselves and their property when threatened, including by using firearms.

3.2.3. Delict in the form of a nuisance

In US law, the institution of a *nuisance* supports the protection of privacy. A nuisance constitutes any activities conducted on neighboring land, the effects of which impact the owner of another property. This interpretation resembles that of indirect immissions in Poland[585]. Traditionally, a claimant is entitled to compensation should there be an "unjustified" amount of damages resulting from such activities. The balancing of interests between the parties involved does not apply here.

A delict in the form of a *nuisance* may take two forms: either the violation of private or public interests. Establishing liability for a *private* nuisance requires unjustified interference with the use and enjoyment of one's own land. On the contrary, a *public* nuisance requires that the damage concerns at least one person. That is, the damage must be "public", having a negative effect on public health or public safety.[586]

Only the person whose right to the property has been infringed may come forward with a claim. Therefore, they must hold the legal title to a property (not necessarily a title deed)[587]. Behavior such as tracking, harassment, and insistent

---

584 The US Court of Appeals for the DC Circuit is currently hearing the case against the FAA. According to the plaintiff, the FAA is responsible for drafting of a comprehensive plan to integrate drones with the US airspace and that it is responsible for ensuring safety in the airspace, including ensuring the protection of privacy. See: Brief for Petitioner at 2, Elec. information on privacy Ctr. against the FAA, no. 15-1075: https://epic.org/privacy/drones/epicvfaa/1581988-FAA-Brief.pdf [access: October 11, 2019].

585 This is also the case with J. Sieńczyło-Chlabicz, Naruszenie prywatności, p. 311.

586 V. Sehrawat, Liability Issue of Domestic Drones. Santa Clara High Technology Law Journal, Vol. 35, No. 1, November 2018, p. 125. See: F.E. Castillo-Ruiz, Property and Privacy Issues Arising from the Integration of Civil and Commercial Drones Into the Domestic Airspace of the United States.

587 J. Sieńczyło-Chlabicz, Naruszenie prywatności, p. 312.

telephone calls have been considered *nuisances*. They all seem to constitute the one same element – an annoyance for the claimant. Taking a single photo is not a *nuisance*[588], but a long-term observation from the sky combined with the capturing of several pictures of a video undoubtedly is.[589]

In 1917, in the case of *Thoenebe v. Mosby*, the court found that running a company that was open in the late hours of the day, which was visited by many cars and which resulted in noise pollution was not a *nuisance*, as the presence of cars on roads, including during the night, was something rather normal. In light of this, can we assume that courts will accept any inconveniences caused by drones in the 21st century as "*noise of progress*"?[590] It seems that courts will be forced to examine whether a given tort in the form of a *nuisance* has a tangible, significant, and troublesome impact on the aggrieved party.

3.2.4. Shooting down UA

Shooting down a drone may expose the property owner to civil and criminal liability. Liability under state tort law could be considerable. Some drones cost tens of thousands of dollars and carry payloads that cost the same or even more. Firing a firearm in violation of firearms regulations may expose the shooter to criminal liability and, if there is an injured party, to civil liability. If the drone crashed, injured someone, or caused damage to property, the shooter could face liability to the injured party and to the drone owner. Under 18 U.S.C. § 32, the sentence may include a fine or imprisonment of up to 20 years.

Shooting down a drone is usually related to issues such as privacy violation, violation of property rights, right to self-help, or self-defense against unlawful interference.[591]

In 2014, a drone operator filed a lawsuit in a small claims court in California for compensation from a neighbor for shooting down a drone while it flying over the operator's family's property. The court found that the defendant acted unreasonably. Regardless of whether it may have been his property or not, the court awarded the drone operator damages of $850 for their losses. In this case, it was noted that the FAA had classified drones as "airplanes", which would mean

---

588 Bernstein of Leigh v Skyviews & General Ltd [1978] QB 479 cited in: J. Sieńczyło-Chlabicz, Naruszenie prywatności, p. 312.

589 Ibidem.

590 V. Sehrawat, Liability Issue of Domestic Drones, p. 126.

591 D.M. Benjamin, Potential Tort Liability for Use of Drone Aircraft. St. Mary's Law Journal, Vol. 46, 2015, p. 573

that they would be subject to the same restrictions as other types of aircraft. This would make shooting down a drone a federal crime.[592]

In 2015, a homeowner in Kentucky was arrested for shooting down a civilian drone that flew over his property. He said it violated his family's privacy, as the homeowner's daughters were sunbathing in the garden. The judge rejected the claimant's allegations, stating that the drone was hovering above people's property, that this constituted an invasion of privacy and that the homeowner had the right to shoot the drone down.[593]

In 2014, in Deer Trail, Colorado, regulations were issued that would allow for the issuing of permits for hunting down drones. In response to this, the FAA issued a statement saying, "shooting at an UA could result in criminal or civil liability, just as would firing at a manned airplane."[594]

In the 2017 case of *Boggs v. Meredith*[595], Boggs filed a lawsuit in a federal court in Kentucky, seeking $1,500 for damage incurred by their drone. To justify jurisdiction in federal rather than state court, Boggs argued that the drone was flying in federal airspace and not over Meredith's property. However, if the drone had been above Meredith's property, he could have had the right under tort law to destroy the drone if "the actor's conduct [shooting down the UA] was, or reasonably believed to be, necessary to protect the actor's land... and the harm inflicted [must] not [be] unreasonable as compared with the harm threatened." Ultimately, the court dismissed the case on the basis of jurisdiction without deciding whether the drone was in federal airspace or on Meredith's property.[596]

There are other ways to destroy a drone without the use of firearms, such as by having a trained animal or through the use of geofencing technology.[597]

---

592 Scott Carr, Samuel L. Felker, Baker Donelson Matthew Grosack, Connie A. Lahn, DRONE ON! Emerging Legal Issues for Commercial Use of Unmanned Aerial Vehicles (UAVs): Will You and Your Clients Be Ready for the Invasion of American Airspace?, ABA Section of Litigation – Environmental, Mass Torts and Products Liability Litigation Committees joint CLE, January 2016.

593 Ibidem.

594 A. M. Froomkin and P. Z. Colangelo, Self-Defense Against Robots and Drones. Connecticut Law Review, Vol. 48, Issue 1, 2015.

595 Boggs v. Meredith, No. 3:16-cv-00006-DJH (W.D. Ky. 2016): https://cases.justia.com/federal/district-courts/kentucky/kywdce/3:2016cv00006/96944/20/0.pdf?ts=1490444322 [access: March 26, 2019].

596 Ibidem.

597 E. Ackerman, Dutch Police Training Eagles to Take Down Drones, IEEE Spectrum, 1 Feb. 2016: http://spectrum.ieee.org/automaton/robotics/drones/dutch-police-train

What's more, property owners have the option of self-defense. In tort law, self-help should be privileged where it is *reasonable*. In the case of drones, there is uncertainty concerning options and intentions, which may make it difficult to determine whether the action was reasonable. Various groups have postulated for states to draft guidelines by enacting self-defense laws against the unlawful use of drones, suggesting that drones are used to monitor people and thus invade their privacy, unless a UA clearly signals that it does not do this[598]. The legislator could order UA operators to give bystanders some sort of a signal whenever video or audio recording takes place, or even impose such an obligation on UA manufacturers. However, given the current dimensions of today's audio and video recording equipment, and considering their long-distance recording capabilities, as well as future technological development, this solution seems rather pointless.

Property owners also have certain options and can act under various state UA laws. At least 13 states have enacted laws restricting drone surveillance of people without their consent, and most states have regulated privacy rights as well.

3.2.5. State law

The FAA has taken the position that federal UA regulations take precedence over all state and local laws, while giving states the opportunity to regulate state and local government issues – including land use, zoning, privacy, misdemeanor, and *law enforcement*. Many states have passed laws that address privacy and UA.

In 2015, the Attorney General noted that states were free to pass laws regulating privacy and property issues related to the use of drones.[599]

One of the biggest concerns about drones is their use by law enforcement agencies (LEA). With privacy and property rights in mind, some states initially banned such authorities from using UA under any circumstances. For example, Virginia temporarily banned using UA except in emergency situations, such as search and rescue operations and training purposes[600]. In 2018, 18 states (Florida, Vermont, Alaska, Illinois, Idaho, Indiana, Iowa, Maine, Montana,

---

ing-eagles-to-take-down-drones [access: March 29, 2019] and G. S. McNeal, Drones & the Future of Aerial Surveillance, 84 Geo. Wash. L. Rev. 354, 394 n. 214 2016.

598 V. Sehrawat,. Liability Issue of Domestic Drones. p. 130.

599 Op. Att'y Gen., Opinion No. 14-051 (Oct. 9, 2014).

600 A. Bohm, Status of Domestic Drone Legislation in the States, ACLU (Feb. 15, 2013), https://www.aclu.org/blog/technology-and-liberty/status-domestic-drone-legislation-states [access: March 1, 2019].

Nevada, North Carolina, North Dakota, Oregon, Tennessee, Texas, Utah, Virginia, and Wisconsin) had regulations that required law enforcement to obtain a court order before using UA.

In addition, states have enacted a number of measures prohibiting the use of UA to spy on, harass, or persecute others. For example, many states had regulations from before drones became so widespread which prohibited photographing or recording other people who might be naked or wearing only underwear[601]. In most cases, these provisions have remained the same. However, in a few cases, states have changed their laws to include crimes committed with the use of UA (e.g. Louisiana[602]). In some states, like Arkansas[603], a new crime of "video voyeurism" was defined. In other states (Mississippi), it is a criminal offense to simply enter someone else's property and use UA to record people without their consent.[604] In Michigan, people who are under the Sex Offender Register are automatically prohibited from using UA.[605]

601 Mich. Comp. Laws Ann. § 750.539j: http://www.legislature.mi.gov/(S(g3r4xyjlnyfbd0egsrdyahua))/mileg.aspx?page=GetObject&objectname=mcl-750-539j [access: March 01, 2019]; Mich. Comp. Laws Ann. § 259.322(1) 2006 https://law.justia.com/codes/michigan/2006/mcl-chap330/mcl-330-1424.html [access: March 1, 2019].

602 LA Rev Stat § 14:283.1 (2016). §283.1. Voyeurism; penalties. A. Voyeurism is the viewing, observing, spying upon, or invading the privacy of a person by looking or using an unmanned aircraft system to look through the doors, windows, or other openings of a private residence without the consent of the victim who has a reasonable expectation of privacy for the purpose of arousing or gratifying the sexual desires of the offender. B.(1) Whoever commits the crime of voyeurism, upon a first conviction, shall be fined not more than five hundred dollars, imprisoned for not more than six months, or both. (2) Upon a second or subsequent conviction, the offender shall be fined not more than one thousand dollars, imprisoned with or without hard labor for not more than one year, or both. C. For purposes of this Section, "unmanned aircraft system" means an unmanned, powered aircraft that does not carry a human operator, can be autonomous or remotely piloted or operated, and can be expendable or recoverable.(Acts 2004, No. 888, §1; Acts 2016, No. 635, §1).

603 Ark. Code Ann. § 5-16- 101(a) 2010: https://law.justia.com/codes/arkansas/2010/title-5/subtitle-2/chapter-16/5-16-101/ [access: March 1, 2019].

604 Miss. Code Ann. § 97-29-61(1)(a) 2013: https://law.justia.com/codes/mississippi/2013/title-97/chapter-29/in-general/section-97-29-61/ (dostęp: March 1, 2019).

605 Mich., Comp. Law, Ann., § 259.322 (4), 2006: https://law.justia.com/codes/michigan/2006/mcl-chap330/mcl-330-1424.html [access: March 1, 2019]. See: K.L. Donohue, A Tale of Two Sovereigns: Federal and State Use and Regulation of Unmanned Aircraft Systems, in: K. P. Valavanis, and G. J. Vachtsevanos (eds.), Handbook of Unmanned Aerial Vehicles, Springer International Publishing, 2018, p. 15.

Conclusions

The main research problem was the legal qualification of drones, which can be perceived in different ways: either as aircraft or as robots. It is important to highlight the confirmed research thesis that a new "branch of law" is emerging, i.e. the Drone law. It is based on the legal approach that UA is considered not as a new type of aircraft, but rather as a new type of device capable of floating in the air, however, in a fundamentally different way from the existing concept of an aircraft. An analysis of regulations and potential scenarios led to the conclusion that it is impossible to unequivocally qualify drones as aircraft or, more broadly, that it is necessary to create a new category in aviation law that would apply to this new technology.

Although public law defines UAVs precisely as aircraft to which the rules resulting from aviation law often apply, there are also specific regulations that go beyond the scope of this area of law. Meanwhile, qualifying drones to one or the other category is of great importance, including from the point of view of private law, especially civil liability. Also from the perspective of public law, the classification of the UA as an aircraft determines the direction of development of legal regulations applicable to dynamically developing technology. Although the starting point in the research was the recognition of the UA as an aircraft, it should be stated that we are dealing with a new type of activity, the central element of which is the UA system. The assumed development of this new technology is aimed at enabling operations beyond visual light of sight, while ensuring a certain degree of automation in the management of the movement of this type of devices. So while the first regulations related to the use of UAs are those that are part of the aviation law, it should be expected that these regulations – along with the development of unmanned aviation – will evolve toward separation from aviation law, becoming part of the new field that is becoming, and in the future, it will probably be the Drone law. This discovery was not preceded by any analogous research works at the national level, but it is in line with the research trends at the European and international level.

As with many other technological advancements, policymakers will need time to understand the scope of UA operations and the liabilities that may result from them. They must be very careful in their actions so as to not hinder innovation by introducing measures that overburden manufacturers when operators (or their insurers) may be better prepared to bear the risk. In the case of drones, as with any new technology, there are many challenges that require discussion and development of solutions. The integration of unmanned aerial vehicles with the manned aviation system is one of the most important challenges of the future of aviation and requires the development of regulations regulating issues related to their use.

Safety regulations are a key element in maintaining the current level of safety in civil aviation. The methods for regulating aviation safety reflect the changes that have taken place over decades in understanding what flight operation safety is and how it can be ensured. Safety is more than just reliable equipment (technical factors) or the way people interact (human factors) – it is also about how regulators and aviation organizations manage the issue of safety at national (regional) and organizational levels. Aviation safety regulations are not confined to just the traditional approach in defining new and more detailed requirements sanctioned by administrative or criminal regulations. They also require systemic management of operational safety at organizational and national levels, which is achieved, for example, by reporting and analyzing aviation incidents. Moreover, we have seen ongoing changes in the approach to regulating requirements for organizations, personnel, or equipment (concerning both its design and production). Traditional regulations, which consist of very detailed descriptions of technical requirements, are being abandoned in favor of regulations that focus on specific goals. The methods by which these goals must be achieved and their subsequent assessment is left up to their addressees or to aviation authorities. What's more, typical administrative regulations are becoming increasingly differentiated depending on the risk associated with a given type of activity. Trends that have emerged over the past several years in the area of aviation safety have contributed to the development of regulations for an entirely new field of aviation – UA operations. However, a fundamental question arises – are these operations just a new type of activity within aviation as we know it? Or are they a completely new category of activity, which requires its own separate regulations?

Time seems crucial in attempting to answer this question. In the **short-term perspective**, it was (and still is) natural to recognize UA as regular aircraft. Consequently, we have the desire to subject both types to the same legal regime built around the main definition of aviation law – the definition of what constitutes an aircraft. However, unmanned and manned aircraft will never meet the same safety requirements since the means in which operational safety is ensured is different for each. One of the key elements of ensuring safety in manned aviation operations is the fact that there is crew on board the aircraft. The technical possibility of operating an aircraft by having its "crew" in a different location gives rise to a number of new challenges. We must look for solutions to overcome these challenges, and these can be found in new technology. How do we ensure reliable data transfer between a control station and an UA? How do we provide UA pilots with situational awareness similar to that of a traditional aircraft pilot? These two fundamental issues will undoubtedly influence the development of the UA sector, including the development of safety requirements within it. Regulators will not be able to specify these requirements without sufficiently mature technical and technological solutions. It will be impossible to have widespread use of UA technology, even just for commercial purposes, without determining the direction for the development of key technologies – including those related to ensuring reliable communications between a pilot and a UA (C2link), traffic detection systems, or collision avoidance systems (DAA). The commercial applications of UA are undoubtedly associated with the possibility of flying beyond an operator's visual line of sight. It is difficult to imagine the economic profitability of parcel delivery without BVLOS operations. Since traditional rules for air traffic management are inadequate for UA sector operations, any advancement on the extensive use of such operations requires the development of a UA traffic management concept, the development of which will be extremely important in the upcoming years. As most available studies indicate, today's concepts are aimed at creating a UTM system based on infrastructure created for a completely different purpose – namely, ICT infrastructure. The assumption is that communications between UA and their operators, as well as the exchange of data between airspace users and the appropriate services, can take place in a completely different manner than in the case of manned aviation. It must be noted that the effectiveness of such a system requires far-reaching automation. In the **long-term perspective**, the direction for the development of the UA sector advocates toward the idea that regulations for this type of activity, including safety regulations, should be created independently or in parallel with aviation law. This is due to the nature of unmanned aviation, which is a completely different type of activity than regular manned flights that usually take off and land at airports in order to transport passengers or cargo.

This difference seems to be reflected in Art. 8 of the Chicago Convention, which states that, when determining the rules for "pilotless aircraft" operations, countries must ensure a certain level of operational control so that the safety of civil aviation is not jeopardized – as through UA flights were not a part of "civil aviation". On a side note, it seems that we should review the traditional division into state and civil aviation, which is rooted precisely in the Chicago Convention, in the case of unmanned aviation. With the broad scope of what constitutes state aviation and the wide-ranging possibilities of exploiting UA in public activities, there is a chance that a significant part of unmanned aviation operations will not be regulated in a manner that adequately reflects their associated risks.

For example, if a national legislator decides not to subject public service UA operations to EU rules (which is an option under EU law), then what safety rules should these operations fall under? And what if their required level of safety is different than that applicable to "civilian" UA?

It seems that unmanned aviation requires a series of new, well-defined regulations; including provisions regulating the principles of UA traffic management. UA traffic will most likely take place at very low altitudes and in urban zones, and must take place at a massive scale in order to be profitable. This will require creating a new traffic management system from scratch. It is difficult to imagine such a system not being based on electronic registration or remote UA identification. Of course, any activity related to the development of unmanned aviation must ensure the current level of safety at the minimum. Therefore, changes to manned aviation safety regulations are inevitable. Even organization of airspace and air traffic management must be altered, so the development of UA regulations will naturally force changes in manned aviation.

In the **mid-term perspective**, UA safety regulations will be a type of "mix" between traditional aviation regulations and an array of new solutions. Whether these will be part of existing safety regulations (and thus aviation law) or become a completely new and separate field – **drone law** – is a different matter.

An analysis of the evolution of UA safety regulations at national, EU, and international levels seems to confirm the above thesis. A given starting point usually determines which solutions are proposed first – if we formally recognize UA as aircraft, then these should meet all the requirements for aircraft and aircraft operations. However, this is not possible in practice. Safety regulations are (mostly) based on the assumption that there is a crew on board an aircraft. Therefore, the initial stage of development of UA regulations allowed them to operate while not necessarily abiding to all applicable rules, while also assuming the segregation of airspace. In the following stages, legislators created detailed regulations applying only to UA. These were usually limited to UA operations within an operator's visual line of sight. These regulations were developed at national levels, as they are of local importance only. Nevertheless, compliance with these rules is not that obvious. Traditional aviation traffic management systems are not prepared for the appearance of a large number of users usually operating at altitudes so low that they are practically excluded from manned aviation. However, the locality of UA operations does not limit the development of safety regulations solely to national solutions. Actually, the situation is quite the opposite. We have observed a visible trend toward the unification of UA operation regulations at a supranational level. However, unification activities are not so obvious, as international organizations responsible for the development of aviation safety regulations mainly focus on the safety of international operations. In practice, local operations are the most important, which result from the degree of technological development of the UA sector. Therefore, the first regulations that apply to UA had to be and were created at national and regional levels. Nonetheless, the process of creating these regulations is not simple, as evidenced in the process of developing regulations at national and EU levels. Usually, the first national regulations to appear were limited to VLOS operations. Working out the rules for BVLOS operations is a much more complex task. The biggest challenge for regulators is finding a compromise between not hampering the development of UA technology and maintaining appropriate levels of safety. The way we assess levels of safety of UA activity is extremely important here. It must be noted that existing rules for reporting and analyzing incidents in aviation are focused on the safety of manned aviation. Thus, reports mainly concern cases where flight crews described potentially dangerous UA sightings. At the same time, there is no obligation to report dangerous incidents involving only UA. As a consequence, we lack data on the basis of which we could assess the safety of this type of activity. We only have access to fragmentary data, which show that technical issues, such as loss of control, are the most common cause in dangerous incidents involving UA. Regulators must be very cautious here, since safety of people on the ground, other airspace users, and critical infrastructure should always be a priority. The best example of such regulator precaution is EASA's idea to amend EU rules, which should have already entered into force, but were postponed after an accident involving a test UA that crashed in close vicinity to a kindergarten.

It is possible to base new UA regulations on certain approaches developed over the years for manned aviation safety regulations. These regulations should, above all, be proportionate. They can and should be differentiated depending on the risk associated with a given operation. However, unlike in the case of traditional safety regulations, for which an aircraft has always been the starting point, UA safety regulations focus more on operations themselves. As of today, there are no commonly accepted standards for designing and manufacturing UA. **An unmanned aircraft is more of a system in which an aircraft (understood as a device capable of sustained flight) is just one of its elements.** The aircraft maintains flight despite lacking a crew on board and therefore – as a system – it must consist of other critical elements such as a remote-control system or traffic detection and avoidance systems. These elements also need to be subject to strict requirements. Unfortunately, legal regulations are always one step behind when it comes to novel technology.

Determining these requirements is not the only challenge here. It is also necessary to develop rules for UA traffic organization and to review the principles of manned aviation traffic and airspace organization.

However, since certain regulatory solutions have proven to be successful in manned aviation, it seems like a good idea to use them as the basis for developing solutions for unmanned aviation. The best example of this are *performance-based regulations*. The key elements in these regulations rely on data that confirms the achievement of a set of goals and the adopted method for such confirmation.

And since collecting and analyzing information in terms of risks and their potential impact on safety are the foundation of manned aviation's approach to systematic safety management, it is worth adopting a similar approach in the case of unmanned aviation. This also requires promoting a culture of safety among UA operators, including raising legal awareness and creating legal solutions to support this ever-growing social group.

This publication also analyzes regulations (national and international, including European) in the field of civil liability for damages caused by UA. Due to the existence of many types of drones, operations, places of operation, a large number of complicated factual circumstances, as well as the problem of their legal qualification, it turns out that the subjective scope can be quite broad since the potential circle of liable entities includes drone operators who are air carriers, drone operators who are not air carriers, drone pilots, State Treasuries (state operations), aviation authorities (CAA) issuing permits, air traffic controllers, and agencies providing air traffic services. The circle of entities can become even broader if we begin considering the U-space concept, smart cities, or autonomous operations, the latter of which can take place without human intervention thanks to the use of complex algorithms.

An issue that required a separate analysis is liability for damages caused by autonomous drones (operating completely without human supervision). It is difficult to obtain public acceptance for such operations in the absence of standardized technical solutions that would guarantee operational safety in all conditions and considering the current level of development of this technology. We can observe a similar phenomenon in the case of autonomous vehicles. In order to sell the autonomous technology idea to the public, it is first necessary to establish and then maintain the highest possible safety and security standards. To ensure such standards, it becomes necessary to develop technological infrastructure (including operation management systems), program interactions between such infrastructure and drones, organize the registration and monitoring of operations, design anti-drone systems, install collision avoidance systems, and, most importantly – from the point of view of liability – define ethical issues (transfer of liability from person to machine).

The widespread availability of advanced technology in UA operations not only concerns the right to privacy and the protection of property rights, but also makes problems related to these issues very complex. Violation of people's rights may take place even without having a drone trespass onto someone else's property, as it could be recording video or audio data while flying over, e.g., a neighbor's garden.

The mere presence of a drone in a park could pose a threat to the privacy of those around it. In addition, the risk is even higher if the drone is equipped with a camera or other devices that collect data.

In many cases, data subjects would not be aware of the drone's presence or of the fact that it may be processing their personal data. Even if a given person is aware of the presence of a UA, they are still deprived of the knowledge of whether there is any data processing equipment onboard, or who is collecting what sort of data and for what purpose[606]. Such situations lead to the feeling of being watched or invigilated, imposing restrictions on civil liberties and rights under what is known as the "*chilling effect*".[607]

The degree of impact of the use of drones on the privacy of individuals depends on a multitude of factors, including the purpose for which the drone is being used, by whom, where, the scope and type of personal data being collected (images or audio of natural persons and their private property), and how this data is then used or processed.

When using UA, the right to respect private life, protected by international public law and especially by human rights law, will always remain valid, as evidenced in Art. 8 sec. 1 of the European Convention on Human Rights and Art. 7 of the Charter of Fundamental Rights (and Art. 47 of the Polish Constitution,). Also, the right to the protection of personal data is laid down in Art. 8 sec. 1 of the Charter (and Art. 51 of the Constitution in Poland). The right to privacy is guaranteed in international, European, and national law. Legal instruments to protect the right to privacy have been significantly developed at all three

606 Opinion 01/2015, op.cit, p. 7.

607 For more on the so-called "chilling effect", see Rachel L. Finn, David Wright and Anna Donovan (Trilateral Research & Consulting, LLP), Laura Jacques and Paul De Hert (Vrije Universiteit Brussel), Privacy, data protection and ethical risks in civil RPAS operations, 7 November 2014, in: http://ec.europa.eu/DocsRoom/documents/7662 [access: June 9, 2020].

levels – at an international level, it is possible to seek redress before the ECtHR for violation of Art. 2 (right to life) and 8 (right to private life) of the European Convention for the Protection of Human Rights and Fundamental Freedoms. At a European level, general principles for the protection of personal data (GDPR) have been enacted (in terms of public law) and may apply to drone operators. On the other hand, the new Drone Regulations (Delegated and Implementing Regulations) are aimed at ensuring the protection of privacy and protection of personal data while allowing free access to airspace for drones.

Citizens' fundamental rights, such as the protection against invasions of privacy and protection of the confidentiality of personal data, must be ensured not only by public authorities (except for areas of national security, public security and order, crime prevention, etc.)[608] but also by private individuals.[609] Claiming for damages (including redress) for the infringement of personal rights in the form of privacy and personal data is usually based on national regulations (civil law), and breaches of the right to privacy can occur in various ways. The *civil law* and *common law* systems present different premises and principles of responsibility.

The problem mainly concerns intrusion, i.e. flying over private property at a level lower than allowed by public law regulations. These are delicts of the so-called *trespass* group, i.e. unauthorized violation of someone else's territory without the owner's consents, the sphere of personal inviolability, or someone's possession[610]. The violation of the right to privacy and personal data is therefore closely related to the issue of violating the possession and limits of protection of the right to property (petition and property protection). Generally, one can start with the principle of *cuius est solum, eius est usque ad coelom et ad inferos*. Although it is limited by allowing passenger flights to take place over private property by commercial aircraft, it can nevertheless be interpreted to prohibit the use of drones over someone's land. A flight over private property at an altitude so low that it constitutes a direct interference with the enjoyment of one's own land is still unacceptable. The *United States v. Causby* judgment was key

608 See: J. Podkowik, Secret Surveillance, National Security and Journalistic Privilege: In Search of a Balance Between Conflicting Values in the Age of New Telecommunications Technologies, [in:] IX World Congress of Constitutional Law (Oslo, 16 20 June 2014). Contributions by Polish Scholars, Wydawnictwa Trybunału Konstytucyjnego, Warsaw, 2015, pp. 171–192.

609 K. Bernauw, Drones: The Emerging Era of Unmanned Civil Aviation, p. 242.

610 See J. Sieńczyło-Chlabicz, Naruszenie prywatności osób publicznych przez prasę, p. 310.

here, as it established a fundamental link between airspace and private property. It is impossible to establish strict vertical boundaries for the protection of the right to property, both in the USA and in Poland. Only the existing interpretative guidelines make it possible *ad casum* to examine whether or not there has been an infringement of property rights. On the one hand, regulations have not yet set a minimum height at which drones can fly. The FAA, on the other hand, seeks a literal interpretation of the concept of "navigable airspace" and the recognition that drones can fly anywhere.

In the era of enormous technological development opportunities for UA, and in order to bring balance to expectations as to their proper use with reasonable assumptions regarding privacy, it is necessary to combine the most appropriate aspects of existing tort law with a modern understanding of appropriate standards of conduct[611] and the auxiliary application of solutions proposed by public law. It is also necessary to apply the provisions of public law when examining the unlawfulness of action or the fault (as in the USA) of a pilot / drone operator as a matter of infringement of personal interest in the form of the right to privacy or personal data. They remain helpful, for example, by requiring that a safe distance be maintained between a drone and people, and because they forbid operations from taking place over assemblies of people. One of the purposes of introducing public law regulations (e.g. Regulation 945/2019) includes privacy protection and the protection of personal data while allowing drones and their operators free access to airspace. These groups must be taken into account when determining an entity's liability for violation of the right to privacy and personal data protection.

It should also be added that the protection of privacy, personal data, and security is the responsibility of not only the legislator, but also of private enterprises that introduce new technological solutions to international markets. For example, one company has already created software that can distinguish drones from other objects and uses a laser scanner to determine a drone's position. A detection module searches for drones using video cameras in combination with radar and laser technology (LIDAR) and audio sensors. If the system recognizes an object to be a UA, then a command is sent to a specialized module to jam communications between that device and its operator, causing the UA to initiate emergency return home protocols or to land on the spot.[612]

---

611 B.D. Mathews, Potential Tort Liability for Personal Use of Drone Aircraft (August 1, 2015). St Mary's Law Journal, Vol. 46, 2015, p. 573.

612 https://www.kaspersky.pl/antidrone [access: November 11, 2019].

"Privacy is to be protected precisely because and only because every person is granted the right to exclusive control over this sphere of their life as it does not concern others, and freedom from the curiosity of others is a unique *conditio sine qua non* allowing for the free development of an individual."[613]

613 M. Safjan, Prawo do ochrony życia prywatnego, [in:] Szkoła Praw Człowieka, Helsinki Foundation for Human Rights, Warsaw, 2006, p. 211 et seq.

Bibliography

Articles and chapters

Ackerman E., Dutch Police Training Eagles to Take Down Drones, IEEE Spectrum, 1 February 2016: http://spectrum.ieee.org/automaton/robotics/drones/dutch-police-training-eagles-to-take-down-drones

Alberstadt R., Drones under International Law. Open Journal of Political Science, Vol. 4, Issue 4, 2014.

Archambault L., Mazous A., L'Envol des Drones Civils: Appréhension par le droit français d'une pratique émergente., 40 Annals of Air and Space Law, 2015.

Autonomiczny Transport Przyszłości. Polish Economic Institute. April 2020.

Barcz J., Traktat z Lizbony. Wybrane aspekty prawne działań implementacyjnych, Warsaw, 2012, Chapter 5.

Bartsch R., Coyne J., Gray K., Drones in Society, Routledge, Abingdon, 2017.

Basic Principles on the Use of Force and Firearms by Law Enforcement Officials, Adopted by the Eighth United Nations Congress on the Prevention of Crime and the Treatment of Offenders, Havana, Cuba, 27 August to 7 September 1990: https://www.ohchr.org/en/professionalinterest/pages/useofforceandfirearms.aspx

Baum M. S., Unmanned Aircraft Systems Traffic Management: UTM.

Bernauw K., Drones: The Emerging Era of Unmanned Civil Aviation., 2015.

Beyer D. K., Dulo D. A., Townsley G. A., Wu S. S., Risk, Product Liability Trends, Triggers, and Insurance in Commercial Aerial Robots, WE ROBOT Conference on Legal & Policy Issues Relating to Robotics University of Miami School of Law, April 4 & 5, 2014.

Biała Księga Rynku Bezzałogowych Statków Powietrznych, Warsaw, 2019.

Blom J. D., Unmanned Aerial Systems: A Historical Perspective, 2010. For Polish publications see e.g. Brzezina J. M., Atak Dronów, Warsaw, 2013.

Bodnar A., Pacho I., Targeted Killings (Drone Strikes) and the European Convention on Human Rights, Polish Yearbook of International Law, 2012.

Bohm A., Status of Domestic Drone Legislation in the States, ACLU (15 February 2013). https://www.aclu.org/blog/technology-and-liberty/status-domestic-drone-legislation-states

Boon K., Lovelace D. C., The Domestic Use of Unmanned Aerial Vehicles, Oxford University Press, 2014.

Bouvé C. L., Private Ownership of Airspace, Air Law Review, Issue 1, 1930.

Brief for Petitioner at 2, Elec. information on privacy Ctr. against the FAA, no. 15-1075: https://epic.org/privacy/drones/epicvfaa/1581988-FAA-Brief.pdf

Bujnowski M., Bezpieczeństwo lotnictwa cywilnego, Aspekty współpracy międzynarodowej, 2016.

Bujnowski M., Integracja bezzałogowych statków powietrznych z unijnym systemem lotnictwa załogowego" IKAR 2017, nr 2(6).

Busti S., Le sanzioni in materia di trasporto marittimo, aereo, terrestre e codice della strada, in: Responsabilità per i danni a terzi dal volo di aeromobile, Cagnazzo A., Toschei S., Pozzi E. C., Giappichelli (ed.), Turin, 2012.

Carey B., Enter the Drones. The FAA and UAVs in America, 2016, p. 55.

Carr S., Felker S. L., Baker Donelson Matthew Grosack, Connie A. Lahn, DRONE ON! Emerging Legal Issues for Commercial Use of Unmanned Aerial Vehicles (UAVs): Will You and Your Clients Be Ready for the Invasion of American Airspace?, ABA Section of Litigation – Environmental, Mass Torts and Products Liability Litigation Committees joint CLE, January 2016.

Cassart A., Droit des drones: Belgique, France, Luxembourg, Bruxelles, 2017.

Castillo-Ruiz F. E., Property and Privacy Issues Arising from the Integration of Civil and Commercial Drones into the Domestic Airspace of the United States, Annals of Air and Space Law, Vol. 40, 2015.

Chechetka S. A., Yu Y., Tange M., Miyako E., Materially Engineered Artificial Pollinators, Chem, Volume 2, Issue 2, 2017.

Cook A. (ed.), European Air Traffic management. Principles, Practice and Research, 2007.

Correia V., Rouissi N., The European Union and Civil Drones: The Riga Declaration and the Future of the European RPAS Industry, w: B. Scott, The Law of Unmanned Aircraft Systems.

Custers B. (ed.), The Future of Drone Use, Springer, 2016.

Dalamagkidis K. et al., On Integrating Unmanned Aircraft Systems into the National Airspace System, 2012.

Darack E., Are Dubai's Drone Taxis For Real?, Air & Space Magazine: https://www.airspacemag.com/articles/fly-through-air-greatest-ease-180962272/

Di Nucci E., Santoni de Sio F., Drones and Responsibility: Legal, Philosophical and Socio-Technical Perspectives on Remotely Controlled Weapons, 2016.

Donohue K. L., A Tale of Two Sovereigns: Federal and State Use and Regulation of Unmanned Aircraft Systems, in: Valavanis K. P., Vachtsevanos G. J. (eds.), Handbook of Unmanned Aerial Vehicles, Springer International Publishing, 2018.

Drone Outlook Study, 2016.

DroneRules PRO, A Privacy Impact Assessment Handbook and Template. https://dronerules.eu/assets/files/DRPRO_Data_Protection_Impact_Assessment_EN.pdf

Eijkman Q., Bakker M., Access to an Effective Remedy and Reparations for Civilian Victims of Armed Drone Strikes, in: Custers B. (ed.), The Future of Drone Use, Information Technology and Law Series, Springer, 2016.

Enemark Ch., Armed Drones and the Ethics of War. Military Virtue in a Post-heroic Age, Routledge, London, 2013.

Fagnant D. J., Kockelman K., Preparing a Nation for Autonomous Vehicles: Opportunities, Barriers and Policy Recommendations, „Transportation Research Part A: Policy and Practice" 2015, Vol. 77.

Farber H., Keep Out! The Efficacy of Trespass Nuisance and Privacy Torts as Applied to Drones, GA. ST. U. L. Rev. 2017, Vol. 33.

Fellner R., Kochańczyk R., Stechnij T., Wilisowski A., Sitko P., Aspekty prawne oraz certyfikacyjne bezzałogowych statków powietrznych w świetle wybranych regulacji międzynarodowych, Katowice, 2019.

Finn R. L., Wright D., Donovan A. (Trilateral Research & Consulting, LLP), Laura Jacques and Paul De Hert (Vrije Universiteit Brussel), Privacy, data protection and ethical risks in civil RPAS operations, 7 November 2014, in: http://ec.europa.eu/DocsRoom/documents/7662

Froomkin A. M., Colangelo P. Z., Self-Defense Against Robots and Drones, Conn. L. Rev. 12015, Vol. 48, Issue 1.

Garlicki L., Commentary to Art. 2 of the ECtHR, in: Garlicki L. (ed.), Konwencja o Ochronie Praw Człowieka i Podstawowych Wolności, Vol. 1, CH Beck, Warsaw, 2010.

Gruber R. H., Commercial Drones and Privacy: Can We Trust States with Drone Federalism, Richmond Journal of Law Technology, Vol. 21, Issue 4, 2014.

Harris K., Drones: Proposed standards of liability. Santa Clara High Technology Law Journal, Vol. 31, Issue 1, 2018.

Hattan T., Lethal Autonomous Robots: Are They Legal under International Human Rights and Humanitarian Law?, Nebraska Law Review, Vol. 93, 2014.

Hawkins A. J., Ehang's passenger-carrying drones look insanely impressive in first test flights, The Verge 5 February 2018, https://www.theverge.com/2018/2/5/16974310/ehang-passenger-carrying-drone-first-test-flight

Heymann B. G., Law and Policy of Targeted Killings. Harvard Journal of National Security, Issue 1, 2012.

Huttunen M., 'Unmanned, Remotely Piloted, or Something Else? Analyzing the Terminological Dogfight', 42 Air & Space Law 3 (2017).

Huttunen M., Drone Operations in the Specific Category: A Unique Approach to Aviation Safety, The Aviation and Space Journal, No. 2, 2019.

Huttunen M., Unmanned, Remotely Piloted or Something Else, Journal of Laws of 2011, No. 80, item 432.

Karnow C. E. A., The application of traditional tort theory to embodied machine intelligence, [in:] Calo R., Froomkin A. M., Kerr I. (ed.), Robot Law, Cheltenham, Northampton, 2016.

Kasprzyk P. „Odpowiedzialność a bezpieczeństwo transportu lotniczego. Kilka uwag o Just Culture" (w) Ius Est Ars Boni Et Aequi, Księga pamiątkowa dedykowana Profesorowi Józefowi Frąckowiakowi, Wrocław, 2018.

Kasprzyk P., Konert A., Bezzałogowe statki powietrzne. Nowa era w dziejach lotnictwa. Nowa era w prawie lotniczym? , księga pamiątkowa XX-lecia Wydziału Prawa i Administracji. Przyszłość prawa, Warsaw, 2017.

Kasprzyk P., Konert A., UAS safety operation – Legal Issues on Reporting UAS Incidents, Journal of Intelligent & Robotic Systems, Issue 2, Vol. 103, 2021

Kasprzyk P., Postępowanie w sprawie badania wypadku lotniczego a postępowanie cywilne, Przegląd Sądowy 2009, no. 4, J. Walulik, Badanie wypadków i incydentów statków powietrznych, Kontrola Państwowa 2011, no. 2.

Kępa L., Ochrona danych osobowych. Praktyczny przewodnik dla przedsiębiorców, Warsaw, 2018, p. 4.

Klich E., Bezpieczeństwo lotów w transporcie lotniczym. Radom, 2010

Knoops G. J. A., Legal, Political and Ethical Dimensions of Drone Warfare under International Law: A Preliminary Survey. International Criminal Law Review, Issue 12, 2012.

Knoops G. J., Drones at Trial. State and Individual (Criminal) Liabilities for Drone Attacks. International Criminal Law Review, Vol. 14, 2014.

Konert A. (ed.), Aspekty prawne badania zdarzeń lotniczych w świetle Rozporządzenia 996/2010, Warszawa, 2013.

Konert A., Kunert-Diallo A., Odpowiedzialność operatora kosmicznego względem turystów kosmicznych, Państwo i Prawo nr 6/2019.

Konert A., in: Żylicz M. (ed.), Prawo lotnicze. Komentarz.

Konert A., Odpowiedzialność cywilna przewoźnika lotniczego, Warsaw, 2010.

Konert A., Smereka, J., Szarpak, L., Morita, S., The Use of Drones in Emergency Medicine: Practical and Legal Aspects, Emergency Medicine International, 2019.

Konert A., Kasprzyk P., Łaciński P., Podstawy prawne zarządzania bezpieczeństwem w lotnictwie cywilnym (in) Zarządzanie Bezpieczeństwem w Lotnictwie Cywilnym, ed. K Łuczak, 2016.

Konert A., Kotliński M., U-space – Civil Liability for Damages Caused by Unmanned Aircraft, INAIR 2020.

Konert A., Odpowiedzialność za szkody spowodowane przez ruch statku powietrznego na ziemi, Warszawa, 2014 (Liability for Damages Caused by Aicraft to Third Parties on the Ground).

Konert A., Prawne aspekty użytkowania bezzałogowych statków powietrznych, Warszawa, 2021.

Konert A., Przetwarzanie danych osobowych przez operatorów bezzałogowych statków powietrznych, Ius Novum 2/2021.

Konert A., Sakowska-Baryła M., Prawne uregulowania w zakresie używania bezzałogowych statków powietrznych przez media, International Journal of Legal Studies 2020, Tom 8, Nr 2.

Konert A., Sakowska-Baryła M., The Impact of the GDPR on the Unmanned Aircraft Sector Air and Space Law, Volume 46, Issue 4/5, (2021).

Konert A., Ubezpieczenia lotnicze, Warsaw, 2014.

Kreps S. E., Drony. Wprowadzenie. Technologie. Zastosowania, PWN, 2019.

Kreuzer M. P., Drones and the Future of Air Warfare: The Evolution of Remotely Piloted Aircraft, Routledge, London, 2016.

Kreuzer M. P., RPAs and Non-International Conflict – A Strategic/Legal Assessment, Cardozo Law Review, Vol. 36, Issue 2, 2014.

Kuchta R., Trzy przykłady nowych robotów, Robotyka, Warsaw, 2015. https://newtech.law/wp-content/uploads/2017/08/Wardynski-i-Wspolnicy_raport-robotyka.pdf

Kunert-Diallo A., "Kontrola tożsamości w przewozie lotniczym", in: Prawo lotnicze i kosmiczne oraz technologie, pub. University of Rzeszów.

Lohsse S., Schulze R., Staudenmayer D. (ed.) Liability for Artificial Intelligence and the Internet of Things Münster Colloquia on EU Law and the Digital Economy IV, 2019.

Lorenc W., Chodnicki M., Kordowski P., Nowakowski M., Drony transportowe – nowa era transportu towarów i ludzi, Efektywność transport, Autobusy: technika, eksploatacja, systemy transportowe no. 6/2016.

Łuczak K. (ed.), Zarządzanie bezpieczeństwem w lotnictwie cywilnym, Uniwersytet Śląski, Katowice, 2016.

Machnikowski P., Perspektywa uegulowania odpowiedzialności cywilnej związanej z nowymi technologiami, in: Dańsko-Roesler A., Leśniak M., Skory

M., Sołtys B., Ius Est Ars Boni et Aequi, Księga pamiątkowa dedykowana Profesorowi Józefowi Frąckowiakowi, Wrocław, 2018.

Maloney W. E., Current Trends in Aviation Product Liability Law, The Journal of Air Law and Commerce,Vol. 36, Issue 3, 1970.

Marr B., 6 Amazing Passenger Drone Projects Everyone Should Know About, Forbes: https://www.forbes.com/sites/bernardmarr/2018/03/26/6-amazing-passenger-drone-projects-everyone-should-know-about/#73a41c9a4ceb

Masutti A., Drones for Civil Use: European Perspective on Third-Party Liability and Insurance, Journal for International Trade and Transport Law, nr 16, 2016.

Masutti A., Tomasello F., International Regulation of Non-Military Drones, Edward Elgar Publishing, Cheltenham, 2018.

Mathews B. D., Potential Tort Liability for Personal Use of Drone Aircraft (August 1, 2015). St. Mary's Law Journal, Vol. 46, p. 573, 2015.

Matiteyahu T., Drone Regulations and Fourth Amendment Rights: The Interaction of State Drone Statutes and the Reasonable Expectation of Privacy, Columbia Journal of Law Social Problems, Vol. 48, 2014.

Matthews M., McNab M., Clarifying the Law Relating to Unmanned Drones and the Use of Force: The Relationships between Human Rights, Self-Defence, Armed Conflict and International Humanitarian Law. Denver Journal of International Law and Policy, Vol. 39, 2011.

Maurer M., Christian Gerdes, J., Lenz, B., Winner, H., Autonomous Driving. Technical, Legal and Social Aspects, Springer OPen, Berlin, 2016.

McCauley L., AI Armageddon and the Three Laws of Robotics, Ethics and Information Technology 9, 2007.

McNabb H., Uber and Hyundai Have Established a Drone Taxi System That Just Might Work, Drone Life: https://dronelife.com/2020/01/10/uber-and-hyundai-have-established-a-drone-taxi-system-that-just-might-work/

McNeal G. S., Drones & the Future of Aerial Surveillance, The George Washington Law Review, 84, n. 214, 354, 394, 2016.

Melzer N., 'Targeted killings in operational law perspective', in: Terry D. Gill and Dieter Fleck (eds.), The Handbook of the International Law of Military Operations, Oxford University Press, Oxford, 2010.

Michaelides-Mateou S., Erotokritou Ch., Flying into the Future with UAVs: The Jetstream 31 Flight, Air and Space Law, Vol. 39, Issue 2, 2014.

Mikromakro Institute's report "Człowiek – maszyna – bezpieczeństwo", 2013.

Mikromakro Institute's report "Roboty w przestrzeni publicznej", 2014.

Mikromakro Institute's report "Rynek dronów w Polsce. Jutrzenka", 2018.

Mikromakro Institute's report "Rynek dronów w Polsce. Księga popytu i podaży", 2015.

Mikromakro Institute's report "Rynek dronów w Polsce. Świt w dolinie śmierci", 2017.

Milde M., Essential Air and Space Law, 2012.

Morales-Ferre R. et al., A Survey on Coping with Intentional Interference in Satellite Navigation for Manned and Unmanned Aircraft, IEEE Communications Surveys & Tutorials, Vol. 22, No. 1, 2020.

Mousazadeh R., Basiri A., Babaee M., Tabasi A., Analyzing the Legal Dimensions of Unmanned Combat Aerial Vehicle in the International Law. Journal of Politics and Law, Vol. 9, Issue 10, 2016.

Newcome L. R., Unmanned Aviation: A Brief History of Unmanned Aerial Vehicles, American Institute of Aeronautics and Astronautics, 2004.

Newstead A., Drones and robots: Liability for Designers, Manufacturers And Insurer. http://www.inhouselawyer.co.uk/legal-briefing/drones-and-robots-liability-for-designers-manufacturers-and-insurers/?pdf=1713

Newstead A., Drones and Robots: Liability for Designers, Manufacturers and Insurer.

Nicas J., Drones Boom Raises New Question: Who Owns Your Airspace?, WALL STREET J. (May 13, 2015, 12:43): https://www.wsj.com/articles/drones-boom-raises-new-question-who-owns-your-airspace-1431535417

O'Connell M. E., Remarks: The Resort to Drones under International Law. Denver Journal of International Law and Policy, Vol. 39, 2011.

Ostrihansky, M., Szmigiero M., Prawo dronów. Bezzałogowe statki powietrzne w prawie Unii Europejskiej oraz krajowym, p. 206 et seq.

Pearl T. H., "Hands on the Wheel: A Call for Greater Regulation of Semi-Autonomous Cars," Indiana Law Journal, Vol. 93, Issue 3, 2018, p. 714.

Perritt Jr. H., Sprague E., Law Abiding Drones, Columbia Scientific & Technology Review, Vol. 16, 2015.

Perritt Jr. H., Eliot O. Sprague, Domesticating Drones: The Technology, Economics, and Law of Unmanned Aircraft, Routledge, London, 2018.

Perritt Jr. H., Who pays when drones crash?, UCLA Journal of Law and Technology, Vol. 21, Issue 1, 2017, p. 7 et seq.

Peterson M., The UAV and the Current and Future Regulatory Construct for Integration into the National Airspace System, Journal of Air Law and Commerce, Vol. 71, 2006. https://www.wsj.com/articles/why-some-drone-makers-hate-the-word-drone-and-want-to-change-it-1412821801

Podkowik J., Secret Surveillance, National Security and Journalistic Privilege: In Search of a Balance Between Conflicting Values in the Age of New Telecommunications Technologies, [in:] IX World Congress of Constitutional Law (Oslo, 16 20 June 2014). Contributions by Polish Scholars, Wydawnictwa Trybunału Konstytucyjnego, Warsaw, 2015.

Poncelet L., L'arsenal législatif relatif à la responsabilité civile en Belgique, est-il suffisant pour pallier aux risques liés à l'utilisation des drones?, These, Université catholique de Louvain, 2016.

Poss J., The "Why's" of the 2018 FAA Reauthorization, https://insideunmanned systems.com/the-whys-of-the-2018-faa-reauthorization-act/

Prigg M., Welcome to drone air: First passenger plane piloted remotely flies across the UK in pioneering trial: https://www.dailymail.co.uk/sciencetech/article-2324358/Welcome-drone-air-First-passenger-plane-pilot-flies-UK-pioneering-trial.html

Prosser W. L., Privacy, California Law Review, Vol. 48, Issue 3, 1960.

Pryciak M., Prawo do prywatności, in Sadowski M., Szymianiec P. (ed.). Prawa człowieka – idea, instytucje, krytyka. Studia Erasmiana Wratislaviensia, Wrocław, 2010.

Pszczoły roboty zapylą kwiaty, a komary drony będą nas szpiegować (Robo-bees will pollinate flowers and mosquito-drones will spy on us), Rzeczpospolita's article: February 15, 2018: https://www.rp.pl/Plus-Minus/302159928-Pszczoly-roboty-zapyla-kwiaty-a-komary-drony-beda-nas-szpiegowac.html

Ratajczyk M., Regional Aviation Safety Organizations. Enhancing Air Transport Safety through Regional Cooperation, Wolters Kluwer, 2015.

Rausch R. L., Reframing ROE: Property Over Privacy, 27 BERKLEY J. GENDER L. & JUST, Vol. 27, 2012.

Regulating emerging robotic technologies in Europe: Robotics facing law and ethics (ROBOLAW). Project URL: http://www.robolaw.eu

Rosen R. D., Drones and the U.S. Courts, William Mitchell Law Review, Vol. 37, Issue, 5, 2011.

Rupprecht J., Drones: Their Many Civilian Uses and the US Laws Surrounding Them, 2015, p. 43

Rutkowski P., Świat dla robotów, Co do zasady. Studia i analizy prawne. 2017: http://www.codozasady.pl/swiat-dla-robotow/

Safjan M., Prawo do ochrony życia prywatnego, [in:] Szkoła Praw Człowieka, Helsinki Foundation for Human Rights, Warsaw, 2006.

Santosuosso A., Boscarato C., Caroleo F., Labruto R., Leroux C., Robots, Market and Civil Liability: A European Perspective, 2012.

Sarnecki P., Art. 47, [in:] Konstytucja Rzeczypospolitej Polskiej. Komentarz, III, ed. GARLICKI L., Warsaw, 2003.

Sarnowski W., Dron poczty spadł 50 metrów od przedszkolaków. Loty wstrzymane: https://cyfrowa.rp.pl/technologie/36293-dron-poczty-spadl-50-metrow-od-przedszkolakow-loty-wstrzymane

Schaerer E. et al., Robots as Animals: A Framework for Liability and Responsibility in Human-Robot Interactions, 18th IEEE International Symposium on Robot and Human Interactive Communication 2009, https://papers.ssrn.com/sol3/papers.cfm?abstract_id=2271466

Scott B. I. (ed.), The Law of Unmanned Aircraft Systems. An Introduction to the Current and Future Regulation under National, Regional and International, Kluwer Law International, The Netherlands, 2016.

Scott B. I., Terminology, Definitions and Classifications, w: B. I. Scott (red.), The Law of Unmanned Aircraft Systems. An Introduction to the Current and Future Regulation under National, Regional and International Law, Kluwer Law International BV, The Netherlands, 2016.

Sehrawat V., Liability Issue of Domestic Drones. Santa Clara High Technology Law Journal, Vol. 35, No. 1, November 2018.

Sieńczyło-Chlabicz J., Naruszenie prywatności osób publicznych przez prasę, Zakamycze, 2006.

Swanson M. A., Comprehensive "FAA Reauthorization Act of 2018" Charts ambitious course forward on drones, article presented at ICUAS 2019.

Szpunar A., The Law of Tort in the Polish Civil Code, The International and Comparative Law Quarterly, Vol. 16, No. 1 (January, 1967).

Szymanski P., Drony w Polsce –szanse i zagrożenia, Civil Aviation Office: https://www.ulc.gov.pl/_download/bezpieczenstow_lotow/prezentacje-2014/07-Drony-w-Polsce-szanse-i-zagrozenia- 18_04_2018_Paweł_Szymanski.pdf

Takahashi T. T., Drones and Privacy, The Columbia Science and Technology Law Review, Vol. 14, 2012.

Tobolewski A., Monetary Limitations of Liability in Air Law: Legal, Economic and Socio-Political Aspects, De Daro Publishing, 1986, p. 40.

Unmanned Aircraft System Handbook and Accident Investigation Guidelines, ISASI, 2015.

Unmanned Aircraft System Handbook and Accident/Incident Investigation Guidelines (International Society of Air Safety Investigators, 2015).

Unmanned Aircraft Systems Traffic Management (UTM) – A Common Framework with Core Principles for Global Harmonization, Edition 3.

Valavanis K. P., Vachtsevanos G. J. (eds.), Handbook of Unmanned Aerial Vehicles, Springer International Publishing, 2018.

Van Rossum C., Liability of robots: Legal responsibility in cases of errors or malfunctioning, thesis Ghent University, 2017.

Vogel R., Drone Warfare & the Law of Armed Conflict. Denver Journal of International Law & Policy, Vol. 39, Issue 1, 2011.

Wallace R. J., Loffi J. M., Evolution of UAS Policy in the Wake of Taylor v. Huerta. International Journal of Aviation, Aeronautics, and Aerospace, 4(3), 2017.

Warre S. D., Brandeis L., The Right to Privacy, Harvard Law Review, Vol. IV, December 1890.

Wild G. et al., A Post-Accident Analysis of Civil Remotely-Piloted Aircraft System Accidents and Incidents, Journal of Aerospace Technology and Management, Vol. 9, No 2, 2017.

Wojdyło K., Kto odpowiada za robota?

Wood S. P., Chang J., Healy T., Wood, J., The Potential Regulatory Challenges of Increasingly Autonomous Motor Vehicles, „Santa Clara Law Review" 2012, Vol. 52, No. 4.

Wu S., Product Liability Issues in the U.S. and Associated Risk Management, in: Maurer M., Gerdes J., Lenz B., Winner H. (eds.), Autonomes Fahren, Springer Vieweg, Berlin, Heidelberg, p. 563–564.

Wu S., Unmanned Vehicles and US Product Liability Law, Journal of Law, Information and Science, Vol. 21, Issue 2, 2012.

Zadura D., Importance of Personal Data Protection Law for Commercial Air Transport, Transactions of the Institute of Aviation, No. 1 (246), Warsaw, 2017.

Završnik A. (ed.), Drones and Unmanned Aerial Systems, 2016.

Zoldi D. M. K., Speirs G. R., Lewber J., Unmanned Aircraft System Legislative Trends in the United States at the State Level, 2013–2016: A Comprehensive Review. https://doi.org/10.1007/978-3-319-32193-6_160-1

Żylicz M., Prawo lotnicze międzynarodowe, europejskie i krajowe, Warsaw, 2011.

Websites

http://aiai.mot.gov.il/NOTES/NAI_1256.pdf

http://avherald.com/h?article=48996163

http://cedd.pl/2019/09/17/spotkieta-dotyczace-c certacji-bsp-z-jednostkami-oceniajacymi-zgodnosc/

http://cedd.pl/start/jak-dziala-cedd/

http://cedd.pl/start/jak-dziala-cedd/

http://di.com.pl/samolot-pasazerski-zderzyl-sie-z-dronem-prawdopodob nie-54803

http://dlapilota.pl/wiadomosci/aero-newsnet/usa-pierwsza-dostawa-paczki-za-pomoca-drona

http://dronealliance.eu/

http://homelandsecuritynewswire.com/canadian-police-push-limits-civil ian-uavs-laws

http://jarus-rpas.org/

http://smalluavcoalition.org/

http://www.bst-tsb.gc.ca/eng/rapports-reports/aviation/2017/a17q0162/a17q0 162.pdf

http://www.icao.int/DCCD2009/

http://www.icao.int/icao/en/leb/rome1952.pdf

http://www.icao.int/publications/Pages/default.aspx

http://www.legislature.mi.gov/(S(g3r4xyjlnyfbd0egsrdyahua))/mileg.aspx-?page=GetObject&objectname=mcl-750-539j

https://aci.aero/about-aci/priorities/safety/drones/

https://app.ntsb.gov/pdfgenerator/ReportGeneratorFile.ashx?EventID=2017092 2X54600&AKey=1&RType=HTML&IType=IA%EF%BB%BF

https://arc.aiaa.org/doi/10.2514/6.2017-4051

https://automatykab2b.pl/prezentacje/51126-autonomiczne-i-wspolpracujace-roboty-mobilne-mir-przyszlosc-transportu-wewnetrznego

https://autonomousweapons.org/ (access: June 16, 2020).

https://cordis.europa.eu/project/rcn/102044/brief/pl

https://dlapilota.pl/wiadomosci/dlapilota/drony-wstrzymaly-ladowa nia-na-epwa

https://dlapilota.pl/wiadomosci/dlapilota/zblizenie-b777-z-dronem-po-star cie-z-epwa

https://dronerules.eu/assets/files/PCC_DR_final-for-printing_9-November-2018.pdf

https://dronerules.eu/pl/

https://dronerules.eu/pl/

https://ec.europa.eu/justice/article-29/documentation/opinion-recommendat ion/index_en.htm

https://ec.europa.eu/transport/modes/air/encasia/activities/opinions_en

https://ec.europa.eu/transport/modes/air/news/2018-10-19-network-u-space-demonstrators_en

https://ec.europa.eu/transport/modes/air/news/2018-11-28-drones_en

https://ec.europa.eu/transport/modes/air/sign-up_en

https://ec.europa.eu/transport/modes/air/studies/support-study-evaluation-regulation-eu-no-9962010-investigation-and-prevention_

https://ec.europa.eu/transport/sites/transport/files/20180515-sesar-ads-b-report.pdf

https://en.wikipedia.org/wiki/Eurocontrol

https://eur-lex.europa.eu/legal-content/EN/TXT/?uri=CELEX%3A32021R0664

https://eur-lex.europa.eu/legal-content/EN/TXT/?uri=uriserv%3AOJ.L_.2021.139.01.0184.01.ENG&toc=OJ%3AL%3A2021%3A139%3ATOC [access: 20 November 2021]

https://eur-lex.europa.eu/legal-content/EN/TXT/?uri=uriserv%3AOJ.L_.2021.139.01.0187.01.ENG&toc=OJ%3AL%3A2021%3A139%3ATOC [access: 20 November 2021]

https://gutma.org/

https://gutma.org/blog/2021/02/25/u-space-regulatory-package-approved-by-easa-member-states-committee/ [access: 21 November 2021]

https://law.justia.com/cases/federal/appellate-courts/cadc/15-1495/15-1495-2017-05-19.html

https://law.justia.com/codes/arkansas/2010/title-5/subtitle-2/chapter-16/5-16-101/

https://law.justia.com/codes/michigan/2006/mcl-chap330/mcl-330-1424.html

https://law.justia.com/codes/michigan/2006/mcl-chap330/mcl-330-1424.html

https://law.justia.com/codes/mississippi/2013/title-97/chapter-29/in-general/section-97-29-61/

https://technode.com/2018/01/03/worlds-top-drone-seller-dji-made-2-7-billion-2017/

https://time.com/collection/genius-companies-2018/5412498/dji/

https://ulc.gov.pl/pl/aktualnosci/5002-przesuniecie-daty-wejscia-w-zycie-przepisow-dotyczacych-dronow

https://wroclaw.wyborcza.pl/wroclaw/1,35771,21282088,dron-uderzyl-w-ostatnie-pieto-sky-tower.html

https://www.5zywiolow.pl

https://www.a6alliance.net/positions/a6-alliance-position-drones/

https://www.airbus.com/newsroom/stories/urban-air-mobility-the-sky-is-yours.html

https://www.airbusutm.com/uam-resources-airbus-blueprint

https://www.altair.com.pl/magazines/article?article_id=4176

https://www.amazon.com/Amazon-Prime-Air/b?ie=UTF8&node=8037720011

https://www.aopa.org/go-fly/aircraft-and-ownership/drones

https://www.arpas.uk/

https://www.assureuas.org/about.php

https://www.astm.org/about/overview.html

https://www.astm.org/COMMITTEE/F38.htm

https://www.auvsi.org/our-impact/waivers-under-Part 107-updated-interactive-report

https://www.aw-drones.eu/

https://www.bbc.com/news/uk-england-sussex-46623754

https://www.bbc.com/news/uk-england-sussex-49846450

https://www.caa.co.uk/Consumers/Unmanned-aircraft/Our-role/Drone-and-model-aircraft-registration/

https://www.canso.org/we-are-all-one-sky-aviation-partners-agree-joint-pri nciples-safe-integration-drones

https://www.casa.gov.au/standard-page/project-us-1418-post-implementation-review-certain-aspects-part-101-casr

https://www.cio.com/article/2383123/geofencing-explained.html

https://www.cnbop.pl/uslugi/c certacja-drony/program-pc-bsp.pdf

https://www.dfs.de/dfs_homepage/en/Press/Press%20releases/2019/12.03.2019.-%20Growing%20risk%20of%20drones%20to%20air%20traffic/

https://www.easa.europa.eu/document-library/agency-decisions/ed-decision-2019021r

https://www.easa.europa.eu/document-library/comment-response-documents

https://www.easa.europa.eu/document-library/general-publications/concept-operations-drones

https://www.easa.europa.eu/document-library/general-publications/european-plan-aviation-safety-2020-2024

https://www.easa.europa.eu/document-library/general-publications/study-and-recommendations-regarding-unmanned-aircraft-system

https://www.easa.europa.eu/document-library/notices-of-proposed-amendm ent/npa-2015-10

https://www.easa.europa.eu/document-library/notices-of-proposed-amendment/npa-2017-05

https://www.easa.europa.eu/document-library/notices-of-proposed-amendment/npa-2020-07

https://www.easa.europa.eu/document-library/opinions/opinion-

https://www.easa.europa.eu/document-library/opinions/opinion-012020

https://www.easa.europa.eu/document-library/opinions/opinion-technical-nature

https://www.easa.europa.eu/document-library/product-certification-consultations/proposed-special-condition-light-uas

https://www.easa.europa.eu/faq/116452

https://www.easa.europa.eu/new-cs-23-%E2%80%93-smart-and-flexible-rules-support-innovation

https://www.easa.europa.eu/newsroom-and-events/events/high-level-conference-drones-leverage-jobs-and-new-business

https://www.easa.europa.eu/newsroom-and-events/events/u-space-draft-opinion-workshop

https://www.easa.europa.eu/newsroom-and-events/news/easa-publishes-proposal-implementation-u-space-europe

https://www.easa.europa.eu/newsroom-and-events/press-releases/regulators-and-industry-unite-need-address-societal-concerns

https://www.easa.europa.eu/sites/default/files/dfu/Opinion%20No%2001-2020.pdf

https://www.easa.europa.eu/sites/default/files/dfu/Opinion%20No%2001-2020.pdf

https://www.easa.europa.eu/sites/default/files/dfu/Opinion%20No%2001-2020.pdf

https://www.easa.europa.eu/system/files/dfu/Explanatory%20Note%20for%20the%20UAS%20Prototype%20regulation%20final.pdf

https://www.easa.europa.eu/system/files/dfu/UAS%20Prototype%20Regulation%20final.pdf and

https://www.easa.europa.eu/the-agency/faqs/drones-uas

https://www.eurocae.net/about-us/our-history/

https://www.eurocae.net/about-us/working-groups/

https://www.eurocockpit.be/campaign/integrating-drones-safely

https://www.eurocontrol.int/event/high-level-workshop-drone-detection-2019

https://www.eurocontrol.int/product/european-network-u-space-demonstrators

https://www.eurocontrol.int/product/european-network-u-space-demonstrators

https://www.eurocontrol.int/project/concept-operations-european-utm-systems

https://www.eurocontrol.int/publication/riga-airspace-assessment

https://www.eurocontrol.int/publication/u-space-services-implementation-monitoring-report

https://www.eurocontrol.int/publication/uas-atm-airspace-assessment

https://www.eurocontrol.int/publication/uas-atm-common-altitude-reference-system-cars

https://www.eurocontrol.int/publication/uas-atm-flight-rules

https://www.eurocontrol.int/publication/unmanned-aircraft-systems-uas-atm-integration

https://www.europarl.europa.eu/RegData/etudes/STUD/2016/571379/IPOL_STU(2016)571379_EN.pdf

https://www.faa.gov/about/office_org/headquarters_offices/ash/ash_programs/investigations/leap/

https://www.faa.gov/about/plans_reports/congress/media/UAS_Comprehensive_Plan.pdf

https://www.faa.gov/airports/airport_safety/media/Updated-Information-UAS-Detection-Countermeasures-Technology-Airports-20190507.pdf

https://www.faa.gov/news/press_releases/news_story.cfm?newsId=16354

https://www.faa.gov/news/press_releases/news_story.cfm?newsId=24956

https://www.faa.gov/news/updates/?newsId=73118

https://www.faa.gov/uas/commercial_operators/part_107_waivers/

https://www.faa.gov/uas/commercial_operators/part_107_waivers/waivers_issued/

https://www.faa.gov/uas/commercial_operators/uas_facility_maps/

https://www.faa.gov/uas/programs_partnerships/data_exchange/

https://www.faa.gov/uas/programs_partnerships/data_exchange/

https://www.faa.gov/uas/programs_partnerships/integration_pilot_program/

https://www.faa.gov/uas/programs_partnerships/test_sites/

https://www.faa.gov/uas/research_development/traffic_management/

https://www.faa.gov/uas/research_development/traffic_management/media/UTM_ConOps_v2.pdf

https://www.faa.gov/uas/research_development/traffic_management/utm_pilot_program/

https://www.faa.gov/uas/resources/policy_library/media/frnotice_uas.pdf

https://www.faa.gov/uas/resources/policy_library/media/UAS_Fact_Sheet_Final.pdf

https://www.faa.gov/uas/resources/policy_library/media/uas_roadmap_2013.pdf

https://www.faa.gov/uas/resources/public_records/uas_sightings_report/

https://www.faa.gov/uas/resources/uas_sightings_report/ (

https://www.federalregister.gov/documents/2015/12/16/2015-31750/registration-and-marking-requirements-for-small-unmanned-aircraft

https://www.federalregister.gov/documents/2016/06/28/2016-15079/operation-and-certification-of-small-unmanned-aircraft-systems

https://www.federalregister.gov/documents/2019/02/13/2019-00732/operation-of-small-unmanned-aircraft-systems-over-people

https://www.federalregister.gov/documents/2019/02/13/2019-00758/safe-and-secure-operations-of-small-unmanned-aircraft-systems

https://www.federalregister.gov/documents/2019/02/13/2019-00765/external-marking-requirement-for-small-unmanned-aircraft

https://www.flightglobal.com/aerospace/bae-joins-high-altitude-race-with-maiden-phasa-35-flight/136767.article

https://www.flightglobal.com/civil-uavs/elbit-to-fly-hermes-900-for-uk-search-and-rescue-trials/136554.article

https://www.flightglobal.com/civil-uavs/jal-trials-transporting-fresh-fish-with-uavs/136922.article

https://www.gao.gov/products/GAO-08-511

https://www.gao.gov/products/GAO-18-110

https://www.gartner.com/en/newsroom/press-releases/2019-12-04-gartner-forecasts-global-iot-enterprise-drone-shipmen

https://www.gov.pl/documents/905843/1047987/20160376RK.pdf

https://www.gov.pl/web/cyfryzacja/grupa-robocza-ds-internetu-rzeczy-internet-of-things-iot

https://www.gov.uk/aaib-reports/aaib-investigation-to-pioneer-300-g-opfa-and-valenta-ray-x-s037996

https://www.gov.uk/aaib-reports/aaib-investigation-to-robin-dr-400-180-f-gsbm-and-sas-wildthing-radio-controlled-model-glider

https://www.gov.uk/government/publications/government-response-to-future-of-drones-in-the-uk-consultation

https://www.govtrack.us/congress/bills/115/hr3388

https://www.huffingtonpost.co.uk/2015/12/01/toddler-drone-eye-blind_n_8686366.html?guccounter=1&guce_referrer=aHR0cHM6Ly93d3cuZ29vZ2xlLmNvbS8&guce_referrer_sig=AQAAACoLIc6Jl3KK7_eTtEWi5ydiOKr4Qr5zFs8cNDzRbawCH-q5wU6OSjs7NJTu25mE1m9rQ9IXad87Uum3N-dWTs6HyHfs59_is94f97HjlVyNPJ39Pcu4LFxmiui1gODZIE2n-Wi67G0Oqm-85pSN7KMK-P-4Ctf3BeEivC2DuVC

https://www.iata.org/contentassets/8c2566421a524258896e89aceb739333/we-are-all-one-in-the-sky-open-letter-to-the-european-commission.pdf

https://www.iata.org/en/programs/safety/drones/

https://www.icao.int/annual-report-2018/Pages/the-world-of-air-transport-in-2018.aspx

https://www.icao.int/Meetings/anconf13/Documents/WP/wp_005_en.pdf

https://www.icao.int/meetings/DRONEENABLE4/Pages/default.aspx

https://www.icao.int/safety/UA/Documents/ICAO%20RPAS%20CONOPS.pdf

https://www.icao.int/safety/UA/Documents/UTM-Framework%20Edition%202.pdf

https://www.icao.int/safety/UA/Pages/ICAO-Model-UAS-Regulations.aspx

https://www.icao.int/safety/UA/Pages/Remotely-Piloted-Aircraft-Systems-Panel-(RPASP).aspx

https://www.icao.int/safety/UA/Pages/Unmanned-Aircraft-Systems-Advisory-Group-(UAS-AG).aspx

https://www.ifalpa.org/news/global-pilots-industry-partners-call-for-new-guidance-on-drone-operations/

https://www.ifatca.org/2020/05/all-one-in-the-sky/

https://www.iso.org/about-us.html

https://www.iso.org/committee/5336224.html

https://www.iso.org/news/ref2461.html

https://www.kaspersky.pl/antidrone

https://www.mckinsey.com/~/media/McKinsey/Business%20Functions/McKinsey%20Digital/Our%20Insights/Disruptive%20technologies/MGI_Disruptive_technologies_Full_report_May2013.ashx

https://www.oig.dot.gov/library-item/35367

https://www.pwc.co.uk/press-room/press-releases/public-concerns-remain-a-barrier-to-drone-adoption-pwc-research.html

https://www.pwc.pl/en/publikacje/2016/clarity-from-above.html

https://www.regulations.gov/document?D=FAA-2019-1100-0001

https://www.sesarju.eu/news/first-drone-test-flights-gof-20-take

https://www.sesarju.eu/news/sesar-u-space-demonstration-gulf-finland-gof-ready-take

https://www.sesarju.eu/node/1510

https://www.sesarju.eu/node/3200

https://www.sesarju.eu/projects/aura

https://www.sesarju.eu/projects/corus

https://www.sesarju.eu/projects/CORUSXUAM

https://www.sesarju.eu/projects/dacus

https://www.sesarju.eu/projects/icarus

https://www.sesarju.eu/projects/podium

https://www.sesarju.eu/projects/podium

https://www.sesarju.eu/sites/default/files/documents/reports/European_Drones_Outlook_Study_2016.pdf

https://www.sesarju.eu/sites/default/files/documents/reports/European%20ATM%20Master%20Plan%20Drone%20roadmap.pdf

https://www.sesarju.eu/sites/default/files/documents/reports/U-space%20Blueprint%20brochure%20final.PDF

https://www.sesarju.eu/sites/default/files/documents/reports/U-space%20Blueprint%20brochure%20final.PDF

https://www.sesarju.eu/U-space

https://www.uavdach.org/

https://www.uk-cpi.com/windowless-plane

https://www.ulc.gov.pl/pl/drony/czesto-zadawane-pytania-faq/493-kategoria-szczegolna/5546-jakie-sa-dostepne-krajowe-scenariusze-standardowe-nsts

https://www.ulc.gov.pl/pl/drony/konwersja-swiadectw-kwalifikacji

https://www.ulc.gov.pl/pl/drony/wdrazanie-przepisow-ue/4717-certyfikacja-bsp-zgodna-z-wymogami-ue

https://www.ulc.gov.pl/pl/zarzadzanie-bezpieczenstwem/program-bezpieczenstwa-w-lotnictwie-cywilnym/krajowy-program-bezpieczenstwa-w-lotnictwie-cywilnym-kpbwlc

https://www.unmannedairspace.info/emerging-regulations/easa-postpones-u-space-draft-opinion-to-february-2020/

https://www.unmannedairspace.info/emerging-regulations/u-space-now-moving-from-research-to-implementation-european-network-of-demonstrators/

https://www4.icao.int/ganpportal/

www.icao.int/icao/en/leb.

Legal documents

39th ICAO Assembly held in September 2016.

A-NPA-2015-10.

A-NPA: 2015-10 — RMT.0230 — 18.12.2015.

AAIB Aviation Safety Report 2018.

AAIU-2016-AII-01.

Advance-Notice of Proposed Amendment (NPA) No 16/2005 Policy for Unmanned Aerial Vehicle (UAV) certification.

AN12/1.1.23-18/11.

Announcement No. 10 of the President of the Polish Civil Aviation Authority, Journal of Laws, April 16, 2013, item 58.

Announcement No. 2 of the President of the Civil Aviation Authority of February 5, 2018 on the publication of the text of Annex 13 to the Convention on International Civil Aviation (Journal of the CAA No. 2 of 2018).

Announcement of the President of the Civil Aviation Authority No. 5, CAA Journal of March 29, 2017, item 471.

Appendix 4, Remotely Piloted Aircraft Systems.

BGBl. no. 253/1957 and BGBl. I, no. 83/2008.

Brussels, May 7, 2018 COM(2018) 246 final.

CAA document LBB-2/811-0006/19 of December 4, 2019.

Cir. 328, note 1.4.

Civil Aviation Safety Regulations 1998 (Cth), reg 101.240.

Commission Implementing Regulation (EU) 2019/947 of 24 May 2019 on the rules and procedures for the operation of unmanned aircraft.

Commission Regulation (EU) No 965/2012 of 5 October 2012 laying down technical requirements and administrative procedures related to air operations pursuant to Regulation (EC) No 216/2008 of the European Parliament and of the Council (Journal of Laws L 296/1 of 25.10.2012).

Commission staff working document "Towards a European strategy for the development of civil applications of Remotely Piloted Aircraft Systems (RPAS). SWD (2012) 259 final.

COMMUNICATION FROM THE COMMISSION On the road to automated mobility: An EU strategy for mobility of the future.

Communication from the Commission to the European Parliament and the Council "A new era for aviation. Opening the aviation market to the civil use of remotely piloted aircraft systems in a safe and sustainable manner" COM (2014) 207 final.

Communication from the Commission to the European Parliament and the Council "A new era for aviation. Opening the aviation market to the civil use of remotely piloted aircraft systems in a safe and sustainable manner" COM (2014) 207 final, Brussels, April 8, 2014; ICAO, Unmanned Aircraft Systems (UAS), Cir 328 AN/190, 2011.

Communication from the Commission to the European Parliament, the Council, The European Economic and Social Committee and the Committee of the Regions An Aviation Strategy for Europe COM/2015/0598 final.

COMMUNICATION FROM THE COMMISSION TO THE EUROPEAN PARLIAMENT, THE COUNCIL, THE EUROPEAN ECONOMIC AND SOCIAL COMMITTEE, THE COMMITTEE OF THE REGIONS On the road to automated mobility: An EU strategy for mobility of the future, Brussels, May 17, 2018 COM(2018) 283 final.

Convention on International Civil Aviation signed on December 7, 1944 in Chicago, ratified by Poland, Journal Of Laws of 1959, No. 35.

Department for Transport, Impact Assessment: Pathway to Driverless Cars — Insurance for Automated Vehicles, 7 October 2016: https://www.parliament.uk/documents/impact-assessments/IA17-008A.pdf

Directive 2006/42/EC of the European Parliament and of the Council of 17 May 2006 on machinery.

Directive 2014/30/EU of the European Parliament and of the Council of 26 February 2014 on the harmonisation of the laws of the Member States relating to electromagnetic compatibility.

Directive 2014/53/EU of the European Parliament and of the Council of 16 April 2014 on the harmonisation of the laws of the Member States relating to the making available on the market of radio equipment and repealing Directive 1999/5/EC.

Drone Safety Risk: An Assessment, CAP 1627.

EASA A-NPA-2015.

EASA Annual Safety Report 2017.

EASA Aviation Safety Report 2006

EASA Aviation Safety Report 2019.

EASA document NPA-2017-05.

EASA Management Board Decision 18-2015 (Rulemaking Procedure).

EASA, Technical Opinion to A-NPA-2015.

EU Regulation 2018/1139, Art. 3.

European ATM Master Plan. Roadmap for safe integration in Europe, SESAR, 2018.

European Parliament resolution of 29 October 2015 on safe use of remotely piloted aircraft systems (RPAS), commonly known as unmanned aerial vehicles (UAVs), in the field of civil aviation (2014/2243(INI)).

FAA Aerospace Forecast 2019-2039.

FAA Aerospace Forecast, Fiscal Years 2019-2039.

FAA Modernization and Reform Act of 2012, Pub. L. No. 112-95, 126 Stat. 11 (2012).

FAA Reauthorization Act of 2018, Pub. L. No. 115-254.

GM1 to UAS.SPEC.050 (1) (b).

ICAO 10019, p. 1-4, JARUS GLOSSARY 0.7.

ICAO Cir 328, note 2.4, ICAO Doc 11019, note 2.3.6.

ICAO Doc 11019, note 2.2.

ICAO Doc 11019, note 2.6.

ICAO Doc. 10019, comments 1.2.5-1.2.6.

ICAO Doc. 9859, Safety Management Manual, annotation 59.

ICAO Doc. 9859, Safety Management Manual, ed. 3, point 2.1.2. Guidelines of the President of the Civil Aviation Authority No. 13, CAA Journal of December 10, 2015, item 66.

ICAO Safety Report 2019.

JARUS, 09 UAS Operational Categorization.

JOEU L 119 of May 4, 2016.

Journal of Laws L 152/45, June 11, 2019.

Journal of Laws of August 12, 2008 L 218.

NPA 2012-10 and NPA 2014-09.

OJEU L 079 of March 19, 2008.

OJEU L 133 of May 6, 2014.

OJEU L 199 of 31.07.2007.

OJEU L 212 of August 22, 2018.

OJEU L 224 of August 21, 2012.

OJEU L 281 of October 13, 2012.

OJEU L 296 of October 25, 2012.

OJEU L 311 of November 25, 2011.

OJEU L 362 of December 17, 2014.

OJEU L 44 of February 14, 2014.

OJEU L 62 of March 8, 2017.

OJEU of August 22, 2002, L 212.

OJEU of June 11, 2019, L 152.

OJEU of May 13, 2020, L 152.

OJEU UE L 63 of March 6, 2015.

Opinion 01/2015 on Privacy and Data Protection Issues relating to the Utilisation of Drones, ARTICLE 29 DATA PROTECTION WORKING PARTY, 01673/15/EN WP 231, p. 7.

Opinion on the draft act amending the Polish Aviation Law Act and some other acts. Legislative Council at the Prime Minister, RL-0303-9 / 15.

Protocol to Amend the Convention for the Unification of Certain Rules Relating to International Carriage by Air signed in Warsaw, Poland on October 12, 1929, signed in Hague, The Netherlands on September 28, 1955.

Regulation (EC) No 1108/2009 of the European Parliament and of the Council of 21 October 2009 amending Regulation (EC) No 216/2008 in the field of aerodromes, air traffic management and air navigation services and repealing Directive 2006/23/EC, OJEU L 309.

Regulation (EC) No 216/2008 of the European Parliament and of the Council of 20 February 2008 on common rules in the field of civil aviation and establishing a European Aviation Safety Agency, and repealing Council Directive 91/670/EEC, Regulation (EC) No 1592/2002 and Directive 2004/36/EC, OJEU L079.

Report from the Commission to the European Parliament and the Council – The European Aviation Safety Programme COM (2015) 599 final.

Report of the Civil Aviation Authority of 2013 http://ulc.gov.pl/pl/drony/409-raporty/2739-raport-o-aktualny-stanie-prawnym-odnoszacym-sie-do-bez-zalogowych-statkow-powietrznych.

Report on Technical Commission (A40-WP/609), https://www.icao.int/Meetings/a40/Documents/WP/wp_609_en.pdf

Report on the State of Civil Aviation Safety for 2017, CAA.

Roadmap for the integration of civil Remotely-Piloted Aircraft Systems into the European Aviation System, http://ec.europa.eu/DocsRoom/documents/10484/attachments/1/translations/en/renditions/native

ruling of the Supreme Administrative Court of October 5, 2018, I OSK 2708/16.

SESAR Drone Outlook Study, 2016.

SESAR Joint Undertaking

SESAR JU. European Drones Outlook Study. Unlocking the value for Europe. 2016.

SESAR, Drone outlook study, 2016

SPEC.UAS.080.

Statement of the President of the Civil Aviation Authority of March 25, 2014 on violations of the rules governing model and UA flights.

Technical Opinion to A-NPA 2015–10.

The Convention for the Unification of Certain Rules Relating to International Carriage by Air signed in Warsaw, Poland on October 12, 1929; Convention for the Unification of Certain Rules for International Carriage by Air signed in Montreal, Canada on May 28, 1999.

The Regulation also introduces requirements for "certified" and "specific" category UAS (Chapter III).

U-space Blueprint, SESAR, 2017.

UAS LUC 030 Regulation 2019/247.

UAS.OPEN.050.

UAS.OPEN.060.

UAV Task-Force Final Report. A Concept for European Regulation for Civil Unmanned Aerial Vehicles.

UK Aviation Safety Review for 2016, CAP 1595.

Unmanned Aircraft Systems (UAS), Cir 328 AN / 190, note 2.2.

US Congress, Public Law 112-95 112th Congress, FAA Modernization and Reform Act of 2012.

US Congress, Public Law 115-254 115th Congress, FAA Modernization and Reform Act of 2018.

Judgements

244 Fed. App'x 944 (11th Cir. 2007).

Allan v. United Kingdom (November 5, 2002, case no. 48539/99).

Assemb. B. 239, 78th Leg., Reg. Sess. (Nev. 2015).

Association for European Integration and Human Rights and Ekimdzhiev v. Bulgaria (June 28, 2007 case no. 62540/ 00).

Boggs v. Meredith, No. 3:16-cv-00006-DJH (W.D. Ky. 2016): https://cases.justia.com/federal/district-courts/kentucky/kywdce/3:2016cv00006/96944/20/0.pdf?ts=1490444322

C. v. Belgium, August 7, 1996, § 25, Reports 1996-III.

Court of Appeal of California, First District, Division Four Jul 9, 1968263 Cal. App.2d 742 (Cal. Ct. App. 1968).

Court of Appeal of Louisiana, Orleans, February 18, 1957, 92 So.2d 593 (1957).

Dougherty v. Stepp, 18 N.C. 371, 372 (1835).

Finogenov and others v Russia (case no. 18299/03 and 27311/03) December 20, 2011. https://hudoc.echr.coe.int/eng#{"fulltext":["001-108231"],"itemid":["001-108231"]}.

Friedl v. Austria (January 31, 1995, case no. 15225/ 89).

Herbecq v. Belgia (January 14, 1998, case no. 32200/96 and 32201/00).

Köpke v. Germany (October 5, 2010, case no. 420/07.

Martin v. United Kingdom (February 19, 2004, case no. 63608/00).

Niemietz v. Germany, December16, 1992, § 29, Series A no. 251-B.

P.G. and J. H. v. United Kingdom (September 25, 2001, case no. 44787/98).

Peck v. United Kingdom (January 28, 2003, case no. 44647/98).

Perry v. United Kingdom (July 17, 2003, case no.63737 / 00).

Pickering v Rudd (1815) 4 Camp 219.

Pretty v. United Kingdom, no. 2346/02, § 61, ECHR 2002-III).

Shorter v. Retail Credit Co., 251 F. Supp. 329, 332 (D.S.C. 1966).

Supreme Court ruling of July 25, 2013, II CSK 613/12.

Supreme Court ruling of September 22, 2005, IV CK 100/05, also see Supreme Court ruling of May 7, 2004 I CK 625/03, LEX no. 479 350.

Szypusz v. United Kingdom (September 21, 2010, case no. 8400/07).

the verdict of the Constitutional Tribunal of September 30th, 2008, file ref. no. K 44/07.

the verdict of the Provincial Administrative Court in Warsaw of October 25th, 2017, file ref. no. VII SA / Wa 2771/16.

U.S. Supreme Court, Dow Chem. Co. v. United States, 476 U.S. at 239.

United States Court of Appeals, Tenth Circuit, Jan 30, 1984, 727 F.2d 917 (10th Cir. 1984).

United States District Court, D. Minnesota Feb 11, 2008, Civil No. 06-2661 (PAM/JSM) (D. Minn. Feb. 11, 2008).

United States District Court, M.D. Florida, Tampa DivisionNov 16, 2005Case No. 8:03-cv-544-T-31MSS, (also docketed in 8:03-cv-539-T-31MSS) (M.D. Fla. Nov. 16, 2005).

United States District Court, N.D. Ohio, E.D Mar 25, 194983 F. Supp. 373 (N.D. Ohio 1949).

United States v. Causby, 328 U.S. 256 (1946), 266.

US Supreme Court, Florida v. Riley, 488 U.S. 445, 450 (1989)

US Supreme Court, Katz v. United States, 389 U.S. 347 (1967).

Index

Ius, Lex et Res Publica
Studies in Law, Philosophy and Political Cultures

Edited by
Anna Jaroń

Vol. 1 Anna Jaroń: Socio-Economic Constitutional Rights in Democratisation Processes. An Account of the Constitutional Dialogue Theory. 2012.

Vol. 2 Stanisław Filipowicz: Democracy – The Power of Illusion. 2013.

Vol. 3 Teresa Dukiet-Nagórska (ed.): The Postulates of Restorative Justice and the Continental Model of Criminal Law. As Illustrated by Polish Criminal Law 2014.

Vol. 4 Agnieszka Kupzok: Enforcement of Patents on Geographically Divisible Inventions. An Inquiry into the Standard of Substantive Patent Law Infringement in Cross-Border Constellations. 2015.

Vol. 5 Alicja Jagielska-Burduk / Wojciech Szafrański: Legal Issues in Cultural Heritage Management. A Polish Perspective. 2016.

Vol. 6 Maciej Mataczyński (ed.): The Takeover of Public Companies as a Mode of Exercising EU Treaty Freedoms. 2017.

Vol. 7 Maciej Barczewski (ed.): Value of Information. Intellectual Property, Privacy and Big Data. 2018.

Vol. 8 Pawel Smoleń, Marcin Burzec: Introduction to Polish Tax Law. 2018.

Vol. 9 Łukasz Pohl, Konrad Burdziak: Judicial Interpretation of the 1997 Criminal Code Provisions on Self-Defence. 2019.

Vol. 10 Adam Szot: Judicial Review of Administrative Discretion. The Influence of Court Decisions on Administrative Actions. 2019.

Vol. 11 Michał Peno / Konrad Burdziak (eds.): The Concept of Modern Law. Polish and Central European Tradition. 2019.

Vol. 12 Leszek Leszczyński / Bartosz Liżewski / Adam Szot (eds.): Potential of Precedent in the Statutory Legal Order. 2019.

Vol. 13 Łukasz Bolesta: In Search of a Model for the Legal Protection of a Whistleblower in the Workplace in Poland. A legal and comparative study. 2020.

Vol. 14 Paweł Chmielnicki / Adam Sulikowski (eds.): New Perspectives on Legislation. A Comparative Approach. 2020.

Vol. 15 Marcin Burzec / Beata Kucia-Guściora / Paweł Smoleń: Agricultural Activity in Poland: A Fiscal and Legal Study. 2020.

Vol. 16 Magdalena Półtorak / Ilona Topa (eds.): Women, Children and (Other) Vulnerable Groups. Standards of Protection and Challenges for International Law. 2021.

Vol. 17 Josef Albert Fox: Die polnische Verfassung vom 3. Mai 1791. Hintergründe der Entstehung und der Außerkraftsetzung. Stellung Polens im Zeitalter der Aufklärung. 2021.

Vol. 18 Barbara Janusz-Pohl (ed.): Juvenile Justice Systems: Poland-Brazil-Portugal. 2021.

Vol. 19 Leszek Leszczyński: General Reference Clauses in the Judicial Process. Context of Legislative Intentions Interpretative Discretion. 2021.

Vol. 20 Francisco J. Campos Zamora: Das Problem der Begründung richterlicher Entscheidungen. Eine Analyse auf der Grundlage der Theorie der juristischen Argumentation. 2021.

Ius, Lex et Res Publica

Studies in Law, Philosophy and Political Cultures

Edited by

Barbara Janusz-Pohl and Anna Jaroń

Vol. 21 Aneta Skorupa-Wulczyńska: Language Rights of the Citizen of the European Union. 2022.

Vol. 22 Mateusz Osiecki: International Legal Aspects of Aerial Terrorism. Methods of Law Enforcement in Avia-tion. 2022.

Vol. 23 Vladimír Sharp / Gabriela Blahoudková / Jakub Handrlica (eds.): Law, Pandemics and Ownership Restrictions. 2022.

Vol. 24 Piotr Kasprzyk / Anna Konert: Drones – Future of Aviation Law? Interference of Public Law in Private Law. 2023.

www.peterlang.com

www.ingramcontent.com/pod-product-compliance
Ingram Content Group UK Ltd.
Pitfield, Milton Keynes, MK11 3LW, UK
UKHW020835290926
15470UKWH00004B/1353

9 783631 895276